Early Ethiopic
An Introduction with Exercises

Robert D. Holmstedt

GlossaHouse
Wilmore, KY
GlossaHouse.com

Early Ethiopic: An Introduction with Exercises

© 2024 *All rights reserved*. No part of this work may be reproduced or transmitted in any form or by any means, electronic or mechanical, including photocopying and recording, or by means of any information storage or retrieval system, except as may be expressly permitted by the 1976 Copyright Act or in writing from the publisher. Requests for permission should be addressed in writing to:

    GlossaHouse, LLC
    110 Callis Circle
    Wilmore, KY 40390

Publisher's Cataloging-in-Publication Data:

Early Ethiopic: An Introduction with Exercises/ Robert D. Holmstedt
Wilmore, KY: GlossaHouse, ©2024

viii, 254 pages ; 21.59 x 27.94 cm

ISBN: 978-1-63663-093-9 (paperback)

1. Non-Fiction, Christian. 2. Author. 3. I. Title. II. Series.

    Library of Congress Control Number:

Cover Design by T. Michael W. Halcomb

Book Layout by Fredrick J. Long

The English font used to create this work are available from www.linguistsoftware.com/lgku.htm

Abba Garima font was created by Daniel Yacob and available at https://github.com/BlackFoundryCom/AbbaGarima

Abba Garima manuscript images used by permission of Michael Gervers.

Gunda Gunde manuscript images courtesy of Michael Gervers and available at http://collections.digital.utsc.utoronto.ca/islandora/object/gundagunde%3Apublic

Images from the 1513 Psalter courtesy of the Foyle Special Collections Library at King's College London

TABLE OF CONTENTS

Preface v
Introduction vii

LESSONS

1—The Writing System 1
     1.1 The Vowels
     1.2 The Consonants
     1.3 Word Stress
     1.4 Root and Pattern Word Structure
     1.5 The Alphabet
2—Common Prepositions 22
3—Forming Clauses without a Verb 26
4—Subject Pronouns 29
5—The Basics of the Perfect Verb 33
6—The Verb ብ-ህ-ል 38
7—(Formally) Introducing Nouns 42
8—The Basics of the Imperfect Verb 47
9—More on Nouns (Plurals) 51
10—Putting Words Together—Basic Syntax 55
11—Beyond the Basics of the Verb 59
12—The Dependent -*a* 65
13—Demonstrative Pronouns 71
14—Verbal Valency 76
15—The Noun with Attached Pronouns 81
16—Adjectives 86
17—Prepositions with Attached Pronouns 92
18—More on Syntax—The መልዓ፡ለንጉሥ Construction 96
19—The Quantifier ኮል- 100
20—Yet More on the Verb—The Verb with Clitic Pronouns 105
21—And More on the Verb—The Subjunctive 110
22—Even More on Syntax 114
     The ቀተሎ፡ለንጉሥ Construction
     Partitive Apposition
23—Still on the Verb—The Converb 118
24—Related to the Verb—The Infinitive 123
25—Relative Clauses 128
26—ለ- and ብ- with Clitic Pronouns 132
27—Finish the Verb! 135
     The Imperative
     Final Verb Note

28—Finishing the Prepositions..138
    More on the Preposition በ-
29—Finishing the Noun..141
    The Agent Noun ቀታሊ
    Nouns of the Pattern ምቅታል
    Nouns of the Pattern መቅተል
30—Finishing the Pronoun..143
    A Special Use of the Third Person Singular Clitic Pronouns
    Clitic Pronouns equivalent to a Prepositional Phrase

APPENDICES
    Appendix A—Noun and Pronoun Paradigms...149
    Appendix B—Strong Verb Paradigms..151
    Appendix C—Weak Verb Paradigms..157
    Appendix D—The Verb with Enclitic Pronouns 168
    Appendix E—Numerals...169
    Appendix F—Manuscript Images and Texts 172
    Appendix G—Vocabulary by Lesson..198

GLOSS LEXICON..209

PREFACE

This textbook owes a great deal to Thomas Lambdin's *Introduction to Classical Ethiopic (Geʿez)*, published in 1978. The earliest version of the present work was a Gəʿəz script revision of Lambdin's. During this process, the felt need to rewrite both grammatical descriptions and language exercises resulted in a product that is quite distinct from the starting point.

Distinctive Features of this New Textbook

There are two obvious features of this textbook, which reflect a very different pedagogy than Lambdin's. First, the student quickly learns the ፊደል *fidal*, that is, the Ethiopic script. This is an essential component for entering the world of Ethiopic manuscripts study, or codicology. To reinforce this, the textbook also has students read directly from images of the Abba Garima III Gospels manuscript, by which they learn the script hand in arguably the earliest Gəʿəz text aside from the limited epigraphic sources.

Second, the grammar and vocabulary are introduced in the context of a coherent running narrative—the first three chapters of the Abba Garima III Gospel of Mark, the first page from the Abba Garima III Gospel of Luke, Psalms 1 and 23 from a 1513 printed Psalter, and the first two pages of the book of Jubilees from a Gunda Gunde manuscript. For the lessons using the Gospel of Mark, the Ethiopic text is provided in an illustrated context. Both features—text and illustration—provide mental structures for aiding the processing and retention of the grammar and vocabulary. The subtle but important grammatical and scribal differences between the Abba Garima III manuscripts and later Ethiopic/Geʿez texts lie behind the choice of "early Ethiopic" for the title of this work rather than "classical Ethiopic."

Beyond the two most obvious features, there are additional, more subtle choices. For example, the grammar is organized in order to move students to textual comprehension as quickly as possible. This includes leaving all weak verb discussions for the appendices, to be referenced at the discretion of instructor and student. The central design principle is one that has also guided other textbooks I have authored: "that language is learned in small chunks of information that alternate through the various aspects of grammar" (Cook and Holmstedt, *Beginning Biblical Hebrew* [Baker Academic, 2013], p. 10).

An additional pedagogical principle is that the tension created by encountering unlearned forms can be useful in the learning process. Thus, it is not until the second or third time a given text is encountered that the student will have learnt all the vocabulary, and even then, there will remain formally unaddressed grammatical concepts until the end of the lessons. The key to using this effectively is to encourage students to recognize what features they can in a given unlearned form (e.g., the root, or the inflectional features) and to remember encountering the item so that when the concept is fully learned, it will have a mental space waiting for it.

Beyond the pedagogical distinctives, this textbook also reflects a number of other departures from existing Ethiopic resources. The English glosses and other lexical information are based not only on Dillmann's *Lexicon linguae aethiopicae* (1865) but also on Leslau's much more recent and impressive *Comparative Dictionary of Geʿez* (1987 [2006]). Additionally, the grammatical descriptions reflect my own research on Semitic linguistic structure.

I am grateful to the students who have dared study Gəʿəz with me, both for increasing my enjoyment of the language and for contributing to the improvement of this teaching tool. I am especially grateful to André Arsenault, one of the first students to study Gəʿəz with me. Not only did he learn so quickly that I could barely keep ahead of him, he turned his excellent linguistic and pedagogical instincts to the task of developing a graded introduction to learning the Ethiopic script. With his kind permission, these exercises are now included in Lesson 1. I am also indebted to Fredrick Long and Michael Halcomb of GlossaHouse (www.glossahouse.com) for giving me permission to use the illustrated pages for Mark chapters 1–3 out of my illustrated Gəʿəz Gospel of Mark volume in their illustrated biblical texts series. Above all, this project would not exist apart from the continual encouragement and sharing of resources by my colleague, Michael Gervers, whose research activity in Ethiopic history is a true Indiana Jones story. Without his timely photographic preservation of manuscripts, the field would be impoverished.

My hope is that it successfully serves many students encountering Gəʿəz for the first time, both to prepare them for reading Gəʿəz texts and to encourage their passion for this beautiful language.

Robert D. Holmstedt
Toronto, Ontario
December 2023

INTRODUCTION

Ancient Ethiopic, or Gəʿəz, is related in some way to an earlier Central West Semitic language that was imported in the first millennium BCE, likely via trade relations, across the Red Sea from ancient Yemen in the South Arabian Peninsula. The exact relationship of Gəʿəz to the group of dialects known as Old South Arabian is unclear, since it does not appear to be directly descended from any one of the attested dialects. It stands to 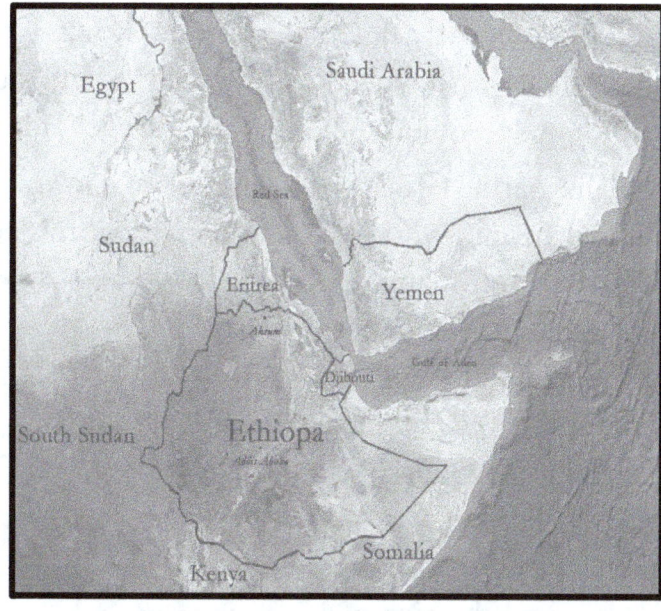 reason that Gəʿəz is descended from an earlier Semitic language that developed alongside these Old South Arabian dialects but was linguistically distinct from them.

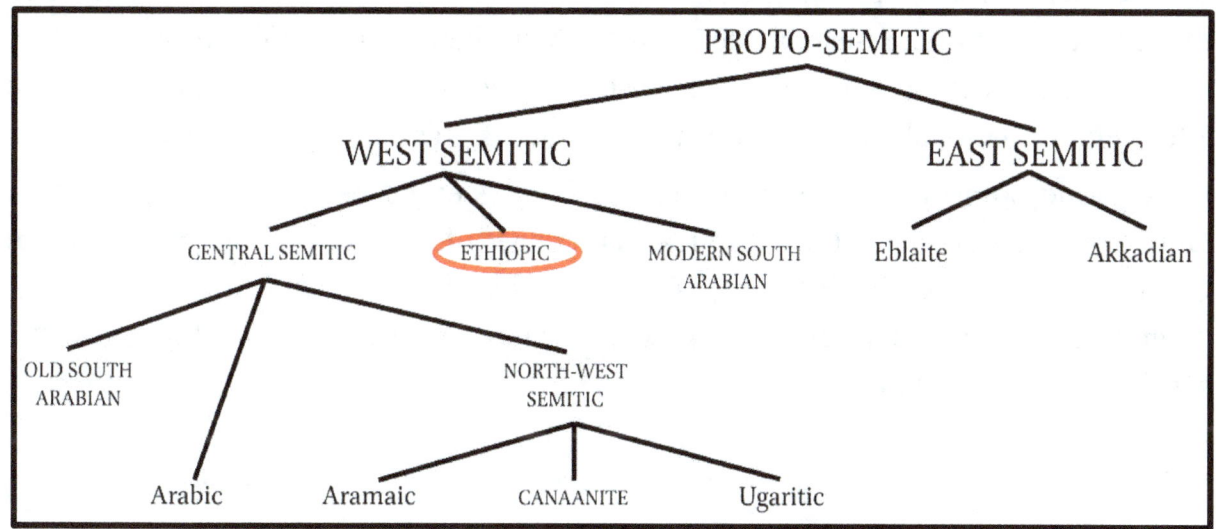

Within the Semitic language family, features of Gəʿəz that were lost, retained, or innovated from earlier Semitic place it as a distinct branch within West division of Semitic, alongside the Modern South Arabian languages and the Central Semitic subgroup. A number of non-Semitic features reflected in Gəʿəz attest to a substratum of Cushitic. That is, some grammatical features and vocabulary from the indigenous Cushitic languages of the area were incorporated into Gəʿəz when it became the dominant language.

Among the Ethiopic language group, Gəʿəz is considered to be a northern dialect, alongside Tigre, spoken in the northern highlands and coastal plain of the Red Sea. The modern dialect Tigrinye, spoken in northern Ethiopia and Eritrea, appears to be a direct linguistic descendant from Gəʿəz. The southern group of Ethiopic consists of Amharic, spoken by the Amhara and nearly 50% of the people in modern Ethiopia, as well as a number of Gurage, Harari, and Argobba languages.

The earliest formal attestation of Gəʿəz appears in the inscriptions of a king named Ezana, who lived and converted to Christianity in the mid-4th century C.E. In the following centuries, Gəʿəz textual evidence consists of translations of the Bible (including the larger canon of the Ethiopic Church), liturgical texts, hagiography, and a monastic rule. The Byzantine retreat and the rise of Islam in the 7th century led to an obscure period for which few Gəʿəz texts exist. But following the year 1000, when the Ethiopian Church re-established contact with the Coptic Church in Alexandria, ecclesiastical texts become numerous, as do non-ecclesiastical texts, such the as the 14th-century national epic, ክብረ ነገሥት *kəbra nagaśt* 'The Glory of the Kings.'

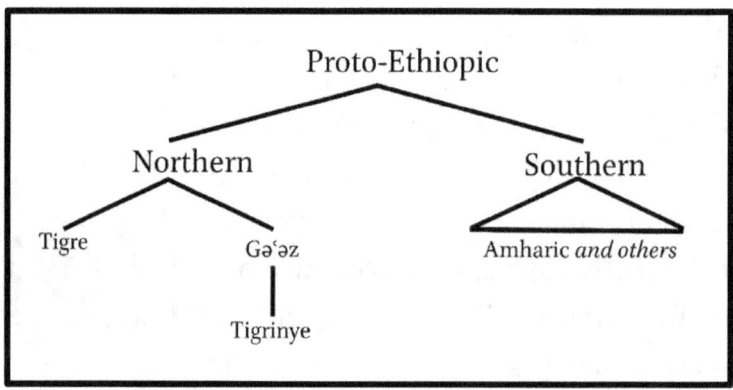

At some point in the medieval period, Gəʿəz ceased being acquired as a first language. However, as the liturgical language of the Ethiopian and Eritrean Orthodox Churches, the Ethiopian Catholic Church, and the Beta Israel Jewish community, Gəʿəz survived as a written language in a manner analogous to the survival of Latin in Europe.

LESSON 1
THE WRITING SYSTEM

1.1 The Vowels

All Semitic languages exhibit a vowel phonology ultimately derived from the common Semitic distinction between three qualities (*a, i, u*) and two quantities (short, long), hence: *a, i, u, ā, ī, ū*. It is likely that the distinction between long and short vowels was mostly lost in Gəʿəz by the period when the language began to be written. The short *i* and *u* had both become *ə*, leaving only the distinction between *ā* and *a*. Additionally, the vowels *e* and *o* represent the typical Semitic contraction of the diphthongs *ay* and *aw*, respectively. The result is a seven vowel system.

> short: *a, ə*
> long: *ā, i, u, e, o*

The pronunciation of these vowels should approximate the following English correspondences:

> *a* as in r*o*t
> *ā* as in f*a*ther
> *e* as in b*ai*t
> *ə* as in d*e*rive
> *i* as in mach*i*ne
> *o* as in b*oa*t
> *u* as in b*oo*t

The most significant difference between the <u>historically reconstructed system</u> above and the <u>traditional received pronunciation</u> is that the latter exhibits the raising and fronting of the short *a* to *ä* (IPA [æ]), as in "rat" (versus the sound in "rot").

	Front	Central	Back
High	i		u
High-Mid	e		o
Mid		ə	
Mid-Low	ä [æ]		
Low		ā [a]	

1.2 The Consonants

Most of the Gəʿəz consonants have an approximate counterpart in English and offer no problems in pronunciation:

b as in *boy*	k as in *king*	t as in *tea*
d as in *dog*	l as in *leaf*	w as in *wall*
f as in *foot*	m as in *man*	y as in *yet*
g as in *goat*	n as in *no*	z as in *zoo*
h as in *hope*	s, ś as in *so*	

Although they had distinct historical origins, the consonants *s* (IPA [s]) and *ś* (probably a lateral, IPA [ɬ]) have merged and both are pronounced as [s].

The five sounds ʾ ʿ h ḥ ḫ will be referred to collectively as gutturals. Three of the gutturals (h ḥ ḫ) are, especially for English speakers, often difficult to distinguish:

h is ordinary [h], as in <u>h</u>ope

ḥ is the voiceless pharyngeal continuant [ħ], that is, an *h* sound accompanied by a tense narrowing between the base of the tongue and the back of the throat.

ḫ is the voiceless velar fricative [x], as in German Ba<u>ch</u>.

The other two gutturals (ʾ ʿ) will be equally difficult for English speakers to master (though not for those who speak, e.g., Arabic) and there will be a temptation to provide neither with a consonantal value (i.e., treating them as silent consonants, or Ø). However, students should strive to give them their historical value and so avoid ambiguity.

ʾ was the glottal stop [ʔ], that is, a momentary cessation of air.

ʿ was the voiced laryngeal (pharyngeal) continuant [ʕ], i.e. the voiced counterpart of *ḥ* above.

The consonants *ṭ ḍ ṣ* and *q* are <u>ejectives</u>: sounds produced by the interruption of the flow of air by raising the glottis followed by a dramatic burst of air. Due to the centrality of the glottis in the sound production, these are also called *glottalized* consonants.

q is glottalized *kʾ* = IPA [kʔ]

ṭ is glottalized *tʾ* = IPA [tʔ]

ṣ is glottalized affricate *tsʾ* = IPA [tsʔ]

ḍ is glottalized lateral affricate, *tlʾ* = IPA [tɬʔ] — note that *ḍ* is traditionally produced like *ṣ*.

There are two *p*-sounds, both of which occur only in words of foreign origin:

ፕሬዝቢጥር *pərezbiṭər* 'priest' (from Gk. *Presbyteros*)

ጳጳስ *pāppās* 'metropolitan, patriarch, bishop'

The labialized sounds k^w $ḫ^w$ g^w q^w are simply k $ḫ$ g q pronounced simultaneously with w, precisely like English [kw] in 'quick' or [gw] in 'Guam'.

The Gəʿəz writing system does not indicate "doubling" or gemination of consonants, which is the lengthened articulation of a single sound (e.g., *bb* or [bː]). However, this feature of Gəʿəz phonology is strongly suggested by the comparative evidence of Semitic languages.

> Note: For further reading on the complexity of reconstructing Gəʿəz phonology, see Stefan Weninger, "Sounds of Gəʿəz—How to Study the Phonetics and Phonology of an Ancient Language," *Aethiopica* 13 (2010): 75–88.

1.3 Word Stress

According to the tradition adopted in this text, word stress follows three simple rules:

(a) All finite verbal forms without cliticized complement pronouns are stressed on the <u>next-to-last syllable</u>.

nabára, qatálat, yəqáttəl, yəqattálu

The sole exception is the 2nd person feminine plural of the Perfect in *-kə́n*:

nabarkə́n

(b) Most non-verbal words, including free form nouns, adjectives, and adverbs, are stressed on the <u>last syllable</u>.

(c) Bound nouns and prepositions, both of which typically end in final *-a*, carry stress on the <u>next-to-last syllable</u>.

Deviations from the three basic rules will be indicated in the lessons and vocabulary by the addition to the Gəʿəz of this mark ˙ over the stressed syllable, e.g., ክቡር.

1.4 Root and Pattern Word Structure

Gəʿəz word formation reflects the typical Semitic root-and-pattern system, in which a consonantal skeleton (e.g., C-C-C) is merged with a pattern of vowels (e.g., *a-a*). Besides variation in the vowel patterns, the triconsonantal root ($C_1C_2C_3$) may also be supplemented by prefixes or suffixes.

		Consonant Base	Vowel Pattern	Additional Elements
nəguś	'king'	ngś	$C_1əC_2uC_3$	none
nəgəśt	'queen'	ngś	$C_1əC_2əC_3$-	suffix *-t*
berhān	'light'	brh	$C_1əC_2C_3$-	suffix *-ān*
manbar	'throne'	nbr	-$C_1C_2aC_3$	prefix *ma-*

Consonantal roots (C₁-C₂-C₃) are often used to create both noun and verb forms, if not multiple types of each, and the core lexical meaning of the forms is typically relatable. For example, *nəguś* 'king', *nəgəśt* 'queen', *nəgś* 'rule, reign', *nagāśi* 'king', *mangəśt* 'kingdom', *nagśa* 'he became king' all sharing a core lexical semantics related to "ruling."

Rather than the cumbersome C₁-C₂-C₃ description of word patterns, Semitists generally employ the root **q-t-l** 'to kill' to refer to the various patterns. Thus,

bəluy 'worn out'	reflects the pattern	**qətul**
bərhān 'light'		**qətlān**
manfas 'spirit'		**maqtal**

Very few root-and-vowel patterns have a completely predictable meaning, but a large number of them belong to the "almost predictable" category. For example, *qətul* is almost always adjectival, though there are always exceptions. Paying attention to the patterns and the semantic trends will give the student insight into the word formation processes at work in the language.

1.5 The Script

The Gəʿəz script was borrowed directly from the Old South Arabic monumental script and gradually modified for book use. Genuine cursive forms are modern. Medieval manuscripts consistently employ a more or less hand-printed form, with separation of all the letters.

The Gəʿəz script is not an *alphabet* or a *syllabary* but an **abugida**. The main difference between the types is that in an abugida the consonant-vowel combinations are based on the same form of the sign. For example, the sign for *ba* and *bi* are both based on the same character.

The Gəʿəz script is divided into seven "orders," each one consisting of a vowel and a consonant. The full seven orders, with the basic consonantal equivalence and the traditional letter name are given in Table A. Note that the letters are presented in the order that Leslau uses in his *Comparative Dictionary of Geʿez* and is common in comparative Semitics (i.e., ʾAlf, ʿAyn, Bet, Dant, etc.). Another ancient order, the *Halḥam* order, is used by some other lexica (e.g., Dillmann's *Lexicon Linguae Aethiopicae*, Leslau's *Concise Dictionary of Geʿez*): ሀ, ለ, ሐ, መ, ሠ, ረ, ሰ, ቀ, በ, ተ, ኀ, ነ, አ, ከ, ወ, ዐ, ዘ, የ, ደ, ገ, ጠ, ጸ, ፀ, ፈ, ፐ.

The forms of the letters in the first order (i.e., the third column of Table A) are read with the vowel *-a* and are considered to be the basic forms. The labialized variants are given in Table B.

Table A. The Gəʿəz Abugida

Base Consonant	Gəʿəz Name	1° Ca	2° Cu	3° Ci	4° Cā	5° Ce	6° C, Cə	7° Co
ʾ	ʾAlf	አ	ኡ	ኢ	ኣ	ኤ	እ	ኦ
ʿ	ʿAyn	ዐ	ዑ	ዒ	ዓ	ዔ	ዕ	ዖ
b	Bet	በ	ቡ	ቢ	ባ	ቤ	ብ	ቦ
d	Dant	ደ	ዱ	ዲ	ዳ	ዴ	ድ	ዶ
ḍ	Ḍappa	ፀ	ፁ	ፂ	ፃ	ፄ	ፅ	ፆ
f	ʾAf	ፈ	ፉ	ፊ	ፋ	ፌ	ፍ	ፎ
g	Gaml	ገ	ጉ	ጊ	ጋ	ጌ	ግ	ጎ
h	Hoy	ሀ	ሁ	ሂ	ሃ	ሄ	ህ	ሆ
ḥ	Ḥawt	ሐ	ሑ	ሒ	ሓ	ሔ	ሕ	ሖ
ḫ	Ḫarm	ኀ	ኁ	ኂ	ኃ	ኄ	ኅ	ኆ
k	Kāf	ከ	ኩ	ኪ	ካ	ኬ	ክ	ኮ
l	Law	ለ	ሉ	ሊ	ላ	ሌ	ል	ሎ
m	Māy	መ	ሙ	ሚ	ማ	ሜ	ም	ሞ
n	Nahās	ነ	ኑ	ኒ	ና	ኔ	ን	ኖ
p	Psa	ፐ	ፑ	ፒ	ፓ	ፔ	ፕ	ፖ
ṗ	Payt	ጰ	ጱ	ጲ	ጳ	ጴ	ጵ	ጶ
q	Qāf	ቀ	ቁ	ቂ	ቃ	ቄ	ቅ	ቆ
r	Rəʾs	ረ	ሩ	ሪ	ራ	ሬ	ር	ሮ
s	Sāt	ሰ	ሱ	ሲ	ሳ	ሴ	ስ	ሶ
ś	Śawt	ሠ	ሡ	ሢ	ሣ	ሤ	ሥ	ሦ
ṣ	Ṣadāy	ጸ	ጹ	ጺ	ጻ	ጼ	ጽ	ጾ
t	Taw	ተ	ቱ	ቲ	ታ	ቴ	ት	ቶ
ṭ	Ṭayt	ጠ	ጡ	ጢ	ጣ	ጤ	ጥ	ጦ
w	Waw	ወ	ዉ	ዊ	ዋ	ዌ	ው	ዎ
y	Yaman	የ	ዩ	ዪ	ያ	ዬ	ይ	ዮ
z	Zay	ዘ	ዙ	ዚ	ዛ	ዜ	ዝ	ዞ

Table B. Labialized Consonants

	1° Ca	3° Ci	4° Cā	5° Ce	6° Cə
g^w	ጐ	ጒ	ጓ	ጔ	ጕ
$ḫ^w$	ኈ	ኊ	ኋ	ኌ	ኍ
k^w	ኰ	ኲ	ኳ	ኴ	ኵ
q^w	ቈ	ቊ	ቋ	ቌ	ቍ

Table C provides the numbers, which are adapted from the Greek alphabet and given numerical value. The numerical values are the same as those known from Greek sources. Note the combinations: *1000 = 10* hundreds; *10,000 = 100* hundreds.

Table C. Numerical Signs

1	6	11	20	70
2	7	12	30	80
3	8	13	40	90
4	9	14	50	100
5	10	15	60	200
	1,000	10,000	100,000	

Table D provides Amharic modifications. Several new letters were developed for the writing of Amharic by modifying certain forms of the Gəʿəz alphabet. These sometimes occur in Gəʿəz manuscripts in writing native personal and place names.

Table D. Amharic Modifications

	1° Ca	2° Cu	3° Ci	4° Cā	5° Ce	6° C, Cə	7° Co
ś							
čʼ							
ñ							
ḳ							
ž							
j							
čʼ							

The Old South Arabic monumental script regularly employed a vertical stroke as a word divider. This too was borrowed and appears after every single word in a Gəʿəz text as ፡ (see the specimen texts for examples). The sign ፡ is used as a colon or semicolon within a sentence, and ። is used as a period. Other more elaborate devices are sometimes used to mark off paragraphs and longer sections. In this textbook, when single words are given in the exercises, they will be separated by ።, and sentences and sentence fragments will appear as they normally would in an Gəʿəz text, with ፡ between words and ። marking the end of the sentence or fragment.

Learning the Gəʿəz Script[1]

1. Signs in the first order (1°)

The traditional first order contains the vowel [a].

አ - ʾa	ገ - ga	ለ - la	ቀ - qa	ተ - ta
ዐ - ʿa	ሀ - ha	መ - ma	ረ - ra	ጠ - ṭa
በ - ba	ሐ - ḥa	ነ - na	ሰ - sa	ወ - wa
ደ - da	ኀ - ḫa	ፐ - pa	ሠ - śa	የ - ya
ፀ - ḍa	ከ - ka	ጰ - ṗa	ጸ - ṣa	ዘ - za
ፈ - fa				

Labialized Consonants

Four of the above consonants can be labialized, where the consonants in question is accompanied by a rounding of the lips. These are represented in transliteration by a superscript *w*. The labialized consonants in the first order are as follows:

ጐ - gʷa   ኈ - ḫʷa   ኰ - kʷa   ቈ - qʷa

EXERCISES

A. Read the following aloud until all signs are memorized (the first line as separate letters, the second and third lines as words):

ከ ረ ቄ ተ ወ ሰ ዐ ጐ ፈ ሀ በ ዘ ሠ ኰ ሐ መ ኀ ቀ የ አ ፐ ጸ ጠ ጕ ደ ነ ፀ ለ ጸ ገ

ነበረ፡፡ወረደ፡፡ነበ፡፡በነበ፡፡ጐየ፡፡ሐነጸ፡፡ቀተለ፡፡ረከበ፡፡ሰደደ፡፡ተከለ፡፡ሰከበ፡፡ሰበከ፡፡ሐነጸ፡፡ነለፈ፡፡በከየ፡፡ዐቀለ፡፡

ቀበረ፡፡ጸሐፈ፡፡ሰአለ፡፡ከመ፡፡ዐደወ፡፡አተወ፡፡ወደየ፡፡ሀለወ፡፡ገሠጸ፡፡ፈጠረ፡፡ገነዘ፡፡ፀረፈ፡፡

B. Write the following words in script:

sadada . ṣaḥafa . ʾatawa . ganaza . ḫaba . baḫaba . ḫalafa . gwaya . saʾala . ḥanaṣa .

qatala .

---

[1] These script exercises in this section were developed by André Arsenault, with funding from a 2008 University of Toronto Excellence Award in the Social Sciences and Humanities. They are used with his permission.

rakaba . nabara . takala .

kama . warada . sabaka . ḍarafa . ḥanada . bakaya . ʿaqala . qabara . ʿadawa .

halawa . gaśaṣa .

faṭara . wadaya .

C. Circle every 1° letter in the manuscript selection below:

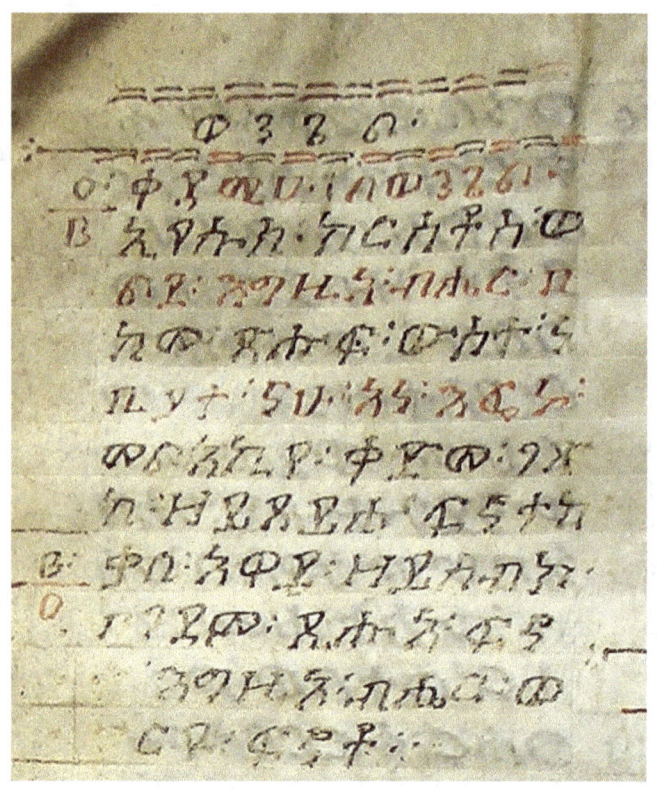

2. Sixth Order (6°)

The 6° is by far the least regular of the orders and also one of the most frequently used in writing due to the fact that it represents both the *shwa* [ə], which reflects the merger of *i* and *u*, and the absence of a vowel [ø].

አ - ʾə/ʾ	ግ - gə/g	ል - lə/l	ቅ - qə/q	ት - tə/t
ዕ - ʾə/ʿ	ህ - hə/h	ም - mə/m	ር - rə/r	ጥ - ṭə/ṭ

8

በ - bə/b   ሐ - ḥə/ḥ   ን - nə/n   ስ - sə/s   ወ - wə/w
ድ - də/d   ኀ - ḫə/ḫ   ፕ - pə/p   ሥ - śə/ś   ይ - yə/y
ḍ - ḍə/ḍ   ክ - kə/k   ጵ - ṗə/ṗ   ጽ - ṣə/ṣ   ዝ - zə/z
ፍ - fə/f

The sixth order is used extremely often in writing so the initial difficulties are soon overcome by repetition. Since there is no one characteristic feature in the sixth order, rote memorization is the only way to learn. There are, however, four different ways that the order is formed and these are outlined below.

The first group exhibits an additional small zig-zag in one of its lines:

አ - ʾə   ሀ - hə   ከ - kə   ፐ - pə   ጠ - ṭə

The second group adds a small stroke on the top left portion of the character:

ዐ - ʿə   ፀ - ḍə   ሕ - ḥə   ን - nə   ቀ - qə   ስ - sə   ት - tə

The third group has a small stroke, similar to that of the 2° and 3°, but here it is on the top-right of the character:

ው - wə   ድ - də   ጵ - ṗə   ጽ - ṣə

The fourth group has a small stroke on its left-hand side:

በ - bə   ዝ - zə

The remaining eight characters are all formed in a rather arbitrary manner and are presented in alphabetical order:

ፍ - fə   ግ - gə   ኅ - ḫə   ል - lə   ም - mə   ር - rə   ሥ - śə   ይ - yə

Labialized consonants

ጉ - g ə/g^w ኁ - ḫ^{w}ə/ḫ^w ኩ - k^{w}ə/k^w ቁ - q^{w}ə/q^w

All the labialized 6° signs have an addition on the right side that consists of a vertical stroke together with a stroke on the right. Note that the vertical portion of the addition is *short.* The reason for making this observation will become clear in due time.

Lesson 1—The Writing System

EXERCISES

A. Read aloud:

ሀገር፡ደብር፡ዐርገ፡እምነ፡ውስተ፡ገብር፡ሐመር፡መጽአ፡ወጸአ፡ሀየ፡ዝየ፡መሥግር፡ሕዝብ፡በጽሐ፡ምስለ፡ ዕፅ፡ዕፀው፡በረድ፡ቄጽል፡አቍጽል፡እንተ፡መኮንን፡ነገር፡መልአክ፡ወልድ፡ዕደው፡እም፡አብ፡ አበው፡ምት፡ንግሥት፡ወይን፡ርእየ፡ገብረ፡በእንተ፡እኍ፡አኅው፡እኅት፡ምድር፡እምዝ፡ድኅረ፡ዕለት፡ እስከ፡ቅድመ፡ሕግ፡ሕገግ፡መጽሐፍ፡ግእዝ፡ኀብስት፡ደም፡እድ፡እደው፡ውሕዘ፡ስሕተ፡ከሐደ፡ነሥአ።

B. Write the following words in script:

wayn . gəʕz . ʾəska . baʾənta . qədma . ḥəgag . badn . targwama . ʾaḫaw . mədr .

ḫəbəst . dam . ʾəd . ʿədaw . wəḥza . ḥəg .

kəḥda . naśʾa . ʾabaw . ʿəlat . mət . nəgəśt . ʿaṣad . rəʾya . gabra . ʾəḫw . ʾəḫt . səḥta .

ʾəmzə . dəḫra . qarba . maṣḥaf

C. Circle every 6° letter in this manuscript selection:

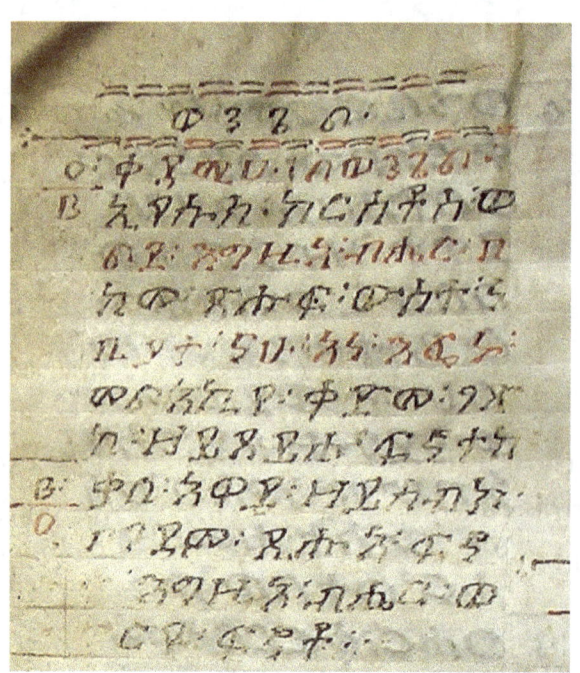

10

3. Second Order (2°)

The 2° consists of the consonants + the vowel [u]. The defining characteristic of this order is a stroke appearing on the right side of the character *in its center*. For example, the sign for *bu* is ቡ and the sign for *hu* is ሁ. Notice that both these characters are identical to their corresponding first order sign (በ for *ba* and ሀ for *ha*) with the addition of the characteristic right-hand stroke in the center of the character.

From the 2° on, some signs are irregular in their formation, going through an additional change in addition to—or instead of—the order's characteristic feature. To facilitate the memorization of these signs—which is the only way they can be learnt—they will be presented separately, after the regular signs. Note that 2° is the most regular.

ኡ - ʼu	ጉ - gu	ሉ - lu	ቁ - qu	ቱ - tu
ዑ - ʽu	ሁ - hu	ሙ - mu	ሩ - ru	ጡ - ṭu
ቡ - bu	ሑ - ḥu	ኑ - nu	ሱ - su	ዉ - wu
ዱ - du	ኁ - ḫu	ፑ - pu	ሡ - śu	ዩ - yu
ዱ - ḍu	ኩ - ku	ጱ - ṗu	ጹ - ṣu	ዙ - zu
ፉ - fu				

Irregular signs

Three of the irregular signs in 2° take an additional 'leg' to stand on in addition to the characteristic right-hand stroke. It is crucial to note that the 'leg' is perfectly vertical in ሩ, but that it *leans towards the left* in ዱ and ፉ. The fourth irregular sign, ዉ, takes the stroke on the *bottom* of the right side of the character:

ዱ - du   ፉ - fu   ሩ - ru   ዉ - wu

Labialized consonants *do not appear in 2°*.

EXERCISES

A. Read aloud:

መኑ:ውእቱ:ዝንቱ:መሠግር፡አንተኑ:መኮንን፡ንጉሥኑ:መጽአ፡ሐመረ:ኢትዮ፡አህገረ:ምድርከሙ።

ለምንት:ቀተሉ:ገብርከ።መኑ:ሰደደ:እምምድርከ።በእንተምንት:በከየ:ዝንቱ:ወልድ።ሀገሩ:ለንጉሥነ።

በደሙ:ለወልድየ፡ንብስት፡ወወይንኣየ:መጽሐፉ:ጸሐፍከ:ለምንት:ገሠጽከሙኑ:ነበርነ:ህየ:ውእተ:ወርኀ።

B. Write the following words in script:

hagarəka . gabru . ʾagbərta . ʾabuka . mədrəkəmu . makwannənəka . ʾəḫuya .

walattu . ʾahgurəya

C. Circle every 2° order letter in the manuscript selection below:

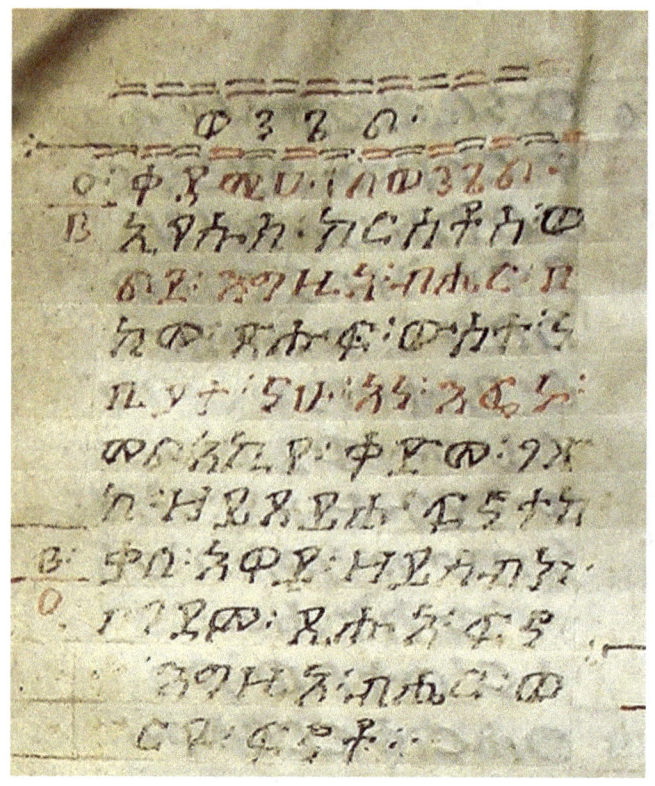

4. Third order (3°)

The 3° is similar to the 2° since its characteristic feature is the same right-hand stroke, but here it is *on the bottom* of the right side of the character. So, where we had ሀ *ba* and ቡ *bu* we now have ቢ *bi*. As with 2o there are irregular characters, but 3° has quite a few more.

ኢ - 'i	ጊ - gi	ሊ - li	ቂ - qi	ቲ - ti
ዒ - 'i	ሒ - ḥi	ሚ - mi	ሪ - ri	ጢ - ṭi
ቢ - bi	ሔ - ḫi	ኒ - ni	ሲ - si	ዊ - wi
ዲ - di	ኺ - ḫi	ፒ - pi	ሢ - śi	ዪ - yi
ዲ - ḍi	ኪ - ki	ጲ - ṗi	ጺ - ṣi	ዚ - zi
ፊ - fi				

Labialized consonants

ጕ - g^wi   ኹ - ḫ^wi   ኩ - k^wi   ቍ - q^wi

All the labialized 3°, the 1° signs have an addition on the right side that consists of a vertical stroke together with the characteristic stroke on the right. The vertical portion of the addition is **long** compared to the short vertical portion of the addition of the 6°.

Irregular signs

The irregulars for 3° fall into two groups: those who take a vertical 'leg' down the center of the sign or *on its right* in addition to the characteristic bottom right stroke, and those who suffer arbitrary changes.

ሒ - hi	ሚ - mi	ሪ - ri	ዊ - wi	ዊ - wi
ዒ - 'i	ዲ - di	ዲ - ḍi	ፊ - fi	ዪ - yi

Note that both ሪ and ፊ see their bottom right extremity curved upwards while ዪ is the 1o plus an addition similar to that of the labials of 3°, except that the vertical portion is *short*.

Lesson 1—The Writing System

EXERCISES

A. Read aloud:

ዲበ፡ብእሲ፡ብእሲት፡ሊቅ፡ነቢይ፡ደቂቅ፡አሚር፡ንጢአት፡ቀሲስ፡ኢቀተሎኒ፡

B. Write the following words in script:

ʾahguriki . bəʾsitəka . ʾabawina . yəʾəti . ʾirakabu . ṣaḥaftina

C. Circle every 3° order letter in the manuscript selection below:

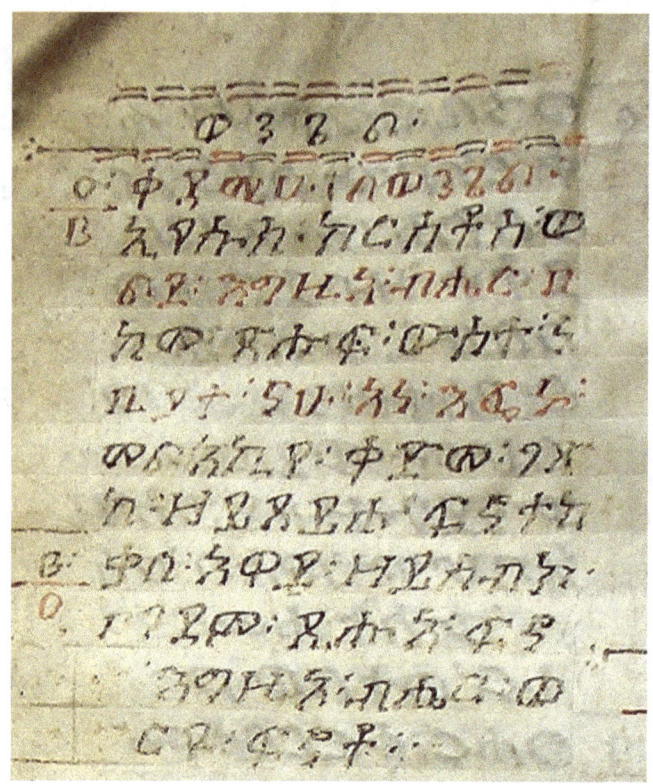

5. Fourth Order (4°)

The fourth order consists of the consonants plus the long vowel [ā]. Before explaining the characteristic feature of this order, it is necessary to step back and consider the basic shapes of the Gəʿəz signs, which can be divided into four categories:

(i) signs with one 'leg'—ገ, ኅ, ነ, ፐ, ቀ, ተ, and የ

(ii) signs with two 'legs'— አ, በ, ከ, ለ, ጸ, ሰ, ደ, and ዘ

(iii) signs with three 'legs'—ሐ and ጠ

(iv) 'legless' signs—ዐ, ደ, ፀ, ፈ, ህ, መ, ረ, ሠ, and ወ

These are represented in the table below:

1 leg	2 legs	3 legs	legless
ገ	አ	ሐ	ዐ
ኅ	በ	ጠ	ደ
ነ	ከ		ፀ
ፐ	ለ		ፈ
ቀ	ጸ		ህ
ተ	ሰ		መ
የ	ደ		ረ
	ዘ		ሠ
			ወ

In general, the legged signs are regular while the legless signs are irregular. It is not always the case that legged/legless and regular/irregular correspond as clearly as in, for example, the 3°, but these distinctions will help in forming the various irregular signs in the remaining orders. Let us now look at the 4°.

አ - ʾā	ጋ - gā	ላ - lā	ቃ - qā	ታ - tā
ዓ - ʿā	ሃ - hā	ማ - mā	ራ - rā	ጣ - ṭā
ባ - bā	ሓ - ḥā	ና - nā	ሳ - sā	ዋ - wā
ዳ - dā	ኃ - ḫā	ፓ - pā	ሣ - śā	ያ - yā
ፃ - ḍā	ካ - kā	ጳ - ṗā	ጻ - ṣā	ዛ - zā
ፋ - fā				

The characteristic feature of the 4° is present in 2- and 3-legged signs and is a lengthening of the *rightmost leg* of the sign—ባ *bā*. The regular signs are as follows:

አ - ʾā   ባ - bā   ሓ - ḫā   ላ - lā   ሳ - sā

ካ - kā   ጳ - ṗā   ጣ - ṭā   ጻ - ṣā   ዛ - zā

The single-legged signs, with the exception of ኒ, form the 4° *by swinging their leg sharply to the left*, e.g., ቃ *qā*.

ጋ - gā   ኃ - ḫā   ና - nā   ፓ - pā   ቃ - qā   ታ - tā

Note: the 4° shape *nā* - ና is completely arbitrary and must simply be memorized:

The remaining signs, all legless, can be further divided into two groups: (i) those who take a leg on their right side or in their center; and

ዓ - ʿā   ዳ - dā   ፃ - ḍā   ሃ - hā   ማ - mā   ሣ - śā   ዋ - wā

(ii) those who have arbitrary shapes:

ፉ - fā   ራ - rā   ያ - yā

Note that ፉ and ፋ are very similar. As was pointed out earlier, the vertical leg on ፋ leans leftward while that of ፉ is perfectly horizontal. This difference should be kept in mind. Also, ያ is somewhat reminiscent of the single-legged 4° with the left-sweeping leg.

Labialized consonants

The labialized consonants in the 4° have an addition similar to that of the 3°, but here it is added to the bottom of the sign. Note that ጓ is slightly deformed because of this addition.

ጓ - $g^w\bar{a}$ ኋ - $\underline{h}^w\bar{a}$ ኳ - $k^w\bar{a}$ ቋ - $q^w\bar{a}$

EXERCISES

A. Read aloud:

አብያት፡አድባር፡አሕማር፡ገዳም፡አሕዛብ፡ፍናው፡ሰማይ፡ታሕተ፡መኳንንት፡ቃል፡መላእክት፡

ጸሐፊ፡አዋልድ፡አምታት፡አላ፡ጽባሕ፡አዕጻደ፡ክርስቲያን፡ለያልይ፡አምዳር፡በሐውርት፡መዓልት

B. Write the following words in script:

mawāʿəl . māʾkal . lāʿla . maṣāḥəft . ləssān . bāraka . ʾəbrāwiyān . ḫabāwəz .

māy . bərhān . ḫaṭāwəʾ . bāḥr . maśāwəʿ . kāhn . p̣āp̣ās .

C. Circle every 4° order letter in the manuscript selection below:

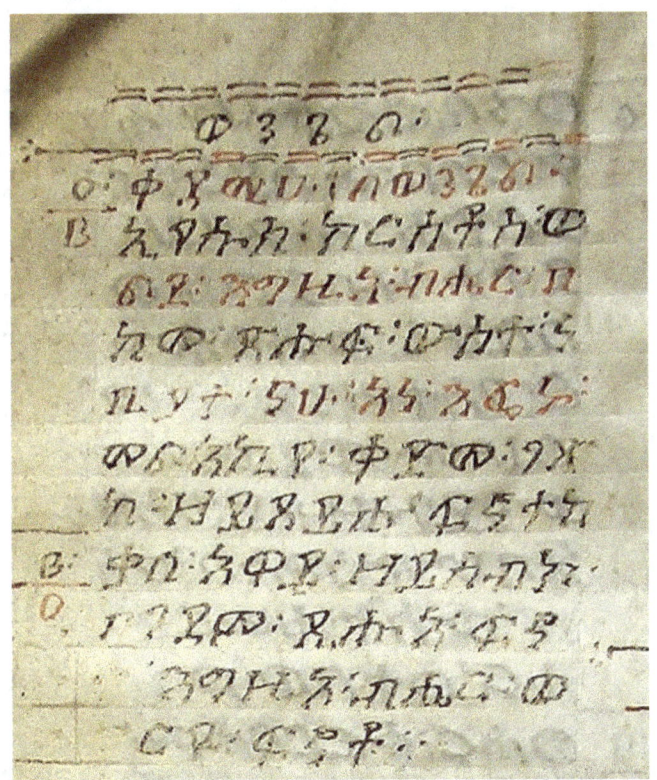

6. Fifth Order (5°)

The 5° poses no problem in that it has hardly any arbitrary variations. The order's characteristic feature—a circular addition to the *bottom right* of the sign is present in all of the 26 signs. The legged signs simply have the addition on their bottom right i.e. ቤ *be*, while the legless signs have the addition on their prosthetic leg i.e. ፄ *we*.

ኤ - ʾe	ጌ - ge	ሌ - le	ቄ - qe	ቴ - te
ዐ̄ - ʿe	ሔ - he	ሜ - me	ሬ - re	ጤ - ṭe
ቤ - be	ሐ̄ - ḥe	ኔ - ne	ሴ - se	ፄ - we
ዴ - de	ኄ - ḫe	ፔ - pe	ሤ - śe	ዬ - ye
ጄ - ḍe	ኬ - ke	ጴ - ṗe	ጼ - ṣe	ዜ - ze
ፌ - fe				

From the legless signs, note that ሬ and ፌ behave rather regularly. The only truly irregular sign in 5° is ዬ which has the addition in the center right rather than on the bottom right.

Labialized consonants

As with the other signs, the labialized consonants have a circular addition on their bottom right, as well as a leftward stroke.

ጔ - g^we ኌ - $ḫ^we$ ኴ - k^we ቌ - q^we

EXERCISES

A. Read aloud:

ቤት፡አርዌ፡እግዚአብሔር፡እስራኤል፡ምሴት፡ሌሊት፡ሤጠ፡ብሔር፡ወንጌል፡ዬገኒ፡ሤመ፡፡

B. Write the following words in script:

wadʾa . malʾak. samāy . bet . wangelu . ʾəmməneki

C. Circle every 5° order letter in the manuscript selection below:

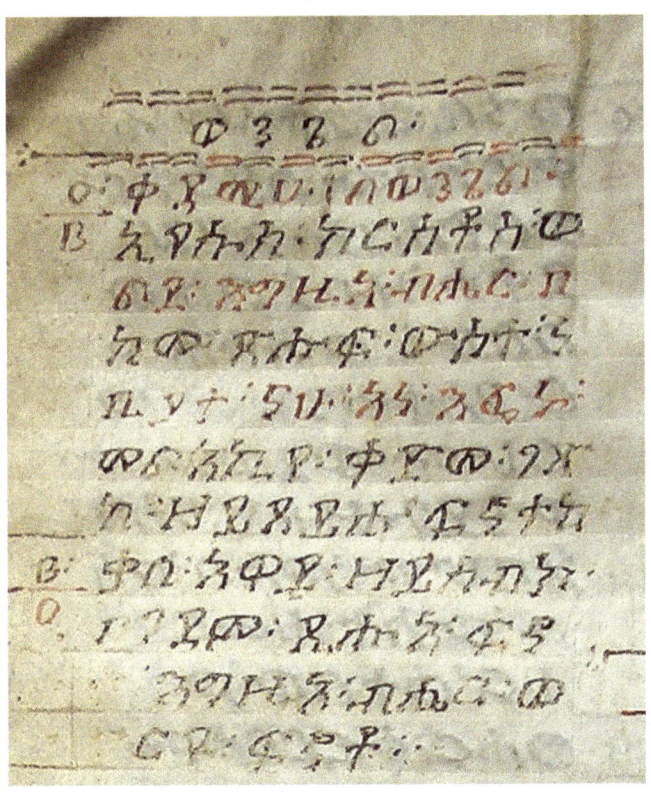

7. Seventh order (7°)

The seventh order represents the consonants plus the long vowel [o]. It is not as irregular as the 6°, but it nonetheless has several modifications.

አ - ʾo	ጎ - go	ሎ - lo	ቆ - qo	ቶ - to
ዖ - ʿo	ሀ - ho	ሞ - mo	ሮ - ro	ጦ - ṭo
ቦ - bo	ሐ - ḥo	ኖ - no	ሶ - so	ዎ - wo
ዶ - do	ኆ - ḫo	ፖ - po	ሦ - śo	ዮ - yo
ዷ - ḍo	ኮ - ko	ጶ - ṗo	ጾ - ṣo	ዞ - zo
ፎ - fo				

Its characteristic feature, present on most characters, is the lengthening of the left leg:

አ - ʾo	ቦ - bo	ሐ - ḥo	ኮ - ko	ሶ - so
ጶ - ṗo	ጾ - ṣo	ጦ - ṭo	ዞ - zo	

Legless characters are divided in their formations, but the majority of them take an additional leg in the center that is straight in the case of ሞ and slanted to the left for the remaining signs:

ዖ - ʿo ዶ - do ዷ - ḍo ሞ - mo ፖ - po ሦ - śo ዎ - wo

A third group of signs take a circular addition, like that of the 5°, but here it is on the top (right) portion of the sign:

ሀ - ho	ሎ - lo	ሮ - ro	ቆ - qo	ቶ - to
ፎ - fo	ኆ - ḫo	ኖ - no		

The two remaining signs do not follow any of these forms, but instead take additions similar to those of the 6°:

ጎ - go   ዮ - yo

Lesson 1—The Writing System

EXERCISES

A. Read aloud:

ሐረ፡በ፡ሮጸ፡ፍኖት፡ዮሐንስ፡ኮነ፡ሞት፡ሞተ፡ዮናዊያን፡ኢትዮጵያ፡ሃይማኖት፡ሰበ፡ኤጲስ፡ቆጶስ፡ዲያቆን፡ ጣያት፡ሞአ፡ቆመ።

B. Write the following words in script:

ḥoru . betomu . soṭa . ʾəmḫabena . ḫabehomu . ʾabdəntihomu . laʾaḫawihomu .

C. Circle every 7° order letter in the manuscript selection below:

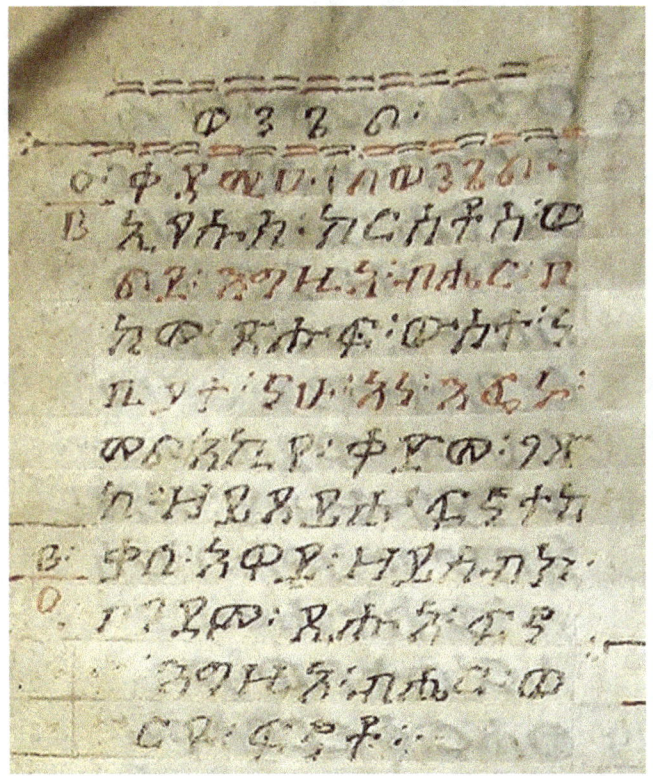

21

LESSON 2
COMMON PREPOSITIONS

Most prepositions are written as free or unbound words:

ውስተ፡ባሕር   'in/into/to the sea'   ምስለ፡ኢየሱስ.   'with Jesus'

A small set of very common prepositions, though, are not free, but cliticized or bound directly to the following noun.

በ   'in, with' (location, agent, manner)
ለ   'to, for' (benefit, advantage)
እም   'from' (source, agent)

The clitic prepositions are always written as a unit with the following word:

በገዳም   'in the wilderness' (Mk 1:3)
ለእግዚአ፡ብሔር   'for God' (Mk 1:24)
እምሰማይ   'from heaven' (Mk 1:11)

The preposition እም also has a free (unbound) form: እምነ. This free form is typically used when the following word begins with a bilabial consonant, such as:

እምነ፡መቃብር   'from the tombs' (Mk 5:2)

However, there also examples of the preposition እም in which the ም combines with the initial ም of the noun, such as:

እምኩራብ   'from the synagogue' (Mk 1:29) [for *እም–ምኩራብ]

Vocabulary 2

በ	in	እግዚአ፡ብሔር	God
ድኅረ	behind, after	ብእሲ	man, person
ኀበ	to, by, near	ብእሲት	woman
ከመ	like, that	ኀጢአት	sin
ለ	to	ልብስ	clothes, garment
ቅድመ	before	ማይ	water
ውስተ	in, into	መንፈስ	spirit
		ወልድ	son
		ወንጌል	gospel

Lesson 2—Common Prepositions

EXERCISES

A. Read aloud the phrases below and then translate them into English.

1. ለማይ፡

2. ቅድመ፡መንፈስ፡

3. ውስተ፡ነጢአት፡

4. ከመ፡እግዚአ፡ብሔር፡

5. ኀበ፡ብእሲ፡

6. ድኅረ፡ወልድ፡

7. በወንጌል፡

8. ውስተ፡ማይ፡

9. ኀበ፡ልብስ፡

10. ለእግዚአ፡ብሔር፡

11. ከመ፡መንፈስ፡

12. ቅድመ፡ልብስ፡

13. በነጢአት፡

14. ድኅረ፡ወልድ፡

15. ለብእሲ፡

B. Produce the phrases below in Gəʿəz.

1. near the water

2. before God

3. after the Spirit

4. into the clothes

5. like the son

6. to the woman

7. like sin

8. behind God

9. in the Gospel

10. near the clothes

C. In the text below, identify each of the prepositions and nouns listed in your vocabulary (in some cases, the word may end slightly differently; don't worry–if it looks close, you're probably correct!).

Note: All proper nouns are in red font and not included in the vocabulary—their meanings can almost always be deduced from their sounds and context.

Lesson 3
Forming Clauses without a Verb

Like many Semitic languages, Gəʿəz allows the creation of a simple copular clause without an overt verb. These clauses are all "copular," that is, verb "be" is simply missing.

ወሲሳዩ፡ ___ አንበጣ፡ወምዐረ፡ጸደና፡ 'and his food (was) locust and wild honey' (Mk 1:6)

እስመ፡መሠግራን፡ ___ እሙንቱ፨ 'because fishermen (were) they' (Mk 1:16)

Vocabulary 3

እም	from, (more) than	ፍኖት	path, road
አመ	at the time of	ገዳም	wilderness
እንበለ	without, except	ገመል	camel
እንተ	through, via, to	ክርስቶስ	Christ
በእንተ	about, because	መልአክ	angel, messenger
ዲበ	upon, over, against	ነቢይ	prophet
ላዕለ	on, above, against	ሲሳይ	food
ምስለ	with	ቃል	voice, sound
ወ-	and		

Exercises

A. Read the phrases below—aloud—and then translate them into English.

1. ወነቢይ፡ነበ፡ገመል፡

2. መንፈስ፡በገዳም፡

3. ሲሳይ፡ምስለ፡ክርስቶስ፡

4. ፍኖት፡ለእግዚአ፡ብሔር፡

5. ጎጢአት፡በእንተ፡ብእሲት፡

6. ቃል፡እምነ፡መልአክ፡

7. ነቢይ፡እንበለ፡ሲሳይ፡

8. ክርስቶስ፡ዲበ፡ኀጢአት፡

9. ማይ፡ድኀረ፡ገመል፡

10. መንፈስ፡እምእግዚአ፡ብሔር፡

B. Produce the phrases below in Gəʿəz.

　1. The prophet is in the water

　2. The Spirit was against the man

　3. Because the angel was on the road

　4. Christ was without sin

　5. A sound was from the camel

　6. Christ was in the wilderness without food

　7. God was with the son

　8. The Gospel was through the Spirit

　9. The food was upon the clothes

　10. God was above the prophet

C. In the text below, identify each of the prepositions and nouns listed in your vocabulary (again, the word may end slightly differently; don't worry—if it looks close, you're probably correct!).

LESSON 4
SUBJECT PRONOUNS

Personal pronouns are essentially a bundle of agreement features that serve to both <u>fill a syntactic position</u> (e.g., subject) and <u>refer back to an established entity</u> (i.e., anaphora).

The personal pronouns below are the basic subject pronouns.

	Singular		**Plural**	
3M	ውእቱ	he, it	እሙንቱ	they
3F	ይእቲ	she, it	እማንቱ	they
2M	አንተ	you	አንትሙ	you
2F	አንቲ	you	አንትን	you
1C	አነ	I	ንሕነ	we

When these pronouns are used with a verb, they duplicate the agreement features of the verb (e.g., a 3MS pronoun goes with a verb that is inflected for 3ms).

ንሕነ፡ሰማዕናሁ፡   '<u>we</u> heard him' (Mk 14:58)

በእፎ፡ስእነ፡<u>ንሕነ</u>፡አውፅአቶ፡፡ 'Why were <u>we</u> unable to drive him out?' (Mk 9:28)

When subject pronouns are used in null copula clauses, the typical word order is often *Noun-Pronoun*:

ወበ፡እለ፡ይቤሉ፡ነቢይ፡ውእቱ፡፡ 'and there were those said, "A prophet (is) <u>he</u>"' (Mk 6:15)

ሰብአ፡ሲሮፌኒቃስ፡ይእቲ፡፡   'of Syro-Phoenician people (was) <u>she</u>' (Mk 7:26)

እስመ፡መሠግራን፡እሙንቱ፡፡   'because fishermen (were) <u>they</u>' (Mk 1:16)

እስመ፡እለ፡ክርስቶስ፡አንትሙ፡፡ 'because those of Christ (are) <u>you</u>' (Mk 9:41)

The opposite order, *Pronoun-Noun*, indicates emphasis on the pronoun.

አንተኑ፡ክርስቶስ፡ወልዱ፡ለቡሩክ፡፡ '(Are) <u>you</u> Christ, the son of the Blessed One?' (Mk 14:61)

አነ፡ውእቱ፡   '<u>I</u> (am) he' (Mk 13:6)

The 3rd person pronouns are also sometimes used as <u>pronominal copulas</u>. That is, the pronoun no longer refers back to another noun; rather, it functions as a substitute for the verb "to be". When they function this way, they typically occur <u>between</u> the subject and the other noun.

አንተ፡ውእቱ፡ወልድየ፡   'you (are) my son' (Mk 1:11)
ዛቲ፡ይእቲ፡ቀዳሚት፡ትእዛዝ፡   'this (is) the first commandment' (Mk 12:30)
መኑ፡ውእቱ እምየ፡ወአኅዊየ፡ 'Who (are) my mother and my brothers?' (Mk 3:33)

Although the pronominal copula sometimes agrees in number and gender with the subject, there is a tendency for the 3MS ውእቱ to be work as an uninflected copula.

Vocabulary 4

እንዘ	while, as	አብ	father
እስመ	because, that	እኁ	brother
ህየ	there	አሚር	day, time
መንገለ	to, toward	ዕለት	day
-ኒ	also, too; even, indeed	ፈለግ	river
ሶበ	if, then, immediately	ሐመር	boat
ዘ-	that, which, who	ሌሊት	night
		መሥግር	fisherman
		ሰማይ	sky, heaven

EXERCISES

A. Read the phrases below—aloud—and then translate them into English.

1. እንዘ፡አንተ፡ህየ፡በሐመር፡

2. ሶበ፡እማንቱ፡በማይ፡

3. እስመ፡ንሕነ፡ውስተ፡ፈለግ፡

4. ውእቱ፡አብ፡

5. እኁ፡ውእቱ፡

6. አንተኒ፡መሥግር፡ከመ፡ነቢይ፡

7. ውእቱ፡ዘመንገለ፡ገዳም፡

8. አነ፡ዲበ፡ፍኖት፡በሌሊት፡

9. አንተ፡እግዚአ፡ብሔር፡ላዕለ፡ሰማይ፡

10. ይእቲ፡በሐመር፡በዕለት፡

B. Produce the phrases below in Gəʿəz.

1. You are a father who is a brother

2. She was upon the camel on the road

3. It is a voice from the heavens

4. Because we were in the boat in the daytime

5. They (M) are without food and without water

6. You (FP) also were with Christ in the wilderness

7. While he was behind the fisherman

8. You are an angel from God through the Spirit

9. It is the gospel about Christ

10. She was against sin

C. In the text below, identify any subject pronoun and any vocabulary you have learned so far.

LESSON 5
THE BASICS OF THE PERFECT VERB

Like most nouns, most Gəʽəz verbs are formed from the three consonant root ($C_1C_2C_3$) overlaid with a pattern of vowels that indicate semantic features and inflectional suffixes that indicate person-gender-number.

There are *six* basic verb conjugations—the Perfect, the Imperfect, the Subjunctive, and Imperative, the Converb, and the Infinitive. Setting aside the Converb and the Infinitive, the other four fall into two groups: 1) the *Perfect* and 2) those based on the *Imperfect* (Imperfect, Subjunctive, and Imperative).

Since the Perfect verb carries along the story line of narrative, we will begin with this conjugation.

Form

The basic form of the Perfect is called the "G" derivation. Even when we learn other derivations, know that all the person-gender-number inflectional endings remain constant. If you learn them well, you will always be able to identify a Perfect verb.

The ten inflected forms of the G Perfect, using the root ን-በ-ረ, are below:

3MS	ውእቱ	ነበረ	he sat	3MP	እሙንቱ ነበሩ	they sat
3FS	ይእቲ	ነበረት	she sat	3FP	እማንቱ ነበራ	they sat
2MS	አንተ	ነበርከ	you sat	2MP	አንትሙ ነበርክሙ	you sat
2FS	አንቲ	ነበርኪ	you sat	2FP	አንትን ነበርክን	you sat
1CS	አነ	ነበርኩ	I sat	1CP	ንሕነ ነበርነ	we sat

Note: Remember that verbs are typically stressed on the next-to-last syllable. Only the 2FP form is stressed on the final syllable, and this is marked by the ˙ mark.

There is a variation on this for some roots—instead of the 3-syllable ነበረ pattern, they follow a two-syllable pattern: ገብረ. This effects only the 3rd person forms: ገብረ, ገብረት, ገብሩ, and ገብራ.

The verb's inflectional endings indicate the person-gender-number features of the implied subject (e.g., 'he, she, they'). A subject pronoun (Lesson 4) or an overt subject noun are unnecessary.

When an overt subject is present, such as a noun ("Jesus") or a subject pronoun ("he"), the verb and its subject normally agree in person, gender, and number features: "Jesus" is matched with a 3MS verb, "kingdom" with a 3FS verb, and "sinners and tax collectors" with a 3MP verb.

መጽአ:ኢየሱስ:እምናዝሬት:. 'Jesus came(3MS) from Nazareth' (Mk 1:9)

ቀርበት:መንግሥተ:ሰማያት:. 'the kingdom of heaven has come near (3FS)' (Mk 1:15)

ብዙኃን:ኃጣአን:ወመጸብሓን:ረፈቁ:ምስለ:ኢየሱስ:ወአርዳኢሁ:

    'many sinners and tax collectors reclined(3MP) with Jesus and his disciples' (Mk 2:15)

Function

The Gəʿəz Perfect signals the "perfective aspect," which means that is takes a whole of view of an action of event (not an "in-process" view, such as 'he was x-ing'). It also defaults to the past temporal setting, and so can often be translated by the English simple past ('he ate, wrote', etc.).

Depending on the surrounding events, the Perfect may also cover what in English is the present perfect ("he has come") or even a past perfect ("it had come near").

Vocabulary 5

አኀዘ	he took, seized	ተለወ	he followed
በጽሐ	he arrived	ወረደ	he went down
ኀደገ	he left; he forgave		
መጽአ[2]	he came, it occurred	አርዌ	animal, wild beast
ነበረ	he sat, dwelt	ባሕር	sea
ሰበከ	he preached	ጊዜ	time, season, hour
ቀርበ	he approached, was near	ሐቅል	plain, wilderness
ርእየ[3]	he saw	መንግሥት	kingdom
ረከበ	he found	ርግብ	dove
ሠምረ	he delighted in, approved of		

---

[2] On verbs whose third root consonant is a guttural, see the Appendix, §C.3.
[3] On verbs whose third root consonant is ው or ይ, see the Appendix, §C.6.

Lesson 5—The Basics of the Perfect Verb

EXERCISES

A. Read the phrases below—aloud—and then translate them into English.

1. መጽአ፡ነቢይ፡ወሰበከ፡በመንፈስ፡

2. ገመል፡ዘሠመረ፡ብእሲ፡

3. ነበረ፡እግዚአ፡ብሔር፡በሰማይ፡

4. ተለዉ፡ድንግረ፡ክርስቶስ፡

5. ሲሳይ፡ውማይ፡ዘረከብነ፡

6. መሥግር፡ዘወረደ፡ውስተ፡ሐመር፡

7. በጽሐ፡በሐቅል፡እንተ፡ፍኖት፡

8. ርግብ፡ዘርእየት፡በሰማይ፡

9. ኃደጉ*፡እምፈለግ፡ወመጻእኩ፡ለባሕር፡

10. ሐመር፡ዘአኀዙ፡አብ፡እኑ፡እምነ፡መሥግር፡

* When the Perfect endings -ከ, -ኪ, -ኩ, -ክሙ, and -ክን, are added to a root ending in ግ or ቅ, the ending assimilates to the root consonant, e.g., ኃደጉ for ኃደግኩ (thus, the form ኃደጉ is ambiguous and may represent 3MP or 1CS).

B. Produce the phrases below in Gəʿəz.

1. They (M) approached near the animal

2. She arrived in the kingdom

3. You (MS) dwelt by the sea

4. The angel that we saw at night

5. The season the prophet preached in the wilderness

6. The spirit left from the man

7. At the time that fisherman went down into the boat

8. The son that God delighted in

9. The wild beast that seized the food

10. They (F) followed after the prophet

Lesson 5—The Basics of the Perfect Verb

C. Locate any Perfect verb in the text below and identify the person-number-gender of the form. If possible, identify the subject of the verb.

LESSON 6
THE VERB ብ-ህ-ል

The Perfect paradigm for the root ብ-ህ-ል 'to say' has been replaced by a unique but frequently occurring form, which we will label the <u>Preterite</u>. The paradigm is below:

3MS	ውእቱ	ይቤ	he said	3MP	እሙንቱ ይቤሉ	they said
3FS	ይእቲ	ትቤ	she said	3FP	እማንቱ ይቤላ	they said
2MS	አንተ	ትቤ	you said	2MP	አንትሙ ትቤሉ	you said
2FS	አንቲ	ትቤሊ	you said	2FP	አንትን ትቤላ	you said
1CS	አነ	እቤ	I said	1CP	ንሕነ ንቤ	we said

The forms reflect two sound losses: 1) the loss of the second root consonant -ህ- between vowels; and 2) the loss of the final root consonant -ል. This verb occurs very often in narrative texts to introduce direct speech and it always has a simple past tense meaning (e.g., "he said").

ወይቤሎሙ፡ኢየሱስ፡ንዑ፡ትልዉኒ፡ 'and Jesus <u>said</u> to them: "Come, follow me."' (Mk 1:17)

ወጸሐፍትኒ፡እለ፡ወረዱ፡እምኢየሩሳሌም፡ይቤሉ፡ብዔል፡ዜቡል፡አኀዞ፡
    'and also scribes who had come down from Jerusalem <u>said</u>: "Beelzebul has seized him!"' (Mk 3:22)

Vocabulary 6

ቦአ [ብ-ው-እ][4]	he came, entered	ብሔር	region, district
ሐረ [ሐ-ው-ር]	he went	ጋኔን	demon
ወፅአ	he left, exited	መሀርት	teaching
ይቤ [ብ-ህ-ል]	he said	መኰንን	judge
		ምኵራብ	synagogue, temple
በበይናቲ	between	ነገር	speech, thing
መኑ	who	ሰንበት	sabbath
ምንት	what, why	ጸሐፊ	scribe
		ትእዛዝ	commandment, law

---

[4] On verbs whose second root consonant is ው or ይ, see the Appendix, §C.5. On verbs that end in a guttural, se Appendix §C.3.

Lesson 6—The Verb ብሁል

EXERCISES

A. Read the phrases below—aloud—and then translate them into English.

1. ሐረ፡ጸሓፊ፡በምኵራብ፡በሰንበት፡

2. ወዕአ፡ጋኔን፡እምብእሲ፡

3. ነገር፡ዘሰበከ፡ነቢይ፡በሐቅል፡

4. ወይቤ፡መኰንን፡መኑ፡በኡ፡በማይ፡

5. ምንት፡በጸሕከሙ፡ምስለ፡ጽሓፊ፡

6. ምንት፡ትቤ፡በእንተ፡መህሮት፡

7. እንዘ፡ነበረ፡ጸሓፊ፡ወወረደ፡መሠግር፡ውስተ፡ሐመር፡

8. ወሰብ፡ወዕአ፡እምብሔር፡

9. ወወረደ፡ርግብ፡እምሰማይ፡ወነበረ፡በበይናቲ፡አብ፡ወእኁ፡

10. ወይቤ፡ክርስቶስ፡ትእዛዝ፡እምእግዚአ፡ብሔር፡

B. Produce the phrases below in Gəʿəz.

1. You (MP) entered into the synagogue before the judge

2. The commandment that the woman delighted in

3. Why did I follow after the prophet?

4. Who went with the scribe?

5. The thing that we found on the Sabbath in the the synagogue

6. The demon said, "Why have you (FP) followed after Christ?"

7. She also entered into the region and immediately went to judge

8. Why did you (MP) go toward the wild beast at night?

9. They (MP) left from the kingdom because of the commandment from God

10. We said, "Because we preached about Christ."

C. Look for each occurrence of the verb ብሀለ below. Also identify each of the new vocabulary words.

LESSON 7
(FORMALLY) INTRODUCING NOUNS

Gəʿəz nouns reflect the common Semitic morphology features of two genders (masculine and feminine) and two numbers (singular and plural).

Gender

The gender features of a given noun may reflect biological sex, so that nouns relating to male creatures are masculine and nouns relating to female creatures are feminine. However, many real-world entities (e.g., city, mountain) lack a biological sex, even though they are assigned a morphological gender feature.

Grammatical gender is thus essentially a morpho-syntactic agreement property of language used to signal relationships between words in a phrase or clause; moreover, it is rarely predictable and can often only be determined by looking for cases where the word is in agreement with a verb or modifier (e.g., adjective, demonstrative pronoun).

ቀርበት፡መንግሥተ፡ሰማያት፡	'the kingdom (FS) of heaven has come (FS)' (Mk 1:15)
ዝንቱ፡ትምህርት፡	'this (MS) teaching (MS)' (Mk 1:27)

Because the gender of nouns is largely unpredictable and also because the gender of a given (inanimate) noun may differ from text to text, it will *not* be noted in vocabulary lists. It is sufficient to understand that gender is a feature of the morpho-syntax of the language.

Number

Many Semitic languages have a three-way number distinction: singular, dual, and plural. The dual ceased to appear in Gəʿəz, leaving only the singular and plural relevant noun features. Grammatical number in nouns typically indicates the singular or plural count of a noun (i.e., is there *just one* or *more than one*?).

ብእሲ	'man'	ሰብእ	'men, people'
ነቢይ	'prophet'	ነቢያት	'prophets'
አርዌ	'animal'	አራዊት	'animals'
መልአክ	'angel'	መላእክት	'angels'
ጋኔን	'demon'	አጋንንት	'demons'

Besides indicating the count feature of a noun, grammatical number also functions as a morph-syntactic agreement feature: a Gəʿəz noun often (but not always!) agrees in number with any modifiers (e.g, adjectives, demonstratives); and if a noun is the subject of a verb, the noun and the verb typically agree in number features.

| አጋንንት፡ርኩሳን፡ | 'unclean (MP) demons (MP)' (Mk 1:27) |
| ጸሐፍት፡ይነብሩ፡ወሐለዩ፡ | 'scribes (MP) were sitting (MP) and thinking (MP)' (Mk 2:6) |

But note that lack of number agreement does occur:

| ዝንቱ፡አሕዛብ፡፡ | 'these (MS!) people (MP!)' (Mk 8:4) |

Finally, as you have undoubtedly already surmised, there is no definite or indefinite article in Gəʿəz. The definiteness of a noun can only be determined from context.

| ወልድ | 'a son' | or | 'the son' |
| ፍኖት | 'a path' | | 'the path' |

Vocabulary 7

አዘዘ	he ordered, commanded	አኮ	no, not
ገሠጸ	he rebuked, chastised	-ኒ	also, too; even, indeed
ሀለወ[5]	he existed, was	ኵል	all, every, each
መሀረ	he taught	-ኑ	[interrogative marker]
		-ስ	but, however; indeed

EXERCISES

A. Read the phrases below—aloud—and then translate them into English.

1. ገሠጸት፡ኵሎ፡ብእሲ፡

2. አዘዝከ፡መሠግረ፡በእንተ፡ሐመር፡

---

[5] On verbs whose third root consonant is ው or ይ, see the Appendix, §C.6. Note that the third singular forms of ሀ-ል-ው often exhibit the contraction of the final syllable, e.g., ሀሎ.

3. ው፡እቴስ፡መኮንን፡አኮ፡ጸሐፊ፡

4. መሀርነ፡ትእዛዘ፡በሰንበት፡

5. መኮንንሂ፡ወፅአ፡እምኮራብ፡

6. ወሀለዉ፡ዮሐንስ፡ወኢየሱስ፡በገዳም፡

7. በጸሕክሙ፡ንብ፡ፈለግ፡በሌሊት፡

8. ወርእዩ፡አርዌ፡በፍኖት፡

9. ወቦአ፡በብሔር፡ምስለ፡ጋኔን፡

10. ነበርኪ፡ምስለ፡ጸሐፊ፡በምኮራብ፡

B. Use the Gloss Lexicon to find and insert the plural forms of the vocabulary nouns below; translate both singular and plural.

Singular	Translation	Plural	Translation
ብእሲ			
ብእሲት			
ኀጢአት			
ልብስ			
ማይ			
መንፈስ			
ወልድ			
ፍኖት			
ገዳም			

Lesson 7—(Formally) Introducing Nouns

ገመል			
መልአክ			
ነቢይ			
ቃል			
አብ			
እኁ			
ዕለት			
ፈለግ			
ሐመር			
ሌሊት			
መሠግር			
ሰማይ			
አርዌ			
ባሕር			
ጊዜ			
ሐቅል			
መንግሥት			
ርግብ			
ምኵራብ			
መኰንን			
ሰንበት			
ብሔር			
ትእዛዝ			
ነገር			
ጸሐፊ			
ጋኔን			

C. Find examples of nouns for which you can clearly determine the gender or number and explain how you determined this.

LESSON 8
THE BASICS OF THE IMPERFECT VERB

As you learned in Lesson 6, four of the six verbal conjugations in Gəʿəz fall into two groups: 1) the Perfect and 2) those based on the Imperfect (Imperfect, Subjunctive, and Imperative). In Lesson 6, you learned the basic Perfect verb. In this lesson you will learn the basic Imperfect verb.

Form

As with the Perfect verb, the basic form of the Imperfect is called the "G" derivation. And also, regardless the derivation of the Imperfect, all the person-gender-number inflectional affixes are identical. So, if you learn them well, you'll always be able to identify an Imperfect verb.

The ten inflected forms of the G Imperfect, using the root ነ-በ-ረ, are below:

3MS	ውእቱ	ይነብር	he will sit	3MP	እሙንቱ	ይነብሩ	they will sit
3FS	ይእቲ	ትነብር	she will sit	3FP	እማንቱ	ይነብራ	they will sit
2MS	አንተ	ትነብር	you will sit	2MP	አንትሙ	ትነብሩ	you will sit
2FS	አንቲ	ትነብሪ	you will sit	2FP	አንትን	ትነብራ	you will sit
1CS	አነ	እነብር	I will sit	1CP	ንሕነ	ንነብር	we will sit

Functions

The Imperfect verb is essentially an imperfective aspect verb, which means that it is typically associated with *durative, habitual, ongoing* events or actions. As the counterpart to the Perfect, the Imperfect has a default setting of the *non-past* (i.e., present or future) time frame. However, when other cues (such as the use of a preceding Perfect verb) set the time of a situation in the past, the Imperfect may continue this but with durative or habitual semantics.

(1) Future:

ወውእቱሰ፡ያጠምቀክሙ፡በመንፈስ፡ቅዱስ፡

'but he <u>will baptize</u> you with the Holy Spirit' (Mk 1:8)

(2) Durative (time setting from context, or by እንዘ 'while'):

ወይነብር፡ሰብእ፡ብዙኅ፡ምስሌሁ፡ 'and many people <u>were sitting</u> with him' (Mk 3:32)

ወይቤልዎ፡ኵሉ፡ይኀሥእከ። 'and they told him, "Everyone <u>is seeking</u> you!" (Mk 1:37)

ወእንዘ፡የኀልፍ፡መንገለ፡ባሕረ፡ገሊላ፡ረከበሙ፡ለስምዖን፡ወለእንድርያስ፨

'and <u>while he was passing</u> toward the Sea of Galilee, he found Simon and Andrew' (Mk 1:16)

(3) Habitual (time setting established from context):

ወስእነ፡በዊአ፡ሀገር፡ክሡተ፨አላ፡አፍአ፡ገዳም፡ይነብር፡ወይመጽኡ፡ኀቤሁ፡እምኵልሄ፨

'and (Jesus) was not able to enter a city openly but <u>would sit</u> out in the country and (people) <u>would come</u> to him from everywhere' (Mk 1:45)

Negated Verb Note

Gəʿəz disprefers two consecutive variations of አ and so whenever a 1CS Imperfect verb (i.e., the form prefixed with እ- or አ-) or any form of a CG (see Lesson 11) Perfect beginning with አ- is also negated by the prefixed neative ኢ-, the እ- of the verb form becomes ይ, የ, or even ያ, resulting in a form that can be confusing and sometimes easily be mistaken for a 3rd-person verb.

ወይቤሎ፡ጴጥሮስ፡ለእመ፡ኵሎሙ፡ክህዱከ፡አንሰ፡ኢይክሕደከ፨

'and Peter said, "Even if all of them deny you, <u>I will not deny you</u>!"' (Mk 14:29)

ወይቤሎሙ፡ግሙራ፡ኢያንበብክሙ፡ዘገብረ፡ዳዊት፡አመ፡ርኅበ፡ውእቱሂ፡ወእለሂ፡ምስሌሁ፨

'and he said to them: <u>Have you never read</u> what David did when he was hungry, he and those who were with him? ' (Mk 2:25)

Vocabulary 8

ፈፀነ	he had a fever	እድ	hand (PL እደው)
ፈወሰ	he cured, he healed	አንቀጽ	door, gate (PL አናቅጽ)
ነገረ	he said, told	ቤት	house (PL አብያት)
		ፀሐይ	sun (PL ፀሐያት)
ኢ-	not	ፈፀንት	fever
ጥቀ	very, extremely	ሀገር	city (PL አህጉር)
ብዙኅ	many, much	ሐማት	mother-in-law (PL ሐማታት)
(F ብዝኅት, MP ብዙኃን, FP ብዙኃት)		ጽባሕ	morning (PL ጽባሓት)

EXERCISES

A. Read the phrases below—aloud—and then translate them into English.

1. ትነብር፡ቤት፨

2. ይበጽሓ፡ውስተ፡ሀገር፨

Lesson 8—The Basics of the Imperfect Verb

3. አንተ፡ትሰብከ፡በአንቀጽ፡

4. ንሕነ፡ንነግር፡ጊዜ፡ለሐማት፡

5. ይአኀዙ፡አርዌ፡

6. ይወርድኑ፡ብእሲ፡ለአንቀጽ፡

7. ይነድግ፡እግዚአ፡ብሔር፡ብዙኅ፡ኀጢአተ፡

8. ኢይመጽእ፡ጽባሕ፡ቅድመ፡ፀሓይ፡

9. ይወፅእ፡መኮንን፡እምብሔር፡

10. ትመጽእ፡ፈፀንት፡በሌሊት፡

B. Produce the phrases below in Gəʿəz.

1. The woman will have a fever many days

2. Christ will heal in the house

3. They will tell the teaching to the scribe

4. The judge will not rebuke the prophet

5. We will preach in very many cities

6. At the time morning arrived, the fever had left

7. I will seize the garment by hand

8. You (FP) will leave from the city through the gate

9. The angel will tell the commandment to the city

10. Why will you (MP) not enter into the house?

C. Find all the Imperfect verbs in the three previous texts and the new one below. Identify the subjects of each verb (some will be overt; some will be implied by the discourse context).

LESSON 9
MORE ON NOUNS (PLURALS)

In general, the plural of a Gəʿəz noun is formed in one of two ways:

a) Pattern replacement ("broken/internal" plurals): ሀገር > አህጉር

b) Addition of a plural suffix ("external" plurals): መሠግር > መሠግራን

Pattern Replacement

There is impossible to predict the plural form based on the singular form. Thus, one must memorize both. The following plural patterns are most common:

qətāl	e.g.,	ፍናው	the plural of	ፍኖት	'road'
qatalt		ጸሐፍት		ጸሓፊ	'scribe'
ʾaqtāl		አሕቃል		ሐቅል	'plain'
ʾaqtul		አህጉር		ሀገር	'city'
ʾaqtəlt		አግብርት		ገብር	'servant'
ʾaqātəl		አባግዕ		በግዕ	'sheep'
maqātəlt		መላእክት		መልአክ	'messenger'

Addition of Plural Suffix

The two endings used to form external plurals are *-ān* and *-āt*. The first, *-ān* is typically restricted to nouns denoting male human beings:

መሠግር	PL	መሠግራን	'fishermen'
ሊቅ		ሊቃን	'elders, chiefs'

The second ending, *-āt*, has no such restriction:

ነቢይ	PL	ነቢያት	'prophets'
ሰማይ		ሰማያት	'heavens'
ነገር		ነገራት	'things'

Several bi-consonantal nouns have plurals ending in -*aw*:

እድ	PL እደው	'hands'	አፍ	PL አፈው	'mouths'
ዕፅ	ዕፀው	'trees'	አብ	አበው	'fathers'
ዕድ	ዕደው	'males'	እኁ	አኀው	'brothers'

The common nouns ብእሲ 'man' and ብእሲት 'woman' have suppletive plurals that are not at all related to the singular forms: ሰብእ 'men' and አንስት 'women'.

Collectives

Some nouns that are morphologically singular may have two lexical uses, one as the typical singular and one as the collective. A collective noun looks singular but refers to a group of items.

ዕፅ	(PL ዕፀው)	SG 'a tree'; PL 'a grove, woods'; 'wood'
ዖፍ	(PL አዕዋፍ)	SG 'a bird'; PL 'fowl'
ሕዝብ	(PL አሕዛብ)	SG 'a people or nation'; PL 'people'
ደቂቅ	(no plural form)	SG 'offspring, progeny, children'

Morphologically singular nouns used collectively are found with both singular and plural verbs in Gəʿəz:

ወይትነሣእ፡ሕዝብ፡ዲበ፡ሕዝብ። 'and <u>people</u> (MS) <u>will rise (3MS)</u> against people' (Mk 13:8)

ዝንቱ፡ሕዝብ፡በከናፍሪሆሙ፡ያኬብሩኒ፡ 'this <u>people (MS)</u> <u>glorifies (3MP)</u> me with their lips' (Mk 7:6)

Vocabulary 9

In the left column are all the nouns from Lessons 2–8 that have plural forms. In the right two columns are their plurals **listed in a different order**. *Match* the singular and plural forms. Check your results using the Gloss Lexicon.

Singular				**Plural**	
ሀገር	_____	ብእሲ	_____	መካንንት	ምኵራባት
ሌሊት	_____	ትእዛዝ	_____	ማያት	ቃላት
ልብስ	_____	ኀጢአት	_____	ትእዛዛት	ነቢያት
ሐመር	_____	ነቢይ	_____	ውሉድ	ነገራት
ሐማት	_____	ነገር	_____	አብያት	በሐውርት
ሕቅል	_____	አርዌ	_____	ፍናው	መንግሥታት
ብእሲት	_____	አብ	_____	ጸሓያት	አልባስ
መልአክ	_____	እጕ	_____	ኢጋንንት	ዕለታት
መሥግር	_____	አንቀጽ	_____	አንሥት	መሥግሪን
መንግሥት	_____	እድ	_____	አግማል	መላእክት
መንፈስ	_____	ወልድ	_____	አኀው	ገዳማት
ምኵራብ	_____	ዕለት	_____	ለያልይ	ጸሐፍት
መኰንን	_____	ገመል	_____	አፍላግ	አህጉር
ማይ	_____	ጋኔን	_____	አናቅጽ	አሕቃል
ርግብ	_____	ገዳም	_____	ሰማያት	ሐማታት
ሰማይ	_____	ጸሐፊ	_____	መንፈሳት	አሕማር
ስንበት	_____	ጽባሕ	_____	ኀጣውእ	አርጋብ
ቃል	_____	ጸሓይ	_____	አራዊት	እደው
ብሔር	_____	ፈለግ	_____	አበው	ጽባሓት
ባሕር	_____	ፍኖት	_____	ባሕርት	ሰናብት
ቤት	_____			ሰብእ	

Lesson 9—More on Nouns (Plurals)

EXERCISES

A. Identify all the plural nouns from your vocabulary that are present in the Mark text of Lessons 2–8, but from the Abba Garima III manuscript pages 1–3 in Appendix F.1.

LESSON 10
PUTTING WORDS TOGETHER — BASIC SYNTAX

In Gəʿəz null copula clauses (Lesson 3), the "default" order when both subject and complement are nouns or when the subject is a demonstrative pronoun is *subject–complement*.

    ወሲሳዩ፡ አንበጣ፡ወምዐረ፡ጸደና፡   'and his food (was) locust and wild honey' (Mk 1:6)

In contrast, when the subject is a <u>pronoun</u> (Lesson 4), the default order is *Noun-Pronoun*:

    ወቦ፡እለ፡ይቤሉ፡ነቢይ፡ውእቱ፡   'and there were those said, "A prophet (is) <u>he</u>"' (Mk 6:15)

And the opposite order, *Pronoun-Noun*, indicates emphasis on the pronoun.

    <u>አንተኑ</u>፡ክርስቶስ፡ወልዱ፡ለቡሩክ፡   '<u>You</u>(!) (are) <u>Christ</u>, the son of the Blessed One?' (Mk 14:61)

In clauses with finite verbs, the default order in Gəʿəz is *Verb-Subject*.

    መጽአ፡ኢየሱስ፡እምናዝሬት፡   '<u>Jesus came</u> from Nazareth' (Mk 1:9)

<u>Note</u> that if a small or "light" prepositional phrase (i.e., a preposition + pronoun) is used, it will typically follow the verb and precede the subject.

    ወይሐውሩ፡ኀቤሁ፡ኵሉ፡ሰብአ፡ይሁዳ፡ወኢየሩሳሌም፡   'all the people of Judah and Jerusalem <u>went to him</u>' (Mk 1:5)

Deviations from this order reflect a desire to introduce a new topic (e.g., a new setting for the action or a new agent in the narrative) or to emphasize, or "focus," some material. This kind of highlighted material is put first in the clause.

For example, while the verb-subject order below is the default, the fronting of the time phrase ይእተ፡አሚረ፡ reflects focus on the time setting, stressing that the very day that John made these comments, Jesus appeared on the scene.

    ወይእተ፡አሚረ፡መጽአ፡ኢየሱስ፡   'On that very day, Jesus came ...' (Mk 1:9)

Similarly, the subject ሐማቱ፡ለስምዖን፡ is fronted as a topic before the verb in the example below to signal the introduction of a new character.

    ወሐማቱ፡ለስምዖን፡ትፈዐን፡   'now Simon's mother-in-law had a fever' (Mk 1:30)

Be sensitive to the use of word order variations to structure Gəʿəz discourse.

Lesson 10—Putting Words Together—Basic Syntax

Vocabulary 10

ፈነወ[6]	he sent (D)	እግዚእ	lord, master (PL ኣጋእዝት)
ፈቀደ	he desired, wanted	ገብር	servant, slave (PL አግብርት)
ገሰሰ	he touched	ካህን	priest (PL ካህናት)
ሐይወ	he lived, recovered	ለምጽ	leprosy
ክህለ	he was able	መባእ	offering (PL መባኣት)
ኮነ [ከ-ው-ን][7]	he/it was, became	ርእስ	head; self (PL አርእስት)
ምሕረ	he had mercy on, pity for		
መልአ[8]	he set out, hurried (D)	አላ	but, except
ስእነ	he was unable	እመ	if
ሰፍሐ	he extended, expanded	እንበይነ	because
		እስከ	up to, until
		ኵልሄ	everywhere, wherever

EXERCISES

A. Read the phrases below—aloud—and then translate them into English.

1. ሐይዉ፡አግብርት፡እምለምጽ፡

2. መልአ፡ካህን፡ለምኵራብ፡

3. እስከ፡ገሰሰ፡ክርስቶስ፡ብእሴሄ፡ዲበ፡ርእስ፡

4. ይፌኑ፡እግዚአ፡ብሔር፡ነቢየ፡እንበይነ፡ኃጢአት፡

5. ምሕረት፡ለገመል፡

6. ኮኑ፡ካህናት፡በሀገር፡

7. ፈቀድነ፡መህሮተ፡እምክርስቶስ፡

8. ሰፍሐ፡እግዚእ፡እድ፡ለብእሲት፡

---

[6] On verbs whose third root consonant is ው or ይ, see the Appendix, §C.6.
[7] On verbs whose second root consonant is ው or ይ, see the Appendix, §C.5.
[8] On verbs whose third root consonant is a guttural, see the Appendix, §C.3.

9. ሐይወ፡ወልድ፡ድኅሬ፡ላምጽ፡አላ፡ስእነ፡እብ፡

10. ይፈውስኑ፡ክርስቶስ፡ብእሴ፡እም፡ኢወፅአ፡ጋኔን፡

B. Produce the phrases below in Gəʿəz.

1. God desired an offering but the man was not able

2. The masters followed after the servants to the temple

3. We went everywhere except the wilderness

4. Christ will come into the house if you (FP) want

5. Will God delight in the offerings

6. But God will also have pity for fishermen

7. She hurried through the city to the house

8. The prophets will rebuke the women because they would not leave from the region

9. Leprosy expanded everywhere except in the wilderness

10. The woman lived because she touched Chris

C. Identify any word you know in the text below. If it is a noun, indicate whether it is singular or plural and what syntactic role (e.g., subject) is has. If it is a verb, indicate the root and person-gender-number, and whether it is a Perfect or Imperfect.

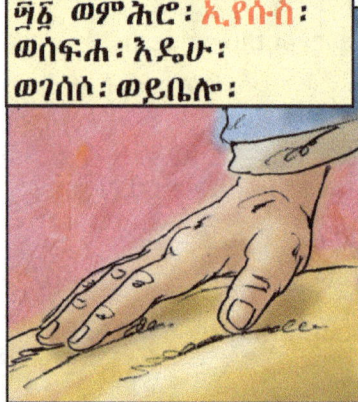

LESSON 11
BEYOND THE BASICS OF THE VERB

Overview

Gəʿəz verbs build upon the basic three consonants and vowel pattern system of word formation (see Lesson 1.4). A system of inflectional affixes is used to indicate person-number-gender features. And a set number of derivational patterns, either gemination within the root or lengthening of a vowel, is used to form an inter-relating word-formation system. These <u>verb-related root derivations</u> are often referred to by the labels *G*, *D*, *L*, and *Q*:

G verbs   simple root+vowel pattern: ነበረ 'he sat' (root ን-በ-ር)

D verbs   "doubling" (D) 2nd root consonant: ነጸረ 'he looked' (root ን-ጸ-ር)

L verbs   lengthening (L) vowel after 1st root consonant: ባረከ 'he blessed' (root በ-ር-ከ)

Q verbs   simple 4-consonant root: ተርጐመ 'he translated' (root ት-ር-ጐ-ም)[9]

For any given verbal root, only one of the above basic patterns is normally used, though some roots exist in both the G and D without any appreciable semantic difference. In Gəʿəz, these basic derivations are no longer semantically related (as they are in many other ancient Semitic languages), but are simply a discrete class of unrelated derivational word-formation processes, turning roots into inflected verbs.

The basic derivations, G, D, L, Q, each have a causative-resultative (CX) counterpart and each of these two counterparts have reflexive-passive (Xt, CXt), reciprocal (Xlt, Cxlt) sub-types, resulting in the following system:

BASE	*Reflexive-Passive*	*Reciprocal*	CAUSATIVE-RESULTATIVE	*Reflexive-passive*	*Reciprocal*
G	Gt	Glt	CG	CGt	CGlt
D	Dt		CD	CDt	
L	Lt		CL	CLt	
Q	Qt	Qlt	CQ	CQt	CQlt

---

[9] When the second consonant of a quadra-consonantal (Q) root is a ው or a ይ, there is a regular contraction of *aw* > *o* and *ay* > *e*, producing such forms as ዶገነ (from *ደየነ 'he pursued') and ሞቅሐ (from *መወቅሐ 'he imprisoned'). These verbs look like the L derivation, with the long vowel after the first root consonant.

Form

3ms Perfect and Imperfect Representative Forms

Though there are few (if any) verbs that occur thru an entire related derivational sequence, the chart below illustrates the forms of the verbs even for derivations that are unattested.

Note well!—The chart below presents the relationship through the sequence as a neat system, as an ideal; in many cases, the meanings for the Xt, Xlt, CXt, and CXlt derivations do not reflect a neat system and must simply be memorized.

SIMPLE	*Reflexive-Passive*	*Reciprocal*	CAUSATIVE-RESULTATIVE	*Reflexive-passive*	*Reciprocal*
G PERF ነገረ IMPF ይነግር 'he told X'	Gt ተነግረ ይትነገር 'X was told'	Glt ተናገረ ይትናገር 'he spoke with X'	CG አንገረ ያነግር 'he made X tell Y'	CGt አስተነገረ ያስተነግር 'X was made to tell Y'	CGlt አስተናገረ ያስተናግር 'he caused X and Y to speak with each other'
D PERF መህረ IMPF ይሜህር 'he taught X'	Dt ተመህረ ይትሜህር 'X was taught'		CD አምህረ ያምህር 'he made X teach Y'	CDt አስተመህረ ያስተሜህር 'X was made to teach Y'	
L PERF ባረh IMPF ይባርh 'he blessed X'	Lt ተባረh ይትባርh 'X was blessed'		CL አባረh ያባርh 'he made X bless Y'	CLt አስተባረh ያስተባርh 'X was made to bless Y'	
Q PERF ገፍትአ IMPF ይገፍትአ 'he destroyed X'	Qt ተገፍትአ ይትገፍትአ 'X was destroyed'	Qlt ተገፋትአ ይትገፋትአ 'he destroyed with X'	CQ አገፍትአ ያገፈትአ 'he had X destroy Y'	CQt አስተገፍትአ ያስተገፈትአ 'X was made to destroy Y'	CQlt አስተገፋትአ ያስተገፋትአ 'he caused X and Y to destroy each other'

Note: Deviations from the norm may occur due to a gutturals (አ,ዐ,ህ,ሐ,ገ) or semivowels (ይ,ወ) in the root; for these, see the "weak" verb paradigms in Appendix B.

Brief Notes on the Key Characteristics of the Derivations

The **G** is the simple derivation and the patterns in all verbs must be memorized.

The **D derivational sequence** is characterized by gemination of the middle root consonant, e.g., *mahhara*, *yəmehhər*, even though this is not reflected in the Ethiopic script, i.e., መህረ, ይሜህር, respectively. Thus, in strong verbs of the Perfect, the D is indistinguishable in writing from the G. In contrast, if the root has a middle ወ or ይ, then the G and D differ: for example, compare ሐረ 'he went' to ፈወስ 'he healed'. Finally, the D Imperfect is characterized by the first root consonant in the 5°, e.g., ይሜህር.

The **L derivational sequence** is characterized by the "long" $\bar{a}$ (the 4° form) for the first consonant of the root, e.g., ባረከ and ይባርክ.

The **Q derivational sequence** is characterized by a root that has four consonants instead of three, e.g., ግ-ፍ-ት-አ 'to destroy'.

The **Xt derivational subtype** is characterized by the addition of ተ as a prefix at the front of the Perfect form (ተ-ነገረ) and between the inflectional prefix and the word stem in the Imperfect (ይ-ት-ነገር). The Xt often reflects *passivization*, that is, the patient or goal of the action in the X derivation (They followed Jesus) is promoted to the subject of the Xt (Jesus was followed). The original agent of the X derivation is omitted, unless it is re-inserted with a prepositional phrase (e.g., with በ-, በኅበ, or እምኅበ). Some Xt verbs reflect a reflexive meaning, by which the verbal action is turned back on the subject (ተአሰረ 'he tied himself up').

> Note: two common verbs are superficially similar but must be distinguished:
>
> ተነሥአ is the Gt passive of ነሥአ 'he took, seized.'
>
> ተንሥአ 'to get up, arise, set out'; 'to rise' (from the dead); 'to rise up against' (ላዕለ)' may look like it is directly related to ነሥአ , it is best understood as a denominative Q verb derived from the noun ትንሣኤ 'ascent, rising, resurrection'.

The **Xlt derivational subtype** combines features of the Xt and L derivations: a ተ is added as a prefix and the first consonant of the root is in the 4° form (i.e., with the "long" $\bar{a}$), as in ተናገረ. This pattern exists for the G and Q sequences, but not for the D or L. Note that in the Qlt pattern, the 4° form occurs on the second root consonant (e.g., ተተራጐሙ). The Xlt pattern typically reflects reciprocity, in which both the subject (first agent) and object (second agent) or two subjects engage in activity with each other; that is, they both function as agents and patients. Often an Xlt verb that has reciprocal meaning is accompanied by a reinforcing prepositional phrase, such as በበይናቲሆሙ 'among themselves' or አሕዱ፡ምስለ፡ካልኡ 'one with the other'.

The **CX derivational subtype** is characterized by an አ- prefix in the Perfect (አንገረ) and a 4° form for the inflectional prefixes of the Imperfect (ያነግር). Semantically the Causative-Resultative derivations either turn a base derivation verb (ነገረ 'he told [something to someone]') into a causative (አንገረ 'he made [someone else] tell [something]') or a base derivation (አከየ 'he was bad') into a resultative (አአከየ '[someone] made him become bad').

> Note: When the negative ኢ- is prefixed to a verb beginning with እ- (any 1st person Imperfect) or አ- (any CX(lt) Perfect), the resulting sequence ኢእ- becomes ኢየ and ኢአ- becomes ኢያ-. What for these in narrative, since the 1st person cases of this phenomenon (e.g., ኢተአአምር 'I do/will not know' > ኢያአምር) look deceptively similar to a negated 3rd person Imperfect!

The **CXt derivational subtype** builds on the CX form by adding a -ስ- to the አ- prefix in the Perfect and (አስተነገረ) and the 4° form for the inflectional prefixes of the Imperfect (ያስተነግር). The CXt is the <u>causative of the reflexive-passive</u>, which means that 'someone is made to be something' or 'someone is made to do something to oneself'.

Finally, the **CXlt derivational subtype** takes the CXt form one step further by putting the first consonant of the root in the 4° form (i.e., with the "long" $\bar{a}$), i.e., Perfect አስተናገረ and Imperfect ያስተናግር. The CXlt is the causative reciprocal, such that someone causes two other parties to engage in activity with each other.

Vocabulary 11

አጥመቀ	he baptized (CG)	አዲም	skin, leather
ደለወ[10]	he was suitable, fitting (G)	ዐዋዲ	messenger (PL ዐዋድያት)
ፈትሐ[11]	he opened, loosed (G)	ገጽ	face (PL ገጻት)
ነስሐ	he repented (D)	ሐቌ	hip, loin (PL ሐቊያት)
ጼሐ [ጽ-ይ-ሕ][12]	he leveled, paved (G)	ቅናት	belt, girdle (PL ቅናውት)
ጻሐፈ	he wrote (G)	ጸጉር	hair
ጸንዐ	he was strong, firm, powerful (G)	ጥምቀት	baptism (PL ጥምቀታት)
ተአመነ	he believed, confessed (Gt)	ቀዳሚ	beginning, first (ADJ)

EXERCISES

A. Read the phrases below—aloud—and then translate them into English.

1. ይፈኑሙ፡እግዚአ፡ብሔር፡ዐዋድያት፡

2. ጻሐፈ፡እግዚእ፡ለጻሐፍት፡

3. ነስሑ፡ሰብእ፡እምኀጢአት፡

4. መኑ፡ተአመነ፡በክርስቶስ፡

---

[10] On verbs whose third root consonant is ው or ይ, see the Appendix, §C.6.
[11] On verbs whose third root consonant is a guttural, see the Appendix, §C.5.
[12] On verbs whose second root consonant is ው or ይ, see the Appendix, §C.5.

5. እስመ፡ፈትሐነኒ፡አናቅጸ፡

6. አመ፡ቀዳሚት፡ዕለት፡አጥመቀ፡ክርስቶስ፡ብዙኃን፡

7. ይጸንዑኑ፡ቅናውት፡እም፡ጽጉር፡

8. ቦአ፡ብእሲ፡ዘይጸንዕ፡ለብሔር፡

9. ገሰሰ፡መልአክ፡ብእሴ፡በገጽ፡ወበሐቄ፡

10. አመ፡ጼሐ፡እግዚአ፡ብሔር፡ፍኖተ፡በገዳም፡

B. Produce the phrases below in Gəʿəz.

1. Shall I send a messenger there?

2. The scribe will go to the temple with the priest.

3. A road was very suitable in the wilderness.

4. While the people went out to the river.

5. Did he repent before the baptism?

6. But he will baptize with the spirit.

7. She believed Christ and entered into the water for baptism.

8. And he said, "If you (MP) will not repent, you will not live."

9. The priests loosed the belt from the first garment.

10. Why would she touch the skin from the animal?

C. Find every verb in the text below and identify person-gender-number, the conjugation (Perfect or Imperfect), and the derivation.

LESSON 12
THE DEPENDENT -A

Noun Cliticization -a

One of the most common strategies for modifying nouns in Gəʿəz is the bound relationship, or noun cliticization. In this relationship, the first noun X "leans" on the second, host noun Y. Semantically, the result is analogous to "of" in English, that is, "X of Y," but without a preposition; a such, the bound construction in Gəʿəz approximates fairly well the range of meanings achievable with English "of" (e.g., possession, authorship, origin, material).

Gəʿəz noun cliticization is indicated by changing the first word's ending to the 1° (i.e., adding -a to the first noun): Noun$_1$-a + Noun$_2$. This is -a has an unclear origin, but should now simply be considered a marker of dependency.

ወልደ:እግዚአ:ብሔር:	'the <u>son of</u> God' (Mk 1:1)
ወንጌለ:መንግሥተ:እግዚአ:ብሔር:.	'the <u>gospel of</u> the <u>kingdom of</u> God' (Mk 1:14)
ቤተ:ስምዖን:	'the <u>house of</u> Simon' (Mk 1:29)
ሊቀ:ካህናት	'the <u>chief of</u> the priests' (Mk 2:26)
ሊቃነ:ካህናት	'the <u>chiefs of</u> the priests' (Mk 15:31)
መላእክተ:ሰማይ:	'<u>angels of</u> the heavens' (Mk 13:32)
ወልደ:እጓለ:እመ:ሕያው:	'the <u>son of</u> the <u>progeny of</u> the <u>mother</u> *of* the living', i.e., the son of Man (Mk 2:10)

Note: the *a-* of cliticization does not carry the word stress, which is moved back to the next-to-last syllable (see above, Lesson 1.3).

Two small variations should be noted:

(a) Most nouns ending in 3° -i have their bound form in 5° -e:

ዐቃቢ 'official, guard' > ዐቃቤ:ሥራይ: '<u>official of</u> medicine', i.e., physician (Mk 2:17)

መጋቢ 'administrator' > መጋቤ:ምኩራብ: '<u>administrator of</u> the synagogue' (Mk 5:22)

(b) Nouns ending in 4° -ā, 5° -e, or 7° -o remain unchanged when bound:

ፍሬ 'fruit' > ፍሬ:ወይን: 'fruit of the vine' (Mk 12:2)

Verbal Complement with Dependent -a

While some complements in Gəʿəz are prepositional (e.g., ሰበከ፡በወንጌል 'he preached በ-the gospel'; see Lesson 14), many that are simply a noun are also marked by the dependent -a.

    ብእሲ፡ተከለ፡ወይነ፡   'a man planted a <u>vineyard</u>' (Mk 12:1)

    ርእየ፡በለሰ፡እምርሑቅ፡   'he saw a <u>fig tree</u> from a distance' (Mk 11:13)

Because a noun in the bound form already has the dependent -a ending, there is no further change when a bound noun is also the verbal complement:

    ሰበከ፡<u>ወንጌለ</u>፡መንግሥተ፡እግዚአ፡ብሔር፡

    'he preached <u>the gospel</u> of the kingdom of God' (Mk 1:14)

As with noun cliticization, two small variations occur:

(a) Most nouns ending in 3° -i have their complement form in 5° -e:

    ትረክቡ፡<u>ብእሴ</u>፡ዘይጸውር፡ጻሕበ፡ማይ፡ 'you will find a <u>man</u> who is carrying a jar of water' (Mk 14:13)

(b) Nouns ending in 4° -ā, 5° -e, or 7° -o remain unchanged:

    እመቦ፡ዘይረክብ፡<u>ፍሬ</u>፡በውስቴታ፡ 'if one could find <u>fruit</u> on it' (Mk 11:13)

A third feature is that that proper nouns are either left unmarked or take the (stressed) ending -ሃ:

    ኀደጉ፡<u>ዘብዴዎስሃ</u>፡   'they left <u>Zebedee</u>' (Mk 1:20)

    አሕየወ፡ሎሙ፡<u> በርባንሃ</u>፡   'he restored to them <u>Barabbas</u>' (Mk 15:15)

The Dependent -A with Verbs of Motion

A noun with -a may be used as the complement of a bivalent verb of motion, instead of a prepositional phrase:

    ሐረ፡ሐቅለ፡   'he went (to) the wilderness' (Mk 1:35)

    ቦአ፡ቤተ፡   'he entered (into) a house' (Mk 7:24)

Rarely the dependent -a is used to indicate static position:

    ነበረ፡<u>ሐቅለ</u>፡አርባዓ፡ዕለተ፡ወአርባዓ፡ሌሊተ፡. 'he dwelt (in) <u>the wilderness</u> forty days and forty nights' (Mk 1:13)

The Dependent -A with Temporal Phrases

Words designating periods of time used adverbially to indicate the time when an action took place may be marked with the dependent -*a*.

ምሴተ = በምሴት   'at evening / in the evening'

ጽባሐ = በጽባሕ   'at morning / in the morning'

ነበረ፡ሐቅለ፡አርብዓ፡ዕለተ፡ወአርብዓ፡ሌሊተ፡

'he dwelt (in) the wilderness forty <u>days</u> and forty <u>nights</u>' (Mk 1:13)

Vocabulary 12

አፍቀረ	he loved, cherished (CG)	ዐሳብ	hireling
አመከረ	he tempted, tested (CD)	ደቂቅ	children
አምነ[13]	he believed, trusted, confessed (G)	መሥገርት	snare, net (PL መሣግር)
አስተሣነየ [ሥ-ን-ይ][14]	he beautified, restored (CGlt)		
አሠገረ	he fished, cast (nets) (CD)	አርብዓ	forty (NUM)
አውፅአ[15]	he took out, expelled (CG)	ሕቀ	little (ADV)
ኃለፈ	he passed by (G)	ቅዱስ	holy (ADJ)
ረስየ	he put, set, made (D)		
ጸውዐ	he summoned, proclaimed (D)	-ሃ	used to mark some proper nouns as a complement
ተሠጠ [ሥ-ጥ-ጥ]	he was torn, split (Gt)		
ተልእከ[16]	he was sent; he served (Gt)		

---

[13] On verbs whose first root consonant is a guttural, see the Appendix, §C.1.
[14] On verbs whose third root consonant is ው or ይ, see the Appendix, §C.6.
[15] On verbs whose third root consonant is a guttural, see the Appendix, §C.3.
[16] On verbs whose second root consonant is a guttural, see the Appendix, §C.2.

Lesson 12—The Dependent -A

EXERCISES

A. Read the phrases below—aloud—and then translate them into English.

1. ልብሰ፡ብእሲት፡

2. መላእክተ፡እግዚአ፡ብሔር፡

3. ሐመረ፡አብ፡ወእኑ፡

4. ደቂቀ፡ሀገር፡

5. ቅናተ፡ጸጉር፡

6. አናቅጸ፡ቤት፡

7. ርእሰ፡አርዌ፡

8. እደው፡ጸሐፊ፡

9. ካህነ፡ምኩራብ፡

10. አጋንንተ፡ሐቅል፡

B. Produce the phrases below in Gəʿəz.

1. God loved the holy man that he sent.

2. The demon tempted the children of the city.

3. If the time has come, you should believe in the Gospel.

4. While the men were restoring the synagogue, the women of the city passed by.

5. Immediately the hireling took the food out of the house and summoned the children.

6. Until the messenger was sent to the master about the law of God.

7. But the leather of the belt will split very much.

8. The prophet put a hand on the face of the woman.

9. The fishermen went into the boat and night and cast nets into the water.

10. An angel of God were sent from the heaven to the holy city.

C. Find every dependent -*a* in the text below and identify whether it is noun cliticization or verbal complement, or both.

LESSON 13
DEMONSTRATIVE PRONOUNS

Demonstratives are deictic ('pointing') words. As such, their properties are closely related to definiteness, which often has to do with identifiability of referents. Pointing to referents is one way to identify them.

Demonstratives often have a 'near' and 'far' deixis, depending on whether the noun and its demonstrative point to something relatively near or far (in space or time) relative to the speaker. The Gəʿəz demonstrative system includes two real demonstrative sets based on ዝ- and ዝኩ, respectively, and one quasi-demonstrative set based on the third-person pronoun.

Form

		Singular			Plural		
this, that	MASC	ዝ-	COMP	ዘ-	እሉ	COMP	
		ዝንቱ		ዘንተ	እሎንቱ		እሎንተ
	FEM	ዛ-			እላ		
		ዛቲ	COMP	ዛተ	እላንቱ	COMP	እላንተ
that yonder	MASC	ዝኩ	COMP	ዝኰ	እልኩ		
		ዝክቱ		ዝክተ	እልክቱ		
		ዝቱ		ዝተ	እልኰቱ	COMP	እልክተ
	FEM	እንትኩ					እልኰተ
		እንታክቲ	COMP	እንታክተ			
"that"	MASC	ውእቱ		ውእተ	እሙንቱ		
	FEM	ይእቲ	COMP	ይእተ	እማንቱ		

Note: ዛ-, እሉ, and እላ as well as a couple of the remote pronouns have no distinct complement forms, nor do the personal pronouns እሙንቱ and እማንቱ when used demonstratively.

The most common demonstrative, the real form based on ዝ-, has both bound and free forms in the singular. The free forms show addition to the ዝ- base: ዝንቱ (MS), ዝንተ (MS COMP) and ዛቲ (FS), ዛተ (FS COMP). The bound forms, ዝ- (MS), ዘ- (MS COMP, and ዛ- (fs and FS COMP) may either be proclitic (i.e., attached to the front of the noun it modifies, as in ዝብእሲ 'this man') or enclitic if the noun is also preceded by a clitic preposition (e.g., ለዝ፡ ብእሲ 'for this man').

71

Note: The proclitic use of ዝ- and ዛ- occurs only twice in AGIII Mark (14:22, 59), but is frequent in subsequent Gəʿəz texts.

Function

The regular ዝ- demonstrative set has both the near and far use, depending on the stance of the speaker with regard to the position of the item pointed to.

    ዝንቱ፡ዓለም፡   '<u>this</u> world' (Mk 4:19)

    ዛቲ፡ነዳይ፡መበለት '<u>that</u> poor widow' (Mk 12:43)

In the first example, the "world" referred to is clearly "near" in the sense that it is the world that the speaker and audience exist within; in contrast, in the second example, the widow to whom Jesus refers is not necessarily near him, since he is sitting across from the alms-treasury and refers to her without ever interacting with her.

Remote deixis places something at a physical or psychological distance and often reflects a distancing (or pejorative) stance taken by the speaker towards the object.

    ለ<u>ዝኩ</u>፡ዘአኀዞ፡ሌጌዎን፡   'to <u>that</u> one whom Legion had seized' (Mk 5:15)

    አሜን፡እብለክሙ፡ኢይሰቲ፡እምዝንቱ፡ፍሬ፡ወይን፡እስከ፡<u>እንታክቲ</u>፡ዕለት፡አም፡አስትዮ፡ሐዲሰ፡በመንግሥተ፡ እግዚአ፡ብሔር።

    'truly I tell you, I will not drink from this fruit of the vine until <u>that (remote)</u> day when I will drink it new in the Kingdom of God'(Mk 14:25)

The third-person pronouns used in a quasi-demonstrative way reflects the difference between *deixis* versus *anaphora*. The regular ዝ- and remote ዝኩ demonstratives are true deictic words, pointing to something in the sense of "that person [over there]" or "this person [over here]." In contrast, the third-person pronouns, when used similarly, do not point in physical or temporal space, but link the item or concept in a previous mention in the discourse, as in "that person [that we both know about]" or "that wilderness [that we just traveled through]."

    አስተራገየ፡<u>ውእቱ</u>፡ጋኔን፡እኩይ፡ '<u>that</u> evil spirit [who Jesus had been speaking to] convulsed him' (Mk 1:26)

    ኢትቀውም፡<u>ይእቲ</u>፡ቤት። '<u>that</u> house [i.e., the one divided against itself] will not stand' (Mk 3:25)

Since the quasi-demonstrative function of the third-person pronouns is used with nouns that have been previously mentioned in the discourse and thus specific and identifiable, this use is limited to definite nouns.

As the examples above illustrate, demonstratives regularly precede the noun they modify (often referred to as the "attributive" use).

The demonstratives may also occur without an overt noun (often referred to as the "substantive" use).

| እንበይነ፡ዝንቱ፡መጻእኩ፡ | 'because of <u>this</u> I came' (Mk 1:38) |
| አኮኑ፡ዝንቱ፡ውእቱ፡ወልደ፡ጸራቢ፡ | 'is <u>that</u> not the son of the carpenter?' (Mk 6:3) |

The complement forms of the demonstrative pronouns are used either when the nouns they modify are verbal complements or when the demonstratives are used without an overt noun to modify (i.e., substantivally) in a complement position. For example,

ገሃደ፡ነገሮሙ፡ዘንተ፡ነገረ፡	'openly he told them <u>this</u> thing' (Mk 8:32)
ተስእልዎ፡አርዳኢሁ፡ዛተ፡አምሳለ።	'his disciples asked him about <u>this</u> parable' (Mk 7:17)
ከመ፡ይርአይ፡ዘገብረ፡ዘንተ፡	'to see who had done <u>this</u>' (Mk 5:32)

Vocabulary 13

አእመረ[17]	he knew, understood (CG)	ትምህርት	teaching (PL ትምህርታት)
አንከረ	he marvelled, was amazed (CG)		
አስተራገጸ	he made kick, convulse (CGlt)	እኩይ	evil, wicked (ADJ)
አውየወ[18]	he wailed, lamented (Q)	ዐቢይ	big (ADJ)
ደንገጸ	he was terrified, astonished (Q)	ሐዲስ	new (ADJ)
		ናዝራዊ	Nazarite (ADJ)
		ርኩስ	unclean, bad (ADJ)

EXERCISES

A. Read the phrases below—aloud—and then translate them into English.

1. ለዝ፡ብእሲ፡

2. ምስለ፡ዝብእሲት፡

3. እሉ፡እኩያን፡

---

[17] On verbs whose first root consonant is a guttural, see the Appendix, §C.1.
[18] On verbs whose third root consonant is ው or ይ, see the Appendix, §C.6.

4. ዝሐዲስ፡ካህን፡

5. ዛቲ፡ትዛዝ፡

6. እላ፡ብዙኃት፡እንሥት፡

7. እሉ፡ብዙኃን፡ሰብእ፡

8. እልኩ፡መላእክት፡

9. ዝኩ፡ርኩስ፡ገብር፡

10. እማንቱ፡ፍናው፡

B. Produce the phrases below in Gəʿəz.

1. The men of the region understood this new thing.

2. Christ came because of this teaching.

3. The time he healed those (women) whom the demon had seized.

4. Until that (remote) time when they will marvel in the Kingdom of God.

5. Because that evil spirit will convulse the unclean man.

6. If she is terrified, she will wail.

7. The Nazirite preached and the people were amazed.

8. The demons were terrified from this prophet.

9. The unclean man said to Christ, "I know who you are."

10. The scribes were amazed at these words.

C. Find the two demonstrative pronouns in the text below. Also identify all new vocabulary, including the verbs (indicating person-gender-number, derivation, and conjugation).

Lesson 14
Verbal Valency

Verbal valency refers to the number of arguments (e.g., a subject, complement) required by the verb. Although verbal valency is related to transitivity, it is a broader category than transitivity, which is concerned only with verbal "objects," which is limited to nouns. Since many Semitic languages, including Gəʿəz, allow prepositional phrases to be the "objects" of various verbs, valency is a more accurate way to describe the system.

The two critical terms in valency are *complement* and *adjunct*. The distinction between complement and adjunct is both syntactic and semantic: *syntactically*, a complement is a licensed element for grammaticality of the expression, while an adjunct is optional; *semantically*, a complement "completes" the meaning of its head, while an adjunct "modifies" its head.

Verbs that do not require any complement, but only a subject (e.g., 'he slept') are labeled <u>monovalent</u>; verbs that require a subject and one complement (e.g., 'he saw the river') are labeled <u>bivalent</u>; and verbs that require a subject and two complements (e.g., 'he guided them into the wilderness') are labeled <u>trivalent</u>.

Consider these examples to see how valency works in Gəʿəz:

ወደንገፁ፡ኵሎሙ፡ 'and all of them were astonished' (Mk 1:27)

Although 'what' the people were astonished at could be added as a prepositional phrase, it is not required; thus, the verb ደ-ን-ግ-ፀ (Q) is **monovalent** since it requires only a subject.

ወአውየወ፡በዐቢይ፡ቃል፡ 'and he wailed with a loud voice' (Mk 1:26)

Similarly **monovalent**, the verb አውየወ (Q) in this example does not require a complement, though the prepositional phrase በዐቢይ፡ቃል፡ is added to provide information about the manner or instrument of the action.

ወሐሩ፡ቅፍርናሐም፡ 'and he went (to) Capernaum' (Mk 1:21)

In this verse, the **bivalent** motion verb ሐ-ዉ-ር (G) requires a locative complement (a place that is the goal of the movement), but it often allows this to be a noun (e.g., ቅፍርናሐም) rather than the prepositional phrase expected in English.

ወቦአ፡በሰንበት፡ምኵራብ፡ 'and he entered the synagogue on the Sabbath' (Mk 1:21)

Similarly, the **bivalent** motion verb ብ-ው-እ (G) allows a noun complement for the goal of movement; the additional element here is the adjunct prepositional phrase በሰንበት, which provides the "optional" time setting.

<blockquote>ወወፅአ፡እምኔሁ። 'and he left from him' (Mk 1:26)</blockquote>

In contrast to the first two examples, this example illustrates a **bivalent** movement verb, here ው-ፅ-እ (G), that takes a prepositional phrase እምኔሁ as its complement.

<blockquote>አምጽኡ፡ኀቤሁ፡ኵሎ፡ድውያነ፡ 'they brought to him all the sick' (Mk 1:32)</blockquote>

Finally, the CG derivation of the verb ም-ጽ-እ is, like many causative-resultatives, **trivalent.** It requires a subject (here, the unnamed people), a complement that is made to act (here, ኵሎ፡ድውያነ፡), and, as a movement verb, a locative goal (here, ኀቤሁ). A more mimetic translation is 'they caused all the sick to come to him'.

Vocabulary 14

አብሐ [ብ-ው-ሕ]¹⁹	he permitted, authorized (CG)	ድዉይ	sick, ill (ADJ)
አሌለየ²⁰	he rose in dark (CL)	ሕሙም	ill, distressed (ADJ)
አንሥአ	he lifted, received (CG)		
ዐረበ²¹	(sun) set, it became evening (G)		
ዴገነ	he chased (L)		
ኀሠሠ	he sought, demanded (G)		
ጸለየ	he prayed (D)		
ተጋብአ²²	it was gathered together (Glt)		
ተንሥአ	he rose, got up (Q)		

---

[19] On verbs whose second root consonant is ው or ይ, see the Appendix, §C.5. For third guttural verbs, see Appendix, §C.3.
[20] On verbs whose third root consonant is ው or ይ, see the Appendix, §C.6.
[21] On verbs whose first root consonant is a guttural, see the Appendix, §C.5.
[22] On verbs whose third root consonant is a guttural, see the Appendix, §C.3.

Lesson 14—Verbal Valency

EXERCISES

A. Read aloud the phrases below that use verbs from past vocabulary, translate them into English, and identify each verb as monovalent, bivalent, or trivalent

Gəʿəz	Translation	Valency
1. አንዘ፡ልብሰ፡		
2. በጽሐት፡ብሀገር፡		
3. ኀደገ፡ኀጢአተ፡		
4. መጽኡ፡እምገዳም፡		
5. ነበረ፡ቤተ፡		
6. ሰበከ፡ወንጌለ		
7. ቀርበት፡ኀበ፡ባሕር፡		
8. ርእዮ፡ፀሐየ፡		
9. ረከብኩ፡ገብረ፡		
10. ሠመረት፡ወልደ፡		
11. ተለዉ፡ነቢየ፡		
12. ወረደ፡ውስተ፡ሐመር፡		
13. ቦአ፡ቤተ፡		
14. ሐርከ፡ምኩራበ፡		
15. ወፅአ፡እምሀገር፡		
16. አዘዘ፡ኢጋንንተ፡		
17. ገሥኩ፡አግብርተ፡		
18. ሀለወት፡በሐቅል፡		
19. መህርት፡ደቂቀ፡		
20. ፈፀኑ፡በስንበት፡		
21. ፈወስኪ፡ብእሲተ፡		
22. ነገረ፡ዘንተ፡ነገረ፡		
23. ፈነውነ፡ዐዋድያተ፡		
24. ፈቀደ፡ጥምቀተ፡		

25. ገሰሰት፡ልብሰ፡		
26. ሓይወ፡እምለምጽ፡		
27. ኮነት፡ሓጣተ፡		
28. ምሕረ፡ርኩሰ፡		
29. ሰፍሐ፡እደ፡		
30. አጥመቀ፡ወልደ፡		
32. ፈትሐ፡አንቀጸ፡		
33. ነስሐ፡እምኃጢአት፡		
34. ጼሑ፡ፍኖተ፡		
35. ጸሐፈኩ፡ትምህርተ፡		
36. ተአመነ፡ኃጢአተ፡		
37. አፍቀሩ፡ደቂቀ፡		
38. አመከረ፡ሰብአ፡		
39. አምነ፡በወንጌል፡		
40. አስተሣነየት፡ቤተ፡		
41. አሠገረ፡ውስተ፡ባሕር፡		
42. አውፅአኩ፡ኢጋንንተ፡		
43. ኃለፈ፡መንገለ፡ሀገር፡		
44. ረሰየ፡ገብረ፡ነቢየ		
45. ጸውዐት፡ሰብአ፡		
46. ተሠጠ፡ብዙኃ፡ጥቀ፡		
47. ተልእከ፡ለምኩራብ፡		
48. አእመረ፡ትምህርተ፡		
49. አንከረ፡ጥምቀተ፡		
50. አስተራገፀ፡ወልደ፡		
51. አውየወት፡በሌሊት፡		
52. ደንገፁ፡በእንተ፡አርዌ፡		

B. Find every verb in the text below and identify its valency.

LESSON 15
THE NOUN WITH ATTACHED PRONOUNS

Possession can be indicated by a bound form of the personal pronoun that attaches (or cliticizes) to the end of a noun. There are slight variations depending on whether the noun stem ends in a vowel or consonant, and there are also complement variations (though not with every form).

(a) Singular Nouns

	Singular noun ending in <u>consonant</u>			Singular noun ending in <u>vowel</u>		
3MS	ሀገሩ	his city	COMP: ሀገሮ	ጸሐፊሁ	his scribe	COMP:
3FS	ሀገራ	her city		ጸሐፊሃ	her scribe	
2MS	ሀገርከ	your city	ሀገረከ	ጸሐፊከ	your scribe	ጸሐፊከ
2FS	ሀገርኪ	your city	ሀገረኪ	ጸሐፊኪ	your scribe	ጸሐፊኪ
1CS	ሀገርየ	my city		ጸሐፊየ	my scribe	
3MP	ሀገሮሙ	their city		ጸሐፊሆሙ	their scribe	
3FP	ሀገሮን	their city		ጸሐፊሆን	their scribe	
2MP	ሀገርክሙ	your city	ሀገረክሙ	ጸሐፊክሙ	your scribe	ጸሐፊክሙ
2FP	ሀገርክን	your city	ሀገረክን	ጸሐፊክን	your scribe	ጸሐፊክን
1CP	ሀገርነ	our city	ሀገረነ	ጸሐፊነ	our scribe	

When the pronoun is attached to a noun ending in a 6° consonant, that final consonant is pronounced as -ə-, which becomes a linking vowel that carries the word stress (e.g., ሀገርየ is pronounced *hagarə́ya*).

For plural nouns, a 3° letter provides a linking vowel -*i*-, between the noun and the attached pronoun. (Note that there are no distinct complement forms.)

(b) Plural nouns

3MS	አህጉሪሁ	his cities
3FS	አህጉሪሃ	her cities
2MS	አህጉሪከ	your cities
2FS	አህጉሪኪ/አህጉርኪ	your cities
1CS	አህጉሪየ/አህጉርየ	my cities
3MP	አህጉሪሆሙ	their cities
3FP	አህጉሪሆን	their cities
2MP	አህጉሪክሙ	your cities
2FP	አህጉሪክን	your cities
1CP	አህጉሪነ	our cities

Some common nouns have slight variations in their forms before the vowels. For example, the four nouns አብ 'father', እኁ 'brother', ሐም 'father-in-law', and አፍ 'mouth' have extended forms that end in 2° (complement, 4°) in the singular before the clitic pronouns.

his father	አቡሁ	COMP:	አባሁ
his brother	እኁሁ		ኤኆሁ
his father-in-law	ሐሙሁ		ሐማሁ
his mouth	አፉሁ		አፋሁ

Finally, the noun እድ 'hand' (singular) appears with a 5° -e- before cliticized pronouns:

my hand	እዴየ
your (MS) hand	እዴከ
you (FS) hand	እዴኪ
his hand	እዴሁ
her hand	እዴሃ
etc.	

A Special Use of the Third Person Singular Clitic Pronouns

The 3rd person cliticized pronouns are sometimes used with the force of a definite article or weak demonstrative.

በእሲሁ 'his man' > 'that man', 'the man in question'

This usage is especially frequent on nouns denoting points or periods of time (e.g., በዕለቱ 'on the day in question') and appears in such fixed expressions, such as:

አሜሃ	'when, at that time'
ቀዳሚሁ	'at the beginning'
ሶቤሃ	'at that time, immediately'
ጊዜሃ	'at that time, right away'
ሳኒታ	'the next day'

Lesson 15—The Noun with Attached Pronouns

Vocabulary 15

አንጽሐ[23]	he purified, cleansed (CG)	ስምዕ	report, testimony (PL ስምዓት)
አስተብቍዐ	he implored (CGt)		
አስተብረከ	he knelt (CGt)	አፍአ/ አፍአ	outside (ADV)
ነጽሐ	he was pure, clean (G)	ክሡት	revealed, uncovered (ADJ)

EXERCISES

A. Read the phrases below—aloud—and then translate them into English.

1. ስምየ

2. ትምህርትየ

3. ደቂቅነ

4. ገጽከ

5. ዐዋዲሃ

6. ርእስኪ

7. እዴሁ

8. አደዊክሙ

9. አብያቲነ

10. አልባሲሃ

---

[23] On verbs whose third root consonant is a guttural, see the Appendix, §C.3.

B. Produce the phrases below in Gəʿəz.

1. He knelt before his lord.

2. The prophet implored the people and they repented.

3. The women purified themselves outside the city.

4. After he repents, he will be clean.

5. When I lift my voice to the heavens.

6. Because she rises in the dark and prays.

7. Her face was uncovered.

8. The priests and the scribes gathered together.

9. Christ chased the evil one from the city.

10. You (MS) will get up immediately and receive the food.

C. Find every attached pronoun on a noun in the text below.

D. Read the last verses of Mark chapter 1 in the Abba Garima III Mark page 4 (chapter 1 ends after the first "paragraph" in the second column, with the word እምኮልሄ).

LESSON 16
ADJECTIVES

Adjectives are content words that do not refer to entities, as nouns do, but properties. Adjectives cannot, therefore, take agent or patient roles, but only serve as modifiers, whether within the domain of a noun (e.g., an <u>evil</u> spirit) or predicated of the noun (e.g., the spirit is <u>evil</u>).

Form

There are two basic types of adjectives in Gəʿəz: (1) those associated with (or derived from) verbs, and (2) those derived from nouns by the addition of the suffixes -āwi and -āy. The second type is used less frequently.

Pattern

qətul	ቅዱስ	holy	>verb:	ቀደሰ (D)	he sanctified, made holy
	ርኩስ	unclean, bad		ርኵሰ (G)	he was unclean, impure
	እኩይ	evil, wicked		እከየ (G)	he was evil, wicked
qətəl	ድዉይ	sick, ill		ደወየ (G)	he was sick, ill
	ፀዉስ	lame, crippled		ፀወሰ (G)	he was lame, crippled
qatil	ጠቢብ	wise, prudent		ጠበበ (G)	he was wise, prudent
	ዐቢይ	big		ዐብየ (G)	he was large, important
	ሐዲስ	new		ሐደሰ (D)	he renewed, repaired
qātəl	ጻድቅ	righteous, just		ጸድቀ (G)	he was righteous, just
qattāl	ነዳይ	poor, needy		ነድየ (G)	he was poor, needy
qətāl	ሕያው	living, alive		ሐይወ (G)	he lived, was healed
-āwi	ሰማያዊ	heavenly	>noun:	ሰማይ	heavens

The two adjective patterns that are related to verbs, the ቅዱስ and ጠቢብ types, are also often used as <u>passive participles</u>, e.g., ቡሩክ 'blessed'.

Most adjectives are inflected for number and gender by the addition of the endings -t (FS), -ān (MP), and -āt (FP) to the masculine singular base; sometimes the internal pattern may change slightly for the FS form, as with ቅዱስ and ቅድስት.

Pattern		MS	FS	MP	FP
qətul	holy	ቅዱስ	ቅድስት	ቅዱሳን	ቅዱሳት
	evil	እኩይ	እኪት	እኩያን	እኩያት
qətəl	sick	ድዉይ	ድዉይት	ድዉያን	ድዉያት
qatil	wise	ጠቢብ	ጠባብ	ጠቢባን	ጠቢባት
	big	ዐቢይ	ዐባይ	ዐበይት	ዐበይት
qātəl	righteous	ጻድቅ	ጻድቅት	ጻድቃን	ጻድቃት
qattāl	poor	ነዳይ	ነዳይት	ነዳያን	ነዳያት
qətāl	living, alive	ሕያው	ሕያውት	ሕያዋን	ሕያዋት
-āwi	heavenly	ሰማያዊ	ሰማያዊት	ሰማያዊያን	ሰማያዊያት

Note: When the stem ends in -ት, -ድ, -ጥ, the -ት of the feminine singular is assimilated and not represented in the script: ባዕድ 'other', FEM ባዕድ (> *ባዕድት).

Note: Some of the adjective patterns also have an internal common plural, e.g., ጠቢብት.

Syntax

Adjectives represent one way that the characteristics of nouns are described in Gəʿəz (the other primary grammatical strategies for this are noun cliticization, apposition, and relative clauses). Adjectives always predicate a property of the noun. The only salient syntactic distinction is whether they do so within the domain of the modified noun or not. The former pattern is typically called "attributive" modification and the latter "predicative."

Attributive

ያጠምቀክሙ፡በመንፈስ፡ቅዱስ፡   'he will baptize you with the <u>holy</u> spirit' (Mk 1:8)

Predicative

ናአምር፡ከመ፡ጻድቅ፡አንተ፡   'we know that you are <u>righteous</u>' (Mk 12:14)

ርኢዮ፡ኢየሱስ፡ከመ፡ጠቢብ፡ውእቱ፡   'Jesus saw him, that he was <u>wise</u>' (Mk 12:34)

Regardless whether the adjective is within the noun phrase or not, if the modified noun refers to a human entity, the adjective normally agrees in number and gender with the noun; if the noun is non-human, the adjective need not agree with the noun in number or gender.

ልብስ፡ብሉይ፡   '<u>old</u> clothes' (Mk 2:21)

| ኣጋንንት፡ርኩሳን፡ | 'unclean (MP) demons (MP)' (Mk 1:27) |
| ሰብእ፡ብዙኅን፡ | 'many (MS) men (MP)' (Mk 3:32) |

If the noun has the dependent -*a*, then so too will its attributive adjective:

| ወይነ፡ሐዲስ፡ | 'new wine' (Mk 2:22) |

When the adjective is within the domain of the noun it modifies, it often follows the noun:

| ትምህርት፡ሐዲስ፡ | 'a new teaching' (Mk 1:27) |
| አሕዛብ፡ብዙኃን፡ | 'many people' (Mk 3:20) |

But adjectives may also precede the noun in order to focus the adjective or if they belong to a small group of quantifying adjectives (e.g., ዐቢይ 'large' and ብዙኅ 'many, much').

| አውየወ፡በዐቢይ፡ቃል፡ | 'he wailed in a loud voice' (Mk 1:26) |
| ፈርሁ፡ዐቢየ፡ፍርሀተ፡ | 'they feared a big fear' (Mk 4:41) |

A final category of adjective usage is what is typically called the "substantive" use, in which an adjective appears in a noun's syntactic role (e.g., as an agent or patient) without an accompanying noun. In reality, these adjectives are attributive—they exist within a noun phrase, though the noun itself is covert or null (recoverable from the context).

| ወፈወሶሙ፡ለብዙኃን፡ድውያን፡ | 'he healed many sick (people)' (Mk 1:34) |

ወነቢረስ፡በየማንየ፡ወበፀጋምየ፡ 'but to sit on my right (hand) and on my left (hand)' (Mk 10:40)

ባዕዳትሂ፡ብዙኃት፡እለ፡ዐርጋ፡ምስሌሁ፡ኢየሩሳሌም፡
'also many other (women) who went down with him to Jerusalem' (Mk 15:41)

Vocabulary 16

አግመረ	he completed, held (CG)	እም	mother (PL እማት)
ሐለየ	he thought, devised (D)	ልብ	heart, mind (PL አልባብ)
ሰምዐ	he heard, listened (G)	ምድር	earth, ground (PL አምዳር)
ጾረ [ጾ-ው-ር]	he bore, carried (G)	መፃጉዕ	paralytic
ጐንዲዮ	after a time (ADV)	ሕያው	alive (ADJ)
ካዕበ	secondly, again (ADV)	ጽፉቅ	crowded, frequent, abundant (ADJ)

Lesson 16—Adjectives

EXERCISES

A. Go back through the vocabulary for Lesson 1–15 and identify any adjectives. List them below.

B. Read aloud the phrases below and then translate them into English.

1. አራዊት፡ሕያዋን፡

2. እም፡ሐዳስ፡

3. ሀገር፡ጽፍቅት፡

4. ትምህርታት፡ቅዱሳን፡

5. አንሥት፡ድውያት፡

6. ጋኔን፡እኩይ፡

7. መዓጕዕ፡ድውይ፡

8. ምድር፡ብዝኅት፡

9. ፈለግ፡ዐቢይ፡

10. አልባብ፡ሐዲሳን፡

C. Produce the phrases below in Gəʿəz.

1. He devised evil in his mind.

2. They heard his testimony about Christ.

3. She will again complete her garment.

4. While we carry water into our crowded city.

5. He will baptize people a second time with the holy spirit.

6. After a time we heard the new teaching by the river.

7. I did not know that my mother was alive.

8. She prayed again for the paralytic.

9. The men rose from the ground and chased the wild animal.

10. The spirit was revealed to his father and his mother.

D. In the text below, identify each verb, noun, and adjective. For each, identify the salient features (for example, verbal derivation and person-gender-number or adjective gender and number).

Lesson 16—Adjectives

LESSON 17
PREPOSITIONS WITH ATTACHED PRONOUNS

Just as clitic pronouns can be added to nouns in Gəʿəz, mostly to express possession, they can also be added to prepositions. With prepositions, though, the attached pronouns are the prepositional complements.

The form of the preposition to which the pronouns attach typically end in 5° (*-e-*) letter forms:

እምነ	እምኔየ	from me
	እምኔከ	from you (MS)
	እምኔኪ	from you (FS)
		etc.
ዲበ	ዲቤየ	upon me
	ዲቤከ	upon you (MS)
	ዲቤኪ	upon you (FS)
		etc.
ታሕተ	ታሕቴየ	under me
	ታሕቴከ	under you (MS)
	ታሕቴኪ	under you (FS)
		etc.

Note: በ- and ለ- with clitic pronouns are covered later in Lesson 26.

The prepositions below rarely allow pronouns to attach directly to the free form, but typically exhibit a distinct bound form (i.e., ending in 5°, *-e*) before attached pronouns:

ኀበ	>	ኀቤየ	to(ward) me
ምስለ	>	ምስሌየ	with me
ቅድመ	>	ቅድሜየ	before me
ማእከለ	>	ማእከሌየ	within me
መንገለ	>	መንገሌየ	toward me
ድኅረ	>	ድኅሬየ	behind me
ላዕለ	>	ላዕሌየ	upon me

A few prepositions, most notably, ውስተ 'into', በእንተ 'about', and ከመ 'like', have distinct stems to which the clitic pronouns are attached:

ውስተ—clitic pronouns are attached to the stem ውስቴት-:
ውስቴትየ, ውስቴትከ, ውስቴትኪ, ውስቴቱ, etc.

በእንተ—clitic pronouns are attached to the stem በእንቲአ-:
በእንቲአየ, በእንቲአከ, በእንቲአኪ, በእንቲአሁ, etc.

ከመ—clitic pronouns are attached to the stem ከማ-:
ከማየ, ከማከ, ከማኪ, ከማሁ, etc.

Vocabulary 17

ነበበ	he spoke, told (G)	እንል	progeny, human (PL እንላት)
ነሠተ	he destroyed, overturned (G)	እንለ:እመ:ሕያው:	human, mankind
ሰከበ	he lay down (G)	ዐራት	bed (PL ዐራታት)
ቀለለ	it was light, easy (G)	ፀርፈት	blasphemy (PL ፀርፈታት)
		ሀይማኖት	faith
አሐዱ	one (ADJ)	ኆኅት	door (PL ኆኃት)
አርባዕቱ	four (ADJ)	ጠፈር	roof, ceiling

EXERCISES

A. Read the phrases below—aloud—and then translate them into English.

1. እምኔከ

2. ዲቤሙ

3. ኀቤሃ

4. ምስሌክን

5. ቅድሜን

6. ማእከሌሁ

7. ድኅሬከሙ

8. መንገሌኪ

9. ታሕቴከ

10. ከማነ

B. Produce the phrases below in Gəʿəz.

1. Her father told Christ about her.

2. Faith will not be easy without the holy spirit.

3. He spoke to the paralytic on his bed and said, "The Son of Man forgives sins."

4. The people destroyed the roof of the house.

5. We listened to the teaching of the prophet four days.

6. The scribes proclaimed that the Nazirite taught blasphemy.

7. After he healed the people, he lay down on his bed that he carried with him.

8. One man can destroy the faith of many.

9. She went out of the house through its door.

10. The sick woman put her head on the ground.

Lesson 17—Prepositions with Attached Pronouns

C. In the text below, find every preposition that has an attached pronoun. Parse the pronoun and identify its referent (i.e., what it is pointing back to).

LESSON 18
MORE ON SYNTAX—THE ወልዱ፡ለንጉሥ CONSTRUCTION

So far, possession has been discussed as one meaning of noun cliticization as well as the use of clitic pronouns attached to nouns.

ወልደ፡እግዚአ፡ብሔር፡	'the son of God' (Mk 1:1)
አንተ፡ውእቱ፡ወልድየ፡	'you are my son' (Mk 1:11)

Gəʿəz has an additional way to indicate possession in the third person, the ወልዱ፡ለንጉሥ or 'son of the king' construction. In this construction, the possessor is indicated first by a clitic pronoun that matches the gender and number of the intended noun, which is then specified inside a following ለ- preposition phrase:

ልብሱ፡ለዮሐንስ፡ 'John's clothes' (Mk 1:6). (*lit.* 'his clothes, belonging to John')

ዮሐንስ፡እኁሁ፡ለያዕቆብ፡ 'John, James' brother' (Mk 3:17)
(*lit.*, 'his brother, belonging to James')

ርእሱ፡ለዮሐንስ፡መጥምቅ፡ 'the head of John the Baptist' (Mk 6:24)
(*lit.*, 'his head, belonging to John the Baptist')

ጸርኀ፡አቡሁ፡ለውእቱ፡ 'the father of that one cried out' (Mk 9:24)
(*lit.*, 'his father, belonging to that one')

አንተኑ፡ክርስቶስ፡ወልዱ፡ለቡሩክ፡ 'Are you the Christ, son of the Blessed One?' (Mk 14:61)
(*lit.* 'his son, belonging to the Blessed One')

መከረ፡ጲላጦስ፡ይግበር፡ፈቃዶሙ፡ለሕዝብ፡ 'Pilate plotted to do the wishes of the people' (Mk 15:15) (*lit.*, their wishes, belonging to the people')

Although the difference between the bound construction, e.g., ወልዳ፡ንጉሥ and the ወልዱ፡ለንጉሥ construction is not fully clear, that the latter may be more specific in that it seems used with when the second noun denotes a definite (specific, identifiable) entity, not an indeterminate (non-specific or non-identifiable) entity. Hence, ወልዳ፡ለንጉሥ does not mean 'son of a king', but 'son of the king'.

Vocabulary 18

አእኰተ[24]	he praised (CG)	ምጽባሕ	tax office
በልዐ[25]	he ate (G)	መጸብሕ	tax collector (PL መጸብሓን)
መስሐ	he dined, supped (G)	ረድእ	disciple (PL አርዳእ)
ረፈቀ	he reclined at meal (G)	ኃጥእ	sinner (ADJ)
ስትየ[26]	he drank (G)	ግሙራ	always, completely (ADV)

EXERCISES

A. Read the phrases below—aloud—and then translate them into English.

1. አርዳኢሁ፡ለዮሐንስ፡

2. ደቂቁ፡ለካህን፡

3. እጎሁ፡ለጸሓፊ፡

4. መላእክቲሁ፡ለእግዚአ፡ብሔር፡

5. ነጋውኢሆሙ፡ለሰብእ፡

6. ምጽባሐሙ፡ለመጸብሓን፡

7. ሐመሩ፡ለመሥግር፡

8. ትምህርታ፡ለመንግሥተ፡እግዚአ፡ብሔር፡

9. ልብሱ፡ለነቢይ፡

10. ቤቶ፡ለመጸብሕ፡

---

[24] On verbs whose first root consonant is a guttural, see the Appendix, §C.1.
[25] On verbs whose third root consonant is a guttural, see the Appendix, §C.3.
[26] On verbs whose third root consonant is ው or ይ, see the Appendix, §C.6.

B. Produce the phrases below in Gəʿəz.

1. They always praised God for his commandments.

2. She rose in the dark and ate her food.

3. The prophet always supped with his disciples.

4. We will drink very much and become ill.

5. The priests reclined at meal and ate with the scribes.

6. The disciples of Christ healed many sinners.

7. Sinners came to the prophet and listened to his teaching.

8. The disciple healed the woman who was a sinner

9. And because of this she praised him and believed in him.

10. Why do you (MS) eat and drink with sinners and tax collectors?

C. Work back through all previous texts to find the cases of the ወልዱ፡ለንጉሥ construction.

D. Read the text below. First read it out loud, trying not to stop (choose whatever speed allows for a smooth reading). Second, read through it again, slowly, trying to recognize as many words as possible without stopping. Finally, go back and identify any words that you could not identify during your readings.

LESSON 19
THE QUANTIFIER ኩል-

The quantifier ኩል-, corresponding to English 'each, every, all', always requires a clitic pronoun.

The quantifier+pronoun may stand alone and function as a clausal subject or complement:

ደንገፁ፡ኩሎሙ፡	'all of them/each of them/everyone was terrified' (Mk 1:27)
ኩልክሙ፡ትክሕዱኒ፡በዛቲ፡ሌሊት።	'all/each of you will deny me on this night' (Mk 14:27)
ይፈክር፡ለአርዳኢሁ፡ኩሎ።	'he would explain everything to his disciples' (Mk 4:34)

Or, the quantifier may be followed by a noun in apposition that matches the 3rd person clitic pronoun on ኩል-:

ኩሉ፡ሀገር፡	'every city' (Mk 1:33)
ኩሎሙ፡ሊቃነ፡ካህናት፡ወጸሐፍት፡	'all the chief priests and scribes' (Mk 14:54)
ኩሉ፡ሰብእ፡	'all the people/every person' (Mk 1:5)
ኩሉ፡በሐውርተ፡ገሊላ።	'all the regions/every region of the Galilee' (Mk 1:28)
ኩሎ፡ድውያነ፡	'all the sick people/every sick person' (Mk 1:32)

Less commonly, the quantifier+pronoun may be in apposition to another pronominal element, as in

እብለክሙ፡ለኩልክሙ፡	'I say to all of you' (*lit.*, 'I say to you, to all of you') (Mk 13:37)

Note: The examples above illustrate that the pronoun attached to ኩል- may or may not match the morphological number of the plural nouns following it.

Vocabulary 19

አዕበየ[27]	he increased (CG)
አንቅዐ[28]	he split, burst (CG)
ጸመ [ጽ-ው-ም][29]	he fasted (G)
ተሐጉለ[30]	he perished, was destroyed (Gt)
ተክዕወ[31]	it was poured out (Gt)
ጠቀበ	he sewed (G)
ወደየ	he put, placed, set (G)
እፎ	why?
አልቦ	there is not
አምጣነ	as long as
ባሕቱ	but, however

ዐቃቢ	guard, official (PL ዐቃቢያን)
ዐቃቤ፡ሥራይ	doctor, physician
ደርግሐ	patch, rag
ግምድ	cut piece, slice (PL ግምዳት)
መዐልት	day, daytime, noontime (PL መዋዕል)
መርዓዊ	groom, son-in-law (PL መርዓዊያን)
ሥራይ	medicine (PL ሥራያት)
ሥጠት	tearing, fragment
ጥቅበት	sewing, stitch
ወይን	vine, wine (PL አውያን)
ዝቅ	wineskin (PL ዝቃት)
ብሉይ	old, worn out (ADJ)
ፈሪሳዊ	Pharisee (ADJ)
ጻድቅ	righteous (ADJ)
ጥዑይ	healthy (ADJ)

EXERCISES

A. Read the phrases below—aloud—and then translate them into English.

1. ኵሉ፡ዐቃቢ፡

2. ኵሎሙ፡ግምዳት፡

3. ኵሉ፡መዐልት፡

4. ኵሉ፡ወይን፡

5. ኵሎ፡ዝቀ፡

---

[27] On verbs whose third root consonant is ው or ይ, see the Appendix, §C.6.
[28] On verbs whose third root consonant is a guttural, see the Appendix, §C.3.
[29] On verbs whose second root consonant is ው or ይ, see the Appendix, §C.5.
[30] On verbs whose first root consonant is a guttural, see the Appendix, §C.1.
[31] On verbs whose second root consonant is a guttural, see the Appendix, §C.2.

6. ኵሉ፡ፈሪሳዊ፡

7. ኵሎሙ፡መርዓዊያን፡

8. ኵሎሙ፡ሥራያት፡

9. ኵሎ፡ሥጠተ፡

10. ኵሉ፡ደርግሐ፡

B. Produce the phrases below in Gəʿəz.

  1. She sewed the new patch on her garment.

  2. Wine will be poured out of the old wineskin.

  3. Why did the physician perish in the sea?

  4. There is no medicine for her ill son.

  5. The hireling split the leather of my wineskin and increased the tear.

  6. The Pharisee fasted all day and did not eat until night.

  7. As long as one righteous man dwells in your city.

  8. Why did the groom not put a roof on his house?

  9. You will not put a cut piece on the garment but a patch.

  10. If the woman is healthy, she can sew a stitch on your new belt.

C. Look back through all the illustrated texts given so far and identify and parse each occurrence of ኵል-.

Lesson 19—The Quantifier ኵሎ-

D. Read the text below. First read it out loud, trying not to stop (choose whatever speed allows for a smooth reading). Second, read through it again, slowly, trying to recognize as many words as possible without stopping. Finally, go back and identify any words that you could not identify during your readings.

LESSON 20
YET MORE ON THE VERB

The Verb with Clitic Pronouns

In Gəʿəz the pronominal complement of a bivalent verb may be attached directly to the verb using the clitic forms of the pronouns.

> Note: for በ-ሀ-ለ: the -ለ of the root is present in the verb form when a cliticized pronoun is added to any of the above forms ending in -e.

Basic Forms

The attached form of most of the pronouns when added to verbs are similar, if not identical, to their forms attached to nouns and prepositions. These will be easy to identify. The forms that are new or that are more difficult to identify due to assimilation are in grey highlighted boxes in the chart.

	Complement		*compare*	Possessive	
3MS	-u/-ሁ/ዎ	him		-u/-ሁ	his
3FS	-ā/-ሃ/ዋ	her		-ā/-ሃ	hers
2MS	-ከ	you		-ከ	your
2FS	-ኪ	you		-ኪ	your
1CS	-ኒ	me		-የ	mine
3MP	-(ሆ)ሙ	them		-ሆሙ	theirs
3FP	-(ሆ)ን	them		-ሆን	theirs
2MP	-ከሙ	you		-ከሙ	your
2FP	-ከን	you		-ከን	your
1CP	-ነ	us		-ነ	our

> Note: The base forms of the 3rd person pronouns begin with -ሀ-. However, in Gəʿəz (as in many Semitic languages), ሀ often either disappears between two vowels or assimilates to one or the other of the vowels. Thus, the following changes occur:
>
> (1) *-ahu > -o
> (2) *-ahā > -ā
> (3) *-uhu > -əwwo
> (4) *-ihu > əyyo
> (5) *-iha > əyyā

Lesson 20—Yet More on the Verb

1. Perfect

	VerbBase	+me	+you(MS)	+you(FS)	+him	+her	+us	+you(MP)	+you(FP)	+them(M)	+them(F)
3MS	ቀተለ	ቀተለኝ	ቀተለህ	ቀተለሽ	ቀተለው	ቀተላት	ቀተለን	ቀተላችሁ	ቀተላችሁ	ቀተላቸው	ቀተላቸው
3FS	ቀተለች	ቀተለችኝ	ቀተለችህ	ቀተለችሽ	ቀተለችው	ቀተለቻት	ቀተለችን	ቀተለቻችሁ	ቀተለቻችሁ	ቀተለቻቸው	ቀተለቻቸው
2MS	ቀተልህ	ቀተልከኝ			ቀተልከው	ቀተልካት	ቀተልከን			ቀተልካቸው	ቀተልካቸው
2FS	ቀተልሽ	ቀተልሽኝ			ቀተልሽው	ቀተልሻት	ቀተልሽን			ቀተልሻቸው	ቀተልሻቸው
1CS	ቀተልኩ		ቀተልኩህ	ቀተልኩሽ	ቀተልኩት	ቀተልኳት		ቀተልኳችሁ	ቀተልኳችሁ	ቀተልኳቸው	ቀተልኳቸው
3MP	ቀተሉ	ቀተሉኝ	ቀተሉህ	ቀተሉሽ	ቀተሉት	ቀተሏት	ቀተሉን	ቀተሏችሁ	ቀተሏችሁ	ቀተሏቸው	ቀተሏቸው
3FP	ቀተሉ										
2MP	ቀተላችሁ	ቀተላችሁኝ			ቀተላችሁት	ቀተላችኋት	ቀተላችሁን			ቀተላችኋቸው	ቀተላችኋቸው
2FP	ቀተላችሁ										
1CP	ቀተልን		ቀተልንህ	ቀተልንሽ	ቀተልነው	ቀተልናት		ቀተልናችሁ	ቀተልናችሁ	ቀተልናቸው	ቀተልናቸው

2. Imperfect

	VerbBase	+me	+you(MS)	+you(FS)	+him	+her	+us	+you(MP)	+you(FP)	+them(M)	+them(F)
3MS	ይቀትል	ይቀትለኝ	ይቀትልህ	ይቀትልሽ	ይቀትለው	ይቀትላት	ይቀትለን	ይቀትላችሁ	ይቀትላችሁ	ይቀትላቸው	ይቀትላቸው
3FS	ትቀትል	ትቀትለኝ	ትቀትልህ	ትቀትልሽ	ትቀትለው	ትቀትላት	ትቀትለን	ትቀትላችሁ	ትቀትላችሁ	ትቀትላቸው	ትቀትላቸው
2MS	ትቀትል	ትቀትለኝ			ትቀትለው	ትቀትላት	ትቀትለን			ትቀትላቸው	ትቀትላቸው
2FS	ትቀትዪ	ትቀትዪኝ			ትቀትዪው	ትቀትያት	ትቀትዪን			ትቀትያቸው	ትቀትያቸው
1CS	እቀትል		እቀትልህ	እቀትልሽ	እቀትለው	እቀትላት		እቀትላችሁ	እቀትላችሁ	እቀትላቸው	እቀትላቸው
3MP	ይቀትሉ	ይቀትሉኝ	ይቀትሉህ	ይቀትሉሽ	ይቀትሉት	ይቀትሏት	ይቀትሉን	ይቀትሏችሁ	ይቀትሏችሁ	ይቀትሏቸው	ይቀትሏቸው
3FP	ይቀትሉ	ይቀትሉኝ	ይቀትሉህ	ይቀትሉሽ	ይቀትሉት	ይቀትሏት	ይቀትሉን	ይቀትሏችሁ	ይቀትሏችሁ	ይቀትሏቸው	ይቀትሏቸው
2MP	ትቀትሉ	ትቀትሉኝ			ትቀትሉት	ትቀትሏት	ትቀትሉን			ትቀትሏቸው	ትቀትሏቸው
2FP	ትቀትሉ	ትቀትሉኝ			ትቀትሉት	ትቀትሏት	ትቀትሉን			ትቀትሏቸው	ትቀትሏቸው
1CP	ንቀትል		ንቀትልህ	ንቀትልሽ	ንቀትለው	ንቀትላት		ንቀትላችሁ	ንቀትላችሁ	ንቀትላቸው	ንቀትላቸው

Lesson 20—Yet More on the Verb

Vocabulary 20

አርመመ	he kept silent, was at rest (CG)	ገራህት	field, arable land (PL ገራውህ)
ገብረ	he did, worked (G)	ኅብስት	bread (PL ኀባውዝ)
ርኅበ[32]	he was hungry (G)	ሊቅ	elder, chief (PL ሊቃን)
ተዐቀበ[33]	he was watched; he was watchful (Gt)	መሥዋዕት	sacrifice (PL መሥዋዕታት)
ተፈጥረ	it was created, produced (Gt)	ሠዊት	ear(s) of grain
ወፈረ[34]	he went out to the countryside (G)		
ወሀበ	he gave (G)	ጽውስ	crippled, lame (ADJ)
የብሰ	it withered, dried up (G)		
		ማእከለ	between; in the middle
እለ	which, that (PLURAL)		

EXERCISES

A. Read the verbal phrases below—aloud—then parse the verbs (root, derivation, conjugation, PNG and pronoun) and translate them into English.

	Parsing	Translation
1. ያጠምቆሙ		
2. ኣጠምቀከሙ		
3. አውፅአኒ		
4. ያሜክራ		
5. አንዝዎ		
6. ረከቦሙ		
7. ትቤሎሙ		
8. ተለዉካ		
9. እሬስየከሙ		
10. ጸውያሙ		

---

[32] On verbs whose second root consonant is a guttural, see the Appendix, §C.2.
[33] On verbs whose first root consonant is a guttural, see the Appendix, §C.1.
[34] On verbs whose first root consonant is ዉ or ይ, see the Appendix, §C.4.

Lesson 20—Yet More on the Verb

11. ትሜህሮን		
12. አአምረከ		
13. ገሠጸነ		
14. አስተራገያ		
15. ይኤዝዘሙ		
16. ነገርዎ		
17. አንዘተኒ		
18. አንሥአ		
19. ፈወሰሙ		
20. ይኅሠከ or ይኅሣሠከ		
21. ምሕሮ		
22. ገሰሶ		
23. ፈነዎ		
24. ሰምዕዋ		
25. ያገምረከን		
26. ይነግሮሙ		
27. ይጸውርዎ		
28. አውረድዎ		
29. አአመሮሙ		
30. አአኮትናሁ		
31. ይፈቅድዎ		
32. ይነሥእዎ		
33. ያነቅያ		
34. ይወድይዎ		
35. ወህብኩከ		
36. ይትዐቀብዎ		

B. Read the text below. Circle every verb that has an attached complement pronoun and identify all the features of the verb and attached pronoun.

LESSON 21
AND MORE ON THE VERB—THE SUBJUNCTIVE

Form (G Imperfect)

The Gəʿəz Subjunctive is a verbal form that is similar to the Imperfect—it uses the very same inflectional affixes.

For a number of derivations (Gt, Glt, CGlt, L, Lt, CL, CLt, Qlt, and CQlt), the Subjunctive form is identical to the Imperfect. In these derivations, the distinction can only be determined from the syntactic context.

In other derivations (G, CG, CGt, D, Dt, CD, CDt, Q, Qt, CQ, and CQt), the Subjunctive differs from the Imperfect by a single vowel change in the form: in G, CG, CGt, Q, Qt, CQ, and CQt the Subjunctive reflects the change of a 1° (*a*) to a 6° (*ə*) in the first root consonant; in the D, Dt, CD, and CDt, the change is from a 5° (*e*) in the Imperfect to a 1° (*a*) in the Subjunctive.

The changes are highlighted in yellow in the chart below; identical forms are greyed.

	G	Gt	Glt	CG	CGt	CGlt
IMPF	ይቀትል	ይትቀተል	ይትቃተል	ያቀትል	ያስተቀትል	ያስተቃተል
SUBJ	ይቅትል	ይትቀተል	ይትቃተል	ያቅትል	ያስተቅትል	ያስተቃተል

	D	Dt	CD	CDt
IMPF	ይቄትል	ይትቄተል	ያቄትል	ያስተቄትል
SUBJ	ይቀትል	ይትቀተል	ያቀትል	ያስተቀትል

	L	Lt	CL	CLt
IMPF	ይቃትል	ይትቃተል	ያቃትል	ያስተቃትል
SUBJ	ይቃትል	ይትቃተል	ያቃትል	ያስተቃትል

	Q	Qt	Qlt	CQ	CQt	CQlt
IMPF	ይቀተልድ	ይትቀተልድ	ይትቀታልድ	ያቀተልድ	ያስተቀተልድ	ያስተቀታለድ
SUBJ	ይቀትልድ	ይትቀትለድ	ይትቀታለድ	ያቀትልድ	ያስተቀትለድ	ያስተቀታለድ

Function

(1) As a main verb

The Subjunctive as the verb of a main clause has a jussive force:

መልኡ፡ንሐር፡ካልአተኒ፡አህጉር፡   'Hurry, <u>let us go</u> to other cities' (Mk 1:38)

The positive form may optionally be preceded by ለ-:

ዘቦ:እዝነ:ሰሚዕ:ሊይስማዕ።   'let he who has ears to hear listen' (Mk 4:9, 23)

The 2nd person forms with the negative ኢ- are equivalent to the negative imperative:

ኢትግባእ:ላዕሌሁ:እንከ።   'do not return upon him anymore!' (Mk 9:25)

(2) As a subordinate verb

The Subjunctive, with or without an overt nominalizer ከመ 'that', may be subordinate to another verb. The semantic result is a purpose or result clause:

ወኢያበውሐሙ:ይንብቡ: 'he would not permit them (that) they should speak' (Mk 1:34)

ዑቅ:ኢትንግር:ወኢለመኑሂ   'Take care not (that) you should not tell even anyone!' (Mk 1:44)

ወይቤሎሙ:ለአርዳኢሁ:ያፅንሑ:ሎቱ:ሐመረ:ከመ:ኢይትጋፍዕዎ:ሰብእ:

'and he told his disciples (that) they should prepare for him a boat that the people should not press on him' (Mk 3:9)

ከመ:ኢ- produces a negative result clause, in English 'lest' or 'so that ... not':

ወይቤሎሙ:ለአርዳኢሁ:ያፅንሑ:ሎቱ:ሐመረ:ከመ:ኢይትጋፍዕዎ:ሰብእ:

'he said to his disciples that they should prepare a boat for him in order that the people would not press upon him' (Mk 3:9)

A number of frequently occurring verbs function as "light" verbs that contribute to the *quality of the action or event* (such as ability or desire) and take a second verb that specifies the lexical content of the action or event. The second verb is in the Subjunctive.

አኀዘ:ይስብክ: 'he took up/began preaching' (Mk 1:45)

The most frequent light verbs in Gəʽəz are:

ፈቀደ   'to want, wish'
አኀዘ   'to begin, take up (activity)'

መከረ   'to decide to'
ኃደገ   'to permit, allow'
አብሐ [ብ-ዉ-ሕ] 'to permit, allow'

Vocabulary 21

አንበበ	he read, recited (CG)	መሐወ	he uprooted, plucked out (G)
አስተዋደየ[35]	he accused, slandered (CGlt)	ቆመ [ቅ-ዉ-ም][36]	he arose, stood (G)

EXERCISES

A. Read the phrases below—aloud—and then translate them into English.

1. ያንብብ

2. ታንብብ

3. ኣስተዋድይ

4. ኢትምሐዊ

5. ኢትቁማ

6. ታስተዋዱ

7. ታንብብ

8. ኢንቁም

9. እምሐዉ

10. ትቁሙ

---

[35] On verbs whose third root consonant is ዉ or የ, see the Appendix, §C.6.
[36] On verbs whose second root consonant is ዉ or የ, see the Appendix, §C.5.

B. Work back through all previous texts to find the occurrences of subjunctive verbs.

C. Now that you have learned all the vocabulary from Mark chapter 2, you may turn to the Abba Garima III manuscript pages 4–7 in Appendix F.1 and practice reading the scribal hand until you achieve fluidity.

LESSON 22
EVEN MORE ON SYNTAX

The ቀተሎ፡ለንጉሥ Construction

A bivalent verb in Gəʿəz requires a complement (Lesson 14). When that complement is a noun, the noun typically has the dependent -a (Lesson 12). Gəʿəz, however, has another common strategy to indicate a noun complement of a verb: the ቀተሎ፡ለንጉሥ 'he killed the king' construction. In this construction, a clitic pronoun indicating the complement is attached to the verb (ቀተሎ 'he killed him'), which is followed a ለ- prepositional phrase with the full noun to which the attached pronoun refers (ለንጉሥ 'regarding the king').

ያጥምቆሙ፡ለኵሎሙ፡በፈለገ፡ዮርዳኖስ።

'he was baptizing all of them (*lit.*, baptized them, ለ- all of them) in the Jordan River' (Mk 1:5)

እለ፡ሰምዕዎ፡ሊቃል፡. 'these hear the word (*lit.*, hear it, ለ- the word)' (Mk 4:18)

The origins of this construction may have been in the use of an appositional phrase following a forward-looking (cataphoric) pronoun: 'him, that is, concerning the king'). Whatever the origin, the construction has become a conventional means of indicating a complement that is specific and definite. (In contrast, the simple complement -*a* may be used to express any nominal complement regardless of its definiteness).

Partitive Apposition

When a part of something is the complement of the bivalent verb, it is often first referred to by an attached pronoun on the verb and then followed by an appositive noun clarifying the whole entity to which the part refers.

አኀዛ፡እዴሃ፡	'he took her, i.e., her hand' (Mk 1:31)
መኑ፡ገሰሰኒ፡ልብስየ፡	'Who touched me, i.e., my clothing?' (Mk 5:30)

Vocabulary 22

አፅንሐ[37]	he prepared, kept ready (CG)	ዑረት	blindness
አሕየወ	he restored to life, healed, cured (CG)	ማዕዶት	opposite side (PL ማዕዶታት)
ገሀደ	be revealed, become visible (G)	ነፍስ	soul (PL ነፍሳት)
ነጸረ	he looked at (G)		
ሰፍሐ	he stretched forth, widened (G)	እኁዝ	seized, possessed (ADJ)
ሰገደ	he bowed down, prostrated himself (G)	ሠናይ	beautiful, proper, good (ADJ)
ቀተለ	he killed (G)		
ጸርኀ	he cried out, shouted (G)		
ተጋፍዐ	oppressed one another, pressed upon (Glt)		
ተግሕሠ[38]	he withdrew, retreated, avoided (Gt)	አው	or
ተከዘ	he was sad, distressed (D)	ሚመ	or
ተምዕዐ	he was angry, indignant (Gt)		
ተማከረ	he counseled together, conspired (Glt)		

EXERCISES

A. Read the phrases below—aloud—and then translate them into English.

1. ሰፍሓ፡ለእዴሁ፡

2. ቀተሎቶሙ፡ለአራዊት፡

3. ነጸሮ፡ለሊቀ፡ካህናት፡

4. ያነብብዎን፡ለትእዛዛት

5. አስተዋደይናሁ፡ለነቢይ፡

6. ትገብሮ፡ለገራህት፡

7. አንዘሙ፡ለፀውሳን፡

8. ትሬክቦ፡ለክርስቶስ፡

---

[37] On verbs whose third root consonant is a guttural, see the Appendix, §C.3.
[38] On verbs whose second root consonant is a guttural, see the Appendix, §C.2.

9. ንስቲሁ፡ለወይን፡ብሉይ

10. አአኮትኮ፡ለእግዚአ፡ብሔር

B. Produce the phrases below in Gəʿəz.

1. His disciples prepared a boat for him.

2. Because he will cure many, the people will press upon him.

3. They accused him because he did good on the Sabbath.

4. She looked at us and was angry and sad because of the blindess of our heart.

5. The Pharisees immediately left and conspired that they would kill him.

6. Will those seized by unclean demons see Christ and bow down to him?

7. The disciples withdrew with Christ towards the sea.

8. I shouted and said, "You are the son of God!"

9. For what would you be revealed to the people?

10. Christ healed his blindness and restored his soul.

C. Work back through all previous texts to find the occurrences of the ቀተሎ፡ለንጉሥ construction.

D. Read the text below. First read it out loud, trying not to stop (choose whatever speed allows for a smooth reading). Second, read through it again, slowly, trying to recognize as many words as possible without stopping. Finally, go back and identify any words that you could not identify during your readings.

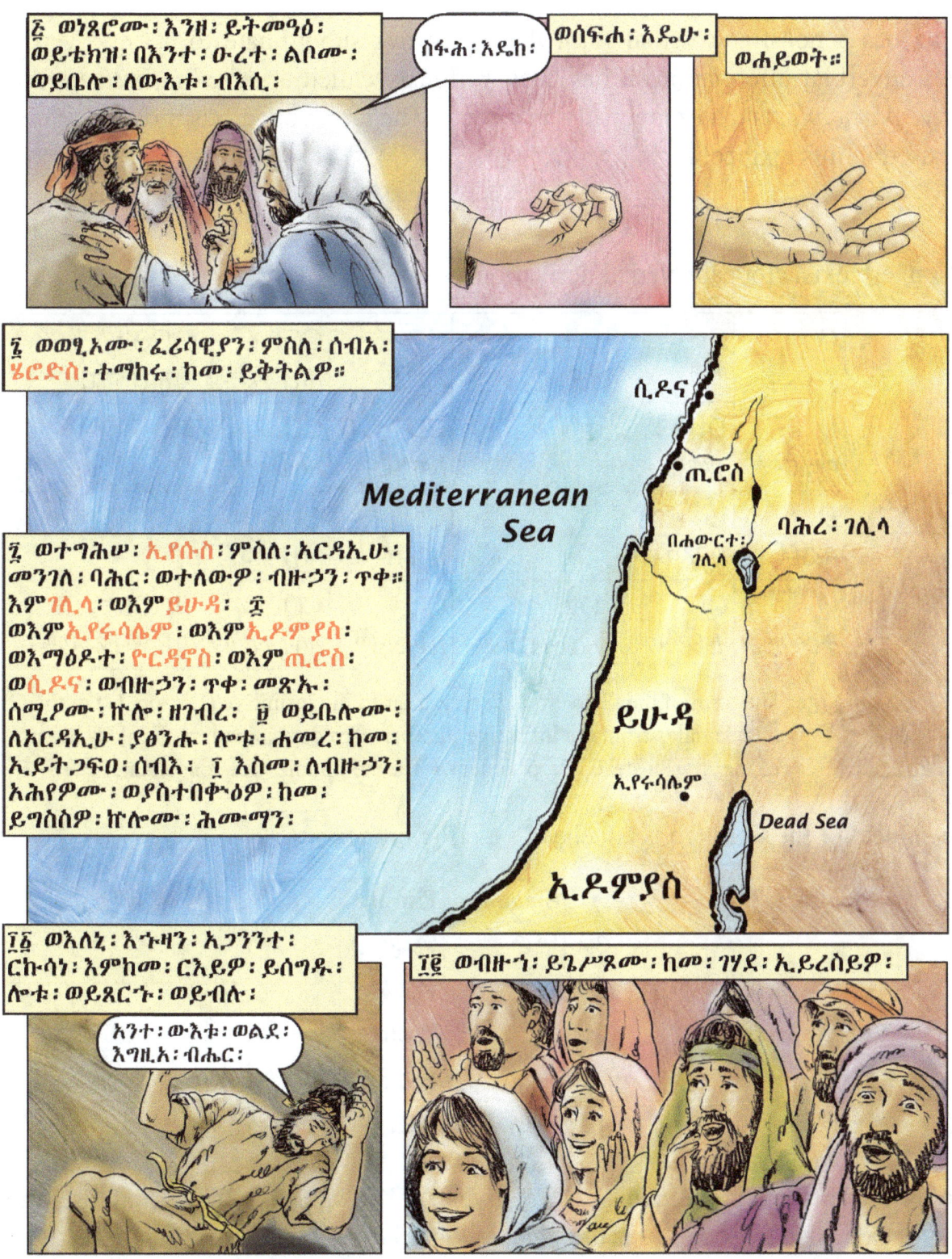

LESSON 23
STILL ON THE VERB—THE CONVERB

Gəʿəz has a non-finite verbal form that is always subordinate to a finite verb and provides adverbial information. It has been variously called a *verbal infinitive, gerund, perfective participle*, and more recently a *converb*. The term converb is most accurate and will be used in this textbook.

Form

A Converb exists for each verbal derivation:

G	Gt	Glt	CG	CGt	CGlt
ነጊር-	ተነጊር-	ተናጊር-	አንጊር-	አስተንጊር-	አስተናጊር-
D	Dt		CD	CDt	
መሂር-	ተመሂር-		አመሂር-	አስተመሂር-	
L	Lt		CL	CLt	
ባሪክ-	ተባሪክ-		አባሪክ-	አስተባሪክ-	
Q	Qt	Qlt	CQ	CQt	CQlt
ተርጉም-	ተተርጉም-	አስተተርጉም-	አተርጉም-	አስተተርጉም-	አስተተራጉም-

Note: The form of the Converb is very similar to the infinitive (Lesson 24) in the G and deviates from the infinitive in other verb derivational patterns by the use of the 3° -i- instead of a 6° order -ə- for the middle root consonant.

The subject of the Converb is attached as a clitic pronoun.

	Singular	Plural
3M	ነጊሮ	ነጊሮሙ
3F	ነጊራ	ነጊሮን
2M	ነጊረከ	ነጊረከሙ
2F	ነጊረኪ	ነጊረክን
1C	ነጊርየ	ነጊረነ

The form of the 1CS pronoun used, ነጊርየ '(when) I had spoken', shows that the form of the pronoun attached to Converbs is the same as those attached to nouns (not those attached to verbs). Moreover, the form of the 3MS pronoun, ቀቲሎ, indicates that the form of the subject pronouns attached to the Converb are actually the complement forms.

The Gəʿəz Converb does not allow attachment of complement pronouns, only subject pronouns. Any complement of the Converb must be expressed as a full noun phrase.

ወርኢዮ፡ኢየሱስ፡ሀይማኖቶሙ፡ይቤሎ፡ለውእቱ፡መፃጉዕ፡

'and he, Jesus, having seen <u>their faith</u>, he said to that paralytic ...' (Mk 2:5)

Function

The Gəʿəz Converb does not have its own tense, but takes it time setting from the finite verb for which it is an adjunct. In terms of aspect, it seems to be perfective, presenting the whole view of an action or event that had occurred prior to the action or event of the main verb.

English lacks a clear converb construction and translating the Gəʿəz Converb typically requires either a temporal clause, such as "when/after going out" or a participial phrase, such as "having left".

ወኂሊፆ፡እምህየ፡ሕቀ፡ረከበሙ፡ለያዕቆብ፡ወለዮሐንስ፡ (Mk 1:19)

'and passing from there a little, he found James and John'

or

'and he, having passed from there a little, found James and John'

or

'and (after) he had passed from there a little, he found James and John'

or

'and (when) he had passed from there a little, he found James and John'

Remember, however, that the use of participial *-ing* forms in these English constructions must not mislead us about the nature of the Gəʿəz Converb.

The cliticized subject pronoun may be followed by an appositional noun phrase that specifies the referent of the pronoun.

ወርኢዮ፡ኢየሱስ፡ሀይማኖቶሙ፡ይቤሎ፡ለውእቱ፡መፃጉዕ፡

'and he, Jesus, having seen <u>their faith</u>, he [i.e., Jesus] said to that paralytic ...' (Mk 2:5)

In the above example, the position of the complement ሀይማኖቶሙ after ኢየሱስ makes it clear that ኢየሱስ belongs within the Converb phrase and cannot be the formal subject constituent of the following main verb ይቤሎ.

As the previous example illustrates, most often the subject of the Converb is also linked referentially to the subject of the main verb.

ወወፂኦሙ፡እሙንቱ፡ኵልሄ፡ሰበኩ፡

'and they having gone out, they preached everywhere' (Mk 16:20)

In the previous examples, the subject of the converb (e.g., "they" in Mk 16:20) and the following main verb (e.g., "they") have the same referent.

Yet, there are cases in which the subject of the Converb is not the same as that of the main verb. In the examples below, the 3MP pronoun on the first Converb and the 3MS pronoun on the second both differ from the subjects of the main verb (አሕዛብ፡ብዙኃን in the first and ዮሴፍ፡እምአርማትያስ in the second).

ወበዊኦሙ፡ቤተ፡መጽኡ፡ካዕበ፡አሕዛብ፡ብዙኃን፡

'and their [Jesus and his disciples] having come home, many people came again' (Mk 3:20)

ወመሲዮ፡ዕርብ፡አሜሁ፡ብአተ፡ሰንበት፡ውእቱ፡ወመጽአ፡ዮሴፍ፡እምአርማትያስ፡

'and Sabbath eve having begun, ... Joseph of Arimathea came' (Mk 15:42–43)

Finally, the Converb cannot be negated. If a negative adjunct clause is desired, then Gə'əz requires the use of a subordinate clause, such as with ሶበ or እንዘ and a finite verb.

Vocabulary 23

አግብአ[39]	he took back; betrayed (CG)	እክል	food
ዐርገ[40]	he ascended, went up (G)	ደብር	mountain (PL አድባር)
ሰመየ[41]	he named, called (G)	ሐዋርያ	apostle (PL ሐዋርያት)
		ዘመድ	kin, family (PL አዝማድ)
ብሂል	that is to say		
		አስቆሮታዊ	Iscariot (ADJ)
		ዐብድ	foolish, insane (ADJ)
		ዐሠርቱ	ten
		ክልኤቱ	two
		ቀናናዊ	Canaanite (ADJ)

---

[39] On verbs whose third root consonant is a guttural, see the Appendix, §C.3.
[40] On verbs whose first root consonant is a guttural, see the Appendix, §C.1.
[41] On verbs whose third root consonant is ው or ይ, see the Appendix, §C.6.

Lesson 23—Still on the Verb—The Converb

EXERCISES

A. Read the phrases below—aloud—and then translate them into English.

1. አግቢአ፡አስቆሮታዊ፡ወልደ፡እጓለ፡እመ፡ሕያው፡

2. ዐሪጋ፡ፅውስት፡ደብረ፡

3. ሰሚየነ፡ክልኤቱ፡ሰብአ፡ሐዋርያተ፡

4. ጸሪነከ፡ለዘመድከ፡

5. ከዊኖ፡ቀናናዊ፡ዐብደ፡

6. ቀዊሞሙ፡ሐዋርያት፡ተግሕሡ፡ለአብያቲሆሙ፡

7. ተማኪረነ፡ዘመድክሙ፡በእንቲአክሙ፡

8. ረኢየ፡ዑረትኪ፡እፌውስኪ፡

9. አስተዋዲየከ፡ሊቀ፡ካህናት፡አርዳኢሁ፡ፀረፈተ፡

10. ርኄባ፡መሐወት፡ሠዊተ፡ወበልዐቶ፡

B. Work back through all previous texts to find the occurrences of a Converb.

C. Read the text below. Identify every Converb and describe how it is functioning in the text.

LESSON 24
RELATED TO THE VERB—THE INFINITIVE

The Form

The infinitives of the verbal derivational patterns of verbs are given in the table below:

G	Gt	Glt	CG	CGt	CGlt
ነጊር	ተነግሮ	ተናግሮ	አንግሮ	አስተንግሮ	አስተናግሮ
D	Dt		CD	CDt	
መህሮ	ተመህሮ		አመህሮ	አስተመህሮ	
L	Lt		CL	CLt	
ባርኮ	ተባርኮ		አባርኮ	አስተባርኮ	
Q	Qt	Qlt	CQ	CQt	CQlt
ተርጉሞ	ተተርጉሞ	አስተርጉሞ	አተርጉሞ	አስተተርጉሞ	አስተተራጉሞ

In the G form, the infinitive has the pattern ነጊር.

- ነቢር 'to sit'
- ገቢር 'to make'
- ዐሪግ 'to ascend'
- ኀሢሥ 'to seek'
- ወሪድ 'to descend'

In all other derivations, the formation of the infinitive follows the basic pattern of the Perfect with two small changes: the vowel before the final root consonant is *-ə-* and the vowel *-o* is added to the end of the word.

When a clitic pronoun is attached as the complement of the infinitive, the ending *-(o)t-* is inserted between the stem and the attached pronoun:

- አንጽሖትየ 'to purify me' (Mk 1:40)
- አብኦቶ 'to bring him in' (Mk 2:4)
- ብሂሎቱ፡ 'to tell him' (Mk 2:9)
- አውፅኦቶ 'to take it/him out' (Mk 9:28)

When a bivalent infinitive is itself the complement of a finite verb, the infinitive's own complement typically lacks the dependent *-a*.

መኑ፡ይክል፡ኃዲገ፡ኃጢአት፡ 'who is able <u>to forgive sin</u>' (Mk 2:7)

ስእነ፡በዊአ፡ሀገር፡ክሡተ። 'he was unable <u>to enter a city</u> uncovered' (Mk 1:45)

Occasionally, the complement of a bivalent infinitive has the dependent *-a*.

ትክሉኑ፡እንከ፡ስቲየ፡ጽዋዐ፡ዘአነ፡እሰቲ፡

'Are you able, then, <u>to drink the chalice</u> that I am drinking' (Mk 10:38)

Functions

The various constructions using an infinitive are described in the sub-points below.

Verbal Complement

The most frequent use of the infinitive is as a complement to another verb, especially verbs like ክህለ 'he was able' and ስእነ 'he was unable'.

ይክሉኑ፡ደቂቁ፡ለመርዓዊ፡<u>ጸዊመ</u>፡አምጣነ፡ሀሎ፡መርዓዊ፡ምስሌሆሙ፡

'Are the children of the bridegroom able <u>to fast</u> as long as the bridegroom is with them?' (Mk 2:19)

ወአልቦ፡ዘይክል፡ቤተ፡ኃያል፡በዊአ፡

'and no one is able <u>to enter</u> the house of a strong man' (Mk 3:27)

Notice that when the G infinitive is a verbal complement, it has the dependent *-a*.

There is discrete group of verbs that provide qualities of events or actions are also used with infinitive as their complements. In these cases, English is largely unable to gloss mimetically the resulting meaning, but requires glossing the infinitive as the finite verb and the finite verb as an adverb. For example, ቀደመ 'he preceded, did first' plus an infinitive (X) results in 'he X-ed first/beforehand'.

ለእመ፡ኢቀደመ፡አሲሮቶ፡ለኃያል፡

'if he does not precede to bind him' → 'bind him first/beforehand' (Mk 3:27)

ዛቲ፡ነድይ፡መበለት፡አብዝኀት፡አብአ፡እምኵሎሙ

'this poor widow has increased to bring in' → 'brought in much' (Mk 12:43)

Though used rarely in AG III Mark, typical verbs of this type in Gəʿəz are:

ቀደመ	'to do [X] first or beforehand'
አፍጠነ	'to do [X] quickly or soon'
ኀብረ	'to do [X] jointly, together'
ደገመ	'to do [X] again, continue to do [X]'
አብዝኀ	'to do [X] a lot, frequently'
ጐንደየ	'to do [X] late, tardily'

Infinitives as Gerunds

Typically, the subject of the action described by the infinitive is inherited from the finite verb that controls the infinitive; in these cases, the subject is not overtly expressed with the infinitive.

But in some cases, the infinitive may be used as a gerund and the subject is signaled by an attached pronoun:

መህሮቶ   'his teaching' (Mk 1:22)

Vocabulary 24

አሰረ[42]	he bound, imprisoned (G)	እኀት	sister (PL አኀት)
አውሥአ[43]	he answered, responded (CG)	ዓለም	world, eternity (PL ዓለማት)
በርበረ	he plundered (Q)	ደይን	judgment
ፀረፈ	he blasphemed (G)	ፈቃድ	desire, wish (PL ፈቃዳት)
ለአከ[44]	he sent a message, messenger (G)	ማኀለቅት	cessation, end
መሰለ	he spoke in parables (D)	ንዋይ	vessel, possessions
ቀደመ	he preceded (G)		(PL ንዋያት)
ተኰነነ	he was judged, condemned (Dt)		
ተናፈቀ	he was torn, divided (Glt)	ኀያል	strong, valiant (ADJ)
አሜን	truly, Amen	አውደ	around
ዝሉፉ	continuously, forever (ADV)	ነ-	behold!

---

[42] On verbs whose first root consonant is a guttural, see the Appendix, §C.1.
[43] On verbs whose third root consonant is a guttural, see the Appendix, §C.3.
[44] On verbs whose second root consonant is a guttural, see the Appendix, §C.2.

Lesson 24—Related to the Verb—The Infinitive

EXERCISES

A. Read the phrases below—aloud—and then translate them into English.

1. አሲር፡ኃያል፡

2. አውሥኦቶ፡ለፈቃዶ፡

3. ፀፈር፡ዲበ፡እግዚአ፡ብሔር

4. ለኢኪ፡በእንተ፡አኃቲከ፡

5. መስሎ፡በእንተ፡ደይን፡

6. ብርብሮሙ፡ለንዋያተ፡ሰብእ፡

7. ተናፈቆ፡ኃበ፡ፈቃዳት፡እኩያን፡

8. ቀዲም፡ማኅለቀተ፡ዓለም፡

9. ተኮኖ፡ኃበ፡ሰብእ፡ጻድቃን፡

10. ሐዊር፡አውደ፡ሀገር፡

B. Work back through all previous texts to find the occurrences of an Infinitive.

Lesson 24—Related to the Verb—The Infinitive

C. Read the texts below. Identify every Infinitive and describe how it is functioning in the text.

LESSON 25
RELATIVE CLAUSES

Relative Clauses

Relative clauses are clauses that modify a noun similar to the way that adjectives do except that the relatives, as clauses, allow greater complexity in the modifying description.

Relative Markers

To introduce relative clauses, Gəʿəz uses a system of relative markers (not pronouns!) that are partially inflected for gender and number to match the noun that the relative clause modifies.

	Singular	**Plural**
MASC	ዘ-	ኡለ
FEM	እንተ	

ቃል፡እምስማይ፡ዘይብል፡	'a voice from heaven <u>that</u> was saying' (Mk 1:11)
ዛቲ፡ጥበብ፡<u>እንተ</u>፡ተውህበት፡ሎቱ፡	'this wisdom <u>that</u> is given to him' (Mk 6:2)
ብዙኃን፡<u>እለ</u>፡የሐውሩ፡	'many <u>who</u> were going' (Mk 6:32)

As the examples illustrate, gender is distinguished in the singular markers, but not in the plural—እለ is the common plural relative marker. Moreover, the proclitic ዘ- is often used as a default marker, regardless of the modified noun's gender or number.

ከመ፡አባግዕ፡ዘአልቦ፡ኖላዌ፡	'like sheep (PL) <u>that</u> (SG) have no shepherd' (Mk 6:34)

Syntax

The examples above demonstrate that Gəʿəz relative clauses are normally *postnominal*, that is, they <u>follow the noun they modify</u>. There are cases of *prenominal* relative clauses, but these reflect the non-Semitic, Cushitic substratum influence on the language.

በ<u>ዘ</u>፡ከመዝ፡<u>አምሳል</u>፡	'with <u>parables that</u> were like this' (Mk 4:33)

The noun modified by a relative clause corresponds to a position within the relative itself, such as the subject or complement.

ቃል፡እምስማይ፡ዘይብል፡	'<u>a voice</u> from heaven that [it] was saying' (Mk 1:11)
አንተ፡ውእቱ፡ወልድየ፡ዘአፈቅር፡	'you are <u>my son</u> who I love [him]' (Mk 1:11)

Gəʿəz allows the noun modified by the relative clause to be "resumed" within the relative clause by means of a pronoun (or, less commonly, by a noun that shares the same reference). Note that this relative resumption is often awkward or simply ungrammatical when translated directly into English.

ዐራቱ፡ዘዲቤሁ፡ይሰክብ፡ 'his <u>bed</u> that he was lying upon <u>it</u>' (Mk 2:4)

ብእሲ፡ዘየብስት፡እዴሁ። 'a <u>man</u> who <u>his</u> hand had withered' (Mk 3:1)

Gəʿəz also allows relative clauses to modify a null (implied) noun.

እለ፡ምስሌሁ። '(the people) <u>who</u> were with him' (Mk 1:36)

ኢርኢነ፡ዘከመዝ። 'we have not seen (a thing) <u>that</u> is like this' (Mk 2:12)

ዘገብረ፡ዳዊት፡ '(the thing) <u>that</u> David did' (Mk 2:25)

Typically, the relative follows immediately after the noun it modifies, but they can also be separated by other words.

ናሁ፡አነ፡እፌኑ፡መልአኪየ፡ቅድመ፡ገጽከ፡ዘይጸይሕ፡ፍኖተከ፡

'behold—I am sending my <u>messenger</u> before you <u>who</u> will level your path' (Mk 1:2)

ሰምዐት፡<u>ብእሲት</u>፡በእንቲአሁ፡<u>እንተ</u>፡ጋኔን፡አኩይ፡አኀዘ፡ላቲ፡ወለታ፡

'a <u>woman</u> heard about him <u>who</u> her daughter had been seized by a demon' (Mk 7:25)

Some uses of the relative clause are very similar to the use of the bound construction or adjectives to modify a noun. For instance, a relative clause (typically with ዘ-, rarely with እንተ or እለ) may contain only one noun indicating a substance that is used to describe some feature of the noun modified. The precise relationship between the noun and the feature inside the relative varies considerably—it may be origin, authorship, material etc.—and must be reconstructed from the context.

ቅናቱ፡ዘአዲም፡ 'his belt was leather (material)' < '(material) that [*consists of*] leather' (Mk 1:6)

ብእሲ፡ዘጋኔን፡ 'a demoniac' < 'a man who was [*seized by*] demon' (Mk 1:23)

ናዝሬት፡ዘገሊላ፡ 'Galilean Nazareth' < 'Nazareth that is [*located in*] Galilee' (Mk 1:9)

ወንጌል፡ዘማርቆስ፡ 'Mark's Gospel' < 'the Gospel that was [*written by*] Mark' (Mk *title*)

When this type of relative is also modifying a null or implied noun, the whole construction is very elliptical:

ዘለምጽ   'a leper' < '(a person) that was [*afflicted by*] leprosy' (Mk 1:40)

ዘጸጕረ፡ገመል፦ 'camel-hair clothes' < '(clothes) that were [*made of*] camel hair' (Mk 1:6)

እለ፡አጋንንት   'demoniacs' < '(people) that are [*seized by*] demons') (Mk 1:32)

እለ፡ክርስቶስ፦   'those of Christ' < '(people) that [*follow*] Christ' (Mk 9:41)

Vocabulary 25

አፍተነ	he handed over for examination (CG)	አንበጣ	locust, grasshopper (PL አናብጥ)
አስተብረከ	he knelt, fell on his knees (CGt)		
አተወ	he went home, departed (for home) (G)	ሕዝብ	people, nation; crowd (PL አሕዛብ, ሕዘብ)
ዐረየ	it was level; he was equal to (D)		
ዴገነ	he pursued, persecuted, tracked (Q/L)	መዐር	honey; honeycomb
ፈጸመ	he completed; accomplished (D)	ሠእን	shoe, sandal (PL አሣእን)
		ጸዴና	wild bee, bee that lives underground
ኪያ-	emphatic complement pronoun base		
ለሊ-	-self	ቲታን	lace, thong, lace (PL ቶታናት)
ናሁ	Behold! Now!	ካልእ	(F ካልእት) other, another, second (ADJ)

EXERCISES

1. Read the phrases below—aloud—and then translate them into English.

   1. ፅውስ፡ዘአፍተኑ፡ለካህን፦

   2. ሕዝብ፡ዘዴገነ፦

   3. እለ፡ይዴግኑ፡ሐዋርያተ፦

   4. ፍኖት፡እንተ፡ዐረገት፦

   5. ጸዴና፡ዘዴገነ፡አንበጠ፦

   6. አሕዛብ፡እለ፡አተዉ፦

7. ብእሲ፡ዘአስተብረከ፡ቅድመ፡ክርስቶስ፡

8. ቶታናት፡እለ፡አኀእኒየ

9. ብእሲት፡እንተ፡በልዐት፡መዐረ፡

10. አኀእን፡እለ፡ፈጸምነ፡

B. Work back through all previous texts to find the occurrences of a Relative Clause.

C. Now that you have learned all the vocabulary from Mark chapters 1–3, you may turn to all the Abba Garima III manuscript pages for that text, given in Appendix F.1, and practice reading the scribal hand until you achieve fluidity.

LESSON 26
ለ- AND በ- WITH CLITIC PRONOUNS

ለ- With Clitic Pronouns

Though many of the pronouns attached to the preposition ለ- are identical to those attached to nouns (Lesson 15) and most other prepositions (Lesson 17), the 3MS, 3FS, and 1CS forms do differ (grey highlighted in the chart below) and must be memorized.

singular		plural	
ሎቱ	to him	ሎሙ	to them (M)
ላቲ	to her	ሎን	to them (F)
ለከ	to you (M)	ለክሙ	to you (M)
ለኪ	to you (F)	ለክን	to you (F)
ሊተ	to me	ለነ	to us

In meaning, the preposition ለ- corresponds to English 'to', 'for', including the sense of 'belonging to' as well as 'with regard to'. However, it is also used to fulfill the valency of many verbs and in such cases is often not mimetically translatable in English.

በ- With Clitic Pronouns

As with the pronouns attached to the preposition ለ-, many of the pronouns attached to the preposition በ- are identical to those attached to nouns and most other prepositions. However, as with ለ-, the 3MS, 3FS forms differ (grey highlighted in the chart below) and must be memorized.

singular		plural	
ቦ, ቦቱ	in him	ቦሙ	in them (M)
ባ, ባቲ	in her	ቦን, ቦንቱ, ቦቶን	in them (F)
በከ	in you (M)	በክሙ	in you (M)
በኪ	in you (F)	በክን	in you (F)
ብየ	in me	በነ	in us

In these forms the preposition may have its core meaning ('in, by, with') or one of the extended uses presented in Lesson 28.

Vocabulary 26

አስተርአየ	it became visible; he made visible (CGt)	እብሬት	alternation; turn of office
ዐጠነ	he burned incense (G)	ዕጣን	incense (PL ዕጣናት)
ረትዐ	it was straight; he was righteous (G)	መቅደስ	temple, sanctuary
		መሥዋዕ	altar (PL ምሥዋዓት)
ተመህረ	he was taught; he learned (Dt)	ስም	name; fame, reputation (PL አስማት)
ጠየቀ	he examined, investigated (D)	ጥንት	beginning
ወጠነ	he began (G=D)	ወለት	daughter, girl, maidservant (PL አዋልድ)
በበ	reduplication = distributive		
በምልኡ-	fully, completely, all together	የማን	the right (side or hand)
ጥዮቀ	precisely, accurately, certainly (ADV)	ዐዚዝ	powerful, strong, excellent (ADJ)
		ልሂቅ	old, grown-up, adult (ADJ)
		መካን	sterile, childless, barren (ADJ)
		መትለው	following; successive (ADJ)
		ንጹሕ	pure, clean; innocent (ADJ)

EXERCISES

A. Read the phrases below—aloud—and then translate them into English.

1. ዐጠነ፡ካህን፡ዕጣነ፡ለነ፡

2. ረትዐት፡ወለታ፡ብከሙ፡

3. መሥዋዕ፡ዘቦቱ፡

4. አስተርአየ፡እግዚአ፡ብሔር፡ብነ፡

5. ጠየቁ፡ጸሐፍት፡ስማ፡ሊተ፡

6. ወጠነት፡እብሬታ፡በሙ፡

7. ተመህረ፡በበ፡መትለው፡ሎቱ፡

8. እጠይቅ፡የማነ፡ጥዩቀ፡ለከሙ፡

9. ረትዕነ፡በምልኡነ፡ብከሙ፡

10. ልሂቃት፡ብነ፡ኮና፡መካናተ፡

B. Work back through all previous texts to find the occurrences of ለ- or በ- with Clitic Pronouns

C. Using all old and new vocabulary and your grammatical knowledge, sight read as much as you can from first from the first page of AG III Luke, given in Appendix F.2.

LESSON 27
FINISH THE VERB!

The Imperative

The Gəʿəz Imperative is related to the shape of the Subjunctive. The difference is that the Imperative lacks an inflectional prefix. The result in the G, D, L, and Q is a form that is identical to the Subjunctive without the 2nd person prefixes:

		G 'say!'	D 'watch!'	L 'bless!'	Q 'be terrified!'
MS	አንተ	ንግር	ነጽር	ባርክ	ደንግፅ
FS	አንቲ	ንግሪ	ነጽሪ	ባርኪ	ደንግፂ
MP	አንትሙ	ንግሩ	ነጽሩ	ባርኩ	ደንግፁ
FP	አንትን	ንግራ	ነጽራ	ባርካ	ደንግፃ

For the other derivations, the Imperative drops the Subjunctive prefix and adds back on the appropriate prefix that marks the derivational type: for causative-resultative derivations, an አ is prefixed to the subjunctive stem; for the passive-reflexive and reciprocal derivations, a ተ is prefixed to the Subjunctive stem. The Gt and CG below should suffice as exemplar paradigms:

		Gt 'say!'	CG 'love!'
MS	አንተ	ተነገር	አፍቅር
FS	አንቲ	ተነገሪ	አፍቅሪ
MP	አንትሙ	ተነገሩ	አፍቅሩ
FP	አንትን	ተነገራ	አፍቅራ

Cliticized complement pronouns of the 1st and 3rd persons may be attached (and are in form like those added as to the Subjunctive and Imperfect). For example,

| ንግሮ | 'tell (ms) him!' |
| ንግርዋ | 'tell (mp) her!' |

Vocabulary 27

ገሐፈ	he removed; he swept away (G)	ዕፅ	tree, shrub; wood (PL ዕፀው)
ተነግፈ	it was knocked off; it lost leaves (Gt)	ፍሬ	fruit (PL ፍሬያት, ፍርያት)
ጠፍአ	it was extinguished; he perished, was lost (G)	ሕግ	law, statute; custom
		ሙሓዝ	aqueduct, channel; river, brook
ዳእሙ	just, merely, only (ADV); furthermore, moreover; rather, but, on the contrary (CONJ)	ምክር	plan, counsel, advice
		መንበር	throne, seat, chair (PL መናብርት)
		መሬት	dirt, dust
		መስተሳልቅ	mocker, scorner (PL መስተሳልቃን)
ብፁዕ	fortunate, blessed; dedicated (ADJ)	ቄጽል	leaf, foliage (PL አቁጽል)
ረሲዕ	godless, impious, sinful (ADJ)		
ትኩል	planted (ADJ)		

EXERCISES

A. Read the phrases below—aloud—and then translate them into English.

1. ገሐፈ፡ዕፀወ፡

2. ነፃሩ፡መሬተ፡

3. ንብሪ፡በመንበር፡

4. ስምዑ፡ምክረ፡

5. ብልዓ፡ፍሬ፡

6. ዬግኑ፡መስተሳልቀ፡

7. መህር፡ሕገ፡

8. ስቲ፡እምሙሓዝ፡

9. ትልዉ፡ድጓረ፡ብዑዕ፡

10. ገሥጺ፡ረሲዓነ፡

B. Work back through AG III Mark 1–3 to find the occurrences of an Imperative

C. Using the new vocabulary, read Psalm 1 from the earliest printed Ge'ez book, a Psalter from 1513. (Don't forget to read it aloud!).

LESSON 28
FINISHING THE PREPOSITIONS

More on the Preposition ብ-

ብ- *Indicating Possession*

Besides the normal meanings, ብ- with an attached pronoun has also developed into a possessive construction, in which the pronoun indicates the possessor and an adjacent noun (often with the dependent -*a*) is the thing possessed.

    ሚመጠነ፡ኅብስት፡ብከሙ። 'how much bread do you have?' (Mk 6:38)
                             (*lit*., 'bread is with you')

    ወበሙ፡ዓሣሂ፡ሕዳጠ። 'and they had a few fish' (Mk 8:7) (*lit*., 'a few fish was with them')

    ወለዘቦ፡ይሁብዎ፡. 'and concerning he who has, they will give him [more]' (Mk 4:25a)
                     (*lit*., 'he who [something] is with him')

    ወአዕይንተ፡ብከሙ፡ወኢትሬእዩ፡ 'and you have eyes and do not see' (Mk 8:18)
                          (*lit*., 'eyes are with you')

The negative is formed by prefixing አል-: አልብየ, አልብከ, etc.

    ወለዘሰ፡<u>አልቦ፡</u>እለሂ፡ይሀይድዎ። 'but concerning him who <u>does not have</u>, even those
                      (things) that he has—they will take it away' (Mk 4:25b)

    <u>አልብከሙ፡</u>ሃይማኖተ፡ 'you <u>do not have</u> faith' (Mk 4:40)

Clauses with the ብ- of possession do not have an inherent time setting; rather, the time setting is determined by the discourse context.

ቦ, ቦቱ *Indicating Existence*

A further development of the ብ- preposition is as an existential marker. ብ- with the 3MS attached pronoun, i.e., ቦ or ቦቱ (negative አልቦ, አልቦቱ), became used to predicate existence. This function likely developed from the spatial use of the preposition, i.e., 'X is in it (e.g., the room)'. When this existential notion of ቦ developed, the location was superfluous to the new construction: 'X exists [in the room]' or 'there is X [in the room]'. The noun following the existential use of ብ- may or may not have the dependent -*a*.

    ወ<u>ቦቱ</u>፡ህየ፡መራዕየ፡አሕርው፡ብዙኅ፡ይትሬዐይ፡መንገለ፡ደብር፡ (Mk 5:11)
    'and <u>there was</u> there a herd of many swine (which was) grazing by the mountain'

ወአልቦ፡ኅቡእ፡. 'there is no hidden thing' (Mk 4:22)

በ ዘ- as the Equivalent of an Indefinite Pronoun

The በ of existence is especially frequent in combination with the relative pronoun ዘ- (the plural እለ is rare in this particular construction). Though grammatically this construction is a null head relative with the existential በ, 'there is (one) who does X', it is often translated in English by the indefinite pronouns 'someone, something', or with the negative, 'no one, nothing'.

ወእንዘ፡ይዘርእ፡በዘወድቀ፡ውስተ፡ፍኖት፡
'and while he was sowing, some [seed] fell on the path' (Mk 4:4)

ወአልቦ፡ዘይክል፡አድክሞቶ።
'and no one was able to weaken him' (Mk 5:3)

Vocabulary 28

አጽሐድ	he caused to be tender; he anointed (CG)	ዕረፍት	rest, peace, quiet, repose
ፈርህ	he was afraid; he feared, revered (G)	በትር	staff, branch, scepter; tribe (PL አብትር)
ሐፀነ	he nursed, reared, trained (G)		
ኀደረ	he resided, dwelt, inhabited (G)	ሕይወት	life, lifetime
ኀጥአ	he lacked, missed, sinned (G)	ማእድ	table, banquet, meal (PL ማእዳት)
መርሐ	he led, guided (G)	ምሕረት	mercy, pity (PL ምሥረታት)
ሜጠ [ም-ይ-ጥ][45] he turned aside; he returned, restored (G)		ሞት	death
		ቅብእ	(olive) oil, ointment, butter
ሣቀየ	he afflicted, tormented (L)	ቀስታም	bow, shepherd's crook, rod
ሠርዐ	he arranged; he established; he made a covenant (G)	ጽድቅ	justice; truth; righteousness (PL ጽድቃት)
		ጽላሎት	shade, shadow(s), darkness
ሥዑር	grassy, covered with vegetation (ADJ)	ጽዋዕ	cup, goblet, chalice (PL ጽዋዓት)
ነዋኅ	high (ADJ)	አንጸረ	opposite, toward, in front of (ADV)
ጽኑዕ	strong (ADJ)		

---

[45] On verbs whose second root consonant is ው or ይ, see the Appendix, §C.5.

Lesson 28—Finishing the Prepositions

EXERCISES

A. Work back through AG III Mark 1–3 to find the special uses of Prepositions covered in this Lesson.

B. Using the new vocabulary, read Psalm 23 (22) from the 1513 Psalter, given in Appendix F.3. (Don't forget to read it aloud!).

LESSON 29
FINISHING THE NOUN

The Agent Noun ቀታሊ

From most active G verbs there may be made the form ቀታሊ (F ቀታሊት; PL ቀታልያን / ቀታልያት or common ቀተልት), an agent noun denoting one who performs, usually habitually or professionally, the action denoted by the verb:

ዐቃቢ	'one who guards', i.e., 'a guard'
ጸሓፊ	'one who writes', i.e., 'a scribe, writer'
ነዳቂ	'one who builds', i.e., 'a builder'

Nouns of the Pattern ምቅታል

There are two principal types of nouns with prefixed ም- derived from G verbs. The most consistently predictable in terms of meaning is ምቅታል, which usually denotes the place where the action of the verb is customarily performed. Below are examples from AG III Mark.

ምኵራብ	'synagogue, temple, sanctuary'
ምጽባሕ	'tax office'
ምርፋቅ	'place for reclining, dining hall, feast, meal'
ምሥያጥ	'marketplace'
ምጽዋት	'alms, charity'

The gender of these nouns is variable; plurals, when attested, are uniformly in -āt.

Nouns of the Pattern መቅተል

The second type of noun with prefixed ም- is መቅተል. Nouns of this formation cover a wide range of meanings (nouns of place, of instrument, of action) and should not be guessed at. For example,

መንፈስ (PL መንፈሳት)	'spirit'
መልአክ (PL መላእክት)	'messenger'
መካን (PL መካናት)	'place'
መንበር (PL መናብርት)	'throne, seat, chair'

For some verbs the form መቅተልት (with final -ት) is used, often along with መቅተል, with the same range of meanings (cf. መሥዋዕት 'sacrifice' from ሠውዐ):

መቅበርት (PL መቃብር)   'grave, tomb, sepulcher'

መንበርት   'state, condition, mode of life'

Vocabulary 29

አንበረ	he set, placed; he settled (CG)	እብን	stone (PL እበን, አእባን)
አስሐተ	he led astray, into sin; he corrupted (CG)	እሳት	fire
		ኢዮቤል	trumpet, jubilee (pl ኢዮቤላውሳት)
ነደደ / ነደ	it burned (G)	ዓለም	world; eternity (PL ዓለማት)
ጸለለ	it shaded, covered	ዓም	year (PL ዓመታት)
አለበወ	he instructed (CD)	ዐሡር	tenth day (of month); ten days
ተናገረ	he spoke to, with (Glt)	ደመና	cloud(s) (PL ደመናት)
ተሰብዐ	it was made seven (times) (Gt)	ፀአት	exit, departure; exodus
		ግብር	deed, act; work, task (PL ግብራት, ግበር)
		ግብጽ	Egypt
መጠነ	during, according to, about, as long as	ኩፋሌ	partition, division, distribution
		መጽሐፍ	writing; book, document (PL መጻሕፍት)
		ስብሐት	praise, glory, majesty (PL ስብሐታት)
		ሰዱስ	sixth day (of week, month); six days
ሳብዕ	seventh (ADJ)	ሥርዐት	order; statue; testament (PL ሥርዐታት)
ሣልስ	third (ADJ)	ጽሌ / ጽላ	tablet (PL ጽላት)
		ወርኅ	moon, month (PL አውራኅ)

EXERCISES

A. Work back through AG III Mark 1–3 to find the Noun Patterns introduced in this Lesson.

B. Using the new vocabulary, read the first page of the Book of Jubilees from a manuscript in the Gunda Gunde monastery collection, given in Appendix F.4. (Don't forget to read it aloud!).

LESSON 30
FINISHING THE PRONOUN

A Special Use of the Third Person Singular Clitic Pronouns

The 3MS cliticized pronouns (-ሁ, -*u*; -ሃ, -*ā*) are sometimes used with the force of a definite article or weak demonstrative.

ብእሲሁ 'his man' > '*that* man' = 'the man in question'

This usage is especially frequent on nouns denoting points or periods of time (e.g., በዕለቱ 'on the day in question') and appears in such fixed expressions, such as:

አሜሃ	'when, at *that* time'
ቀዳሚሁ	'at *the* beginning'
ሶቤሃ	'at *that* time, immediately'
ጊዜሃ	'at *that* time, right away'
ሳኒታ	'*the* next day'

Clitic Pronouns equivalent to a Benefactive Prepositional Phrase

Pronouns attached to verbs as the verbal complement are often used to express various semantic roles other than the complement.

| ወሀበኒ፡ኅብስተ | = | ወሀበ፡ሊተ፡ሕብስተ |
| 'He gave me bread' | = | 'He gave to me bread' (*better*: 'He gave bread to me') |

The enclitic pronoun on the verb in the first example expresses the recipient of the action. This can be expressed in the same way by a prepositional phrase with ለ-. Similarly, consider the next pair:

| ሰአለኒ፡ኅብስተ | = | ሰአለ፡ኅብስተ፡እምኔየ |
| 'He asked me (for) bread' | = | 'He asked (for) bread from me' |

The enclitic pronoun in the first example corresponds to the prepositional phrase with እምኔየ in the second example (note that the prepositional phrase ኀቤየ also works with the verb ሰአለ).

Lesson 30—Finishing the Pronoun

There are only a few categories of verbs where such constructions are frequent, and these are listed below.

a. Verbs of speaking, addressing, telling, and asking:

ይነግሮሙ፡ቃሎ 'He was telling (to) them his message' (Mk 2:2)

b. Verbs of giving:

ወሀበክሙ፡ሙሴ፡ዛተ፡ትእዛዘ. 'Moses gave (to) you this commandment' (Mk 10:5)

c. The verbs of motion — በጽሐ, መጽአ in the sense of 'happen to':

ይምጻእክሙ፡ግብተ 'he comes (to) you suddenly' (Mk 13:36)

Note: With these verbs, the clitic pronouns replace prepositional phrases with, e.g., ላዕለ and ዲበ.

Vocabulary 30

አስምዐ	he made summon; he summoned as a witness (CG)	ዕም/አም	tree(s), dense grove, woods (PL ዕማት)
ድኅነ	he was saved; he escaped safely (G)	አምላክ	the Lord, god; (false) gods (PL አማልክት)
ፀግበ /ጸግበ	he was sated, filled (G)		
ኀብአ	he hid, concealed (G)	ዐይን	eye (PL አዕይንት)
መሐለ	he swore, took an oath (G)	ደብተራ	tabernacle; sanctuary (PL ደብትር)
ቀደሰ	he sanctified, consecrated (D)	ዐዕር / ጻዕር	pain, torment; grief, sorrow
ረስዐ	he forgot; he was negligent; he was impious, godless (G)	ፀር	enemy, adversary (PL አፅራር)
		ፍኖሐት	narrow passage, ravine; elevated shrine (PL ፍኖሐታት)
ሰደደ	he persecuted; he drove out, banished (G)	ፍትሕ	precept, law; judgment, decision
ሰገደ	he bowed down; he worshipped (G)	ግልፅ	carved idol, statue (PL ግልፋት, አግልእት)
ሤመ [ሥ-ይ-ም][46] he appointed; he put, placed (G)		ሐሊብ	milk
		ሒሰት	reviling, blaming
አዕርዐ /አጽርዐ	he ceased; he brought to a stop; he neglected (CG)	ኅሳር / ኅሣር	dishonor, abominable thing, humiliation (PL ኅሳራት)
ተአኀዘ	he was seized, held (Gt)		

---

[46] On verbs whose second root consonant is ው or ይ, see the Appendix, §C.5.

ትሕጕለ / ተሀጕለ he was lost, destroyed (Gt)	ኪዳን pact, covenant; will, testament (PL ኪዳናት)
ተመይጠ he faced about, returned, turned away; he was converted (Gt)	ክሰድ neck (PL ክሰዳት, ክሳውድ)
ተቀንየ he served, ministered (Gt)	ማዕቀፍ obstacle, stumbling block (PL ማዕቀፋት)
ወድቀ he fell (G)	መዓር honey; honeycomb
ውኅዘ/ውሕዘ it flowed (G)	ምግባር action, behavior; workmanship (PL ምግባራት)
ዘብሐ he slaughtered, sacrificed (G)	ምንዳቤ affliction, torment
ዚአ- form of ዘ relative before pronouns	ምረት bitterness, anger, rancor; rebellion
ዘዘ reduplication used for distributive	ቅድሳት holiness, sanctity, sanctuary
ሰማዒ hearing, listening to, obedient (ADJ); as noun: witness, martyr (PL ሰማዕት)	ርኵስ uncleanness; abomination
ነኪር strange, foreign, different; marvelous (ADJ)	ስሒት error, deceit (PL ስሒታት)
ይቡስ dry, arid; paralyzed, stiff (ADJ)	ዘርእ seed; progeny, offspring (pl አዝርእት)

EXERCISES

A. Work back through AG III Mark 1–3 to find the uses of the Pronoun introduced in this Lesson.

B. Using the new vocabulary, read the second page from the Gunda Gunde Book of Jubilees, provided in Appendix F.4. (Don't forget to read it aloud!).

APPENDICES

Appendix A—Noun and Pronoun Paradigms *149*
Appendix B—Strong Verb Paradigms *151*
Appendix C—Weak Verb Paradigms *157*
Appendix D—The Verb with Enclitic Pronouns *168*
Appendix E—Numerals *169*
Appendix F—Manuscripts Images with Texts *172*
Appendix G—Vocabulary by Lesson *198*

APPENDIX A
NOUN AND PRONOUN PARADIGMS

1. Pronouns

A. Personal Pronouns: Subject (Free) Forms and Complement (Enclitic) Forms

SINGULAR			Noun ending w/Consonant	Noun ending w/Vowel	Plural Noun	Verbs	ለ-	በ-
3M	he, it	ወኡቱ	-u/o	ሁ	ሁ	ሁ /-o	ሉቱ	ቦ, ቦቱ
3F	she, it	ይእቲ	-ā	ሃ	ሃ	ሃ /-ā	ላቲ	ባ, ባቲ
2M	you	አንተ	ከ	ከ	ከ	ከ	ለከ	ብከ
2F	you	አንቲ	ኪ	ኪ	ኪ	ኪ	ለኪ	ብኪ
1C	I	አነ	የ	የ	የ	ኒ	ሊተ	ብየ
PLURAL								
3M	they	እሙንቱ	ሙ	ሆሙ	ሆሙ	(ሆ)ሙ	ሎሙ	ቦሙ
3F	they	እማንቱ	ን	ሆን	ሆን	(ሆ)ን	ሎን	ቦን, ቦንቱ
2M	you	አንትሙ	ከሙ	ከሙ	ከሙ	ከሙ	ለከሙ	ብከሙ
2F	you	አንትን	ከን	ከን	ከን	ከን	ለከን	ብከን
1C	we	ንሕነ	ነ	ነ	ነ	ነ	ለነ	ብነ
EXAMPLES			ሀገሩ 'his city'	ጸሐፊሁ 'his scribe'	አህጉሪሁ 'his cities'	ቀተሎ 'he killed him'		

B. Demonstrative Pronouns

		Singular			Plural		
this	MASC	ዝ-, ዝንቱ		COMP ዘ-, ዘንተ	እሉ, እሎንቱ	COMP	እሎንተ
	FEM	ዛ-, ዛቲ		COMP ዛተ	እላ, እላንቱ	COMP	እላንተ
that	MASC	ወእቱ		ወእተ	እሙንቱ		
	FEM	ይእቲ		COMP ይእተ	እማንቱ	COMP	እልክተ, እልተ
that yonder	MASC	ዝኩ, ዝክቱ, ዝቱ		COMP ዝኮ, ዝክተ, ዝተ	} እልኩ, እልክቱ, እልቱ		
	FEM	እንትኩ, እንታክቲ		COMP እንታክተ			

C. Emphatic and Possessive Personal Pronouns

Emphatic—Subject

		Singular		Plural	
3M	he, it	ለሊሁ	they	ለሊሆሙ	
3F	she, it	ለሊሃ	they	ለሊሆን	
2M	you	ለሊከ	you	ለሊከሙ	
2F	you	ለሊኪ	you	ለሊከን	
1C	I	ለሊየ	we	ለሊነ	

These subject pronouns are employed only when a strong emphasis or contrast is required. They are usually appositional to other subject constituents (e.g., the null subject of a verb or overt pronouns) and correspond to English intensive pronouns, e.g., 'I myself saw it')

Emphatic—Complement

		Singular		Plural
3M	him, it	ኪያሁ	them	ኪያሆሙ
3F	her, it	ኪያሃ	them	ኪያሆን
2M	you	ኪያከ	you	ኪያከሙ
2F	you	ኪያኪ	you	ኪያከን
1C	me	ኪያየ	us	ኪያነ

The complement forms are either employed in the place of a regular pronoun (e.g., attached to the verb as its complement) for emphasis or used to express the complement of the Converb.

Possessive

	MASC SG item	FEM SG item	Plural item
his	ዚአሁ	እንቲአሁ	እሊአሁ
hers	ዚአሃ	እንቲአሃ	እሊአሃ
yours	ዚአከ	እንቲአከ	እሊአከ
yours	ዚአኪ	እንቲአኪ	እሊአኪ
mine	ዚአየ	እንቲአየ	እሊአየ
theirs	ዚአሆሙ	እንቲአሆሙ	እሊአሆሙ
theirs	ዚአሆን	እንቲአሆን	እሊአሆን
yours	ዚአከሙ	እንቲአከሙ	እሊአከሙ
yours	ዚአከን	እንቲአከን	እሊአከን
ours	ዚአነ	እንቲአነ	እሊአነ

A noun must be bound to the possessive forms (e..g, በስም፡ዚአየ፡ 'with the name of mine'), unless they are used predicatively as true pronouns (e.g., ዝንቱ፡ስም፡ዚአየ፡ውእቱ 'this name is mine').

D. Interrogative Pronouns

These words establish the clause in which the occur to be an interrogative clause. There are three types: pronouns, adverbs, and one adjective.

Type			COMP	Examples
Pronoun	who?	መኑ	መነ	መኑ፡ውእቱ፡እምየ፡ወአኀዊየ፡
	what?	ምንት	ምንተ	'who is my mother and my brothers' (Mk 3:33)
Adverb	where?	አይቴ, በአይቴ		በአይቴ፡ትፈቅድ፡ናስተዳሉ፡ለከ፡ፍስሐ፡
	how?	እፎ		'where do you want us to prepare Passover for you?'
	from where?	አምአይቴ		
	why?	ለምንት, በእንተ፡ምንት		
	when?	ማእዜ		
Adjective	which?	አይ (PL አያት)	አየ (PL አያተ) not attested in AG III Mark	

2. Nouns

A. Most Common Internal Plural Patterns

qətāl	ፍናው	the plural of	ፍኖት	road
qatalt	ጸሐፍት		ጸሐፊ	scribe
ʾaqtāl	አሕቃል		ሕቅል	plain
ʾaqtul	አህጉር		ሀገር	city
ʾaqtəlt	አብሕርት		ብሐር	region
ʾaqātəl	ለያልይ		ሌሊት	night
maqātəlt	መላእክት		መልአክ	messenger

B. External Plural Endings

The two endings used to form external plurals are *-ān* and *-āt*.

	Singular	Plural	
-ān	መሠግር	መሠገራን	fishermen
	ሊቅ	ሊቃን	elders, chiefs
-āt	ነቢይ	ነቢያት	prophets
	ሰማይ	ሰማያት	heavens
	ነገር	ነገራት	things

APPENDIX B
STRONG VERB PARADIGMS

1. Representative Forms (using ቅ-ት-ል q-t-l for all root derivations even though it is not attested in each)

	G	Gt	Glt	CG	CGt	CGlt
PERF	ቀተለ	ተቀትለ	ተቃተለ	አቅተለ	አስተቀተለ	አስተቃተለ
IMPF	ይቀትል	ይትቀተል	ይትቃተል	ያቀትል	ያስተቀትል	ያስተቃትል
SUBJ	ይቅትል	ይትቀተል	ይትቃተል	ያቅትል	ያስተቅትል	ያስተቃትል
IMPV	ቅትል	ተቀተል	ተትቃተል	አቅትል	አስተቅትል	አስተቃትል
INF	ቀቲል/ቀቲሎት-	ተቀትሎ / ተቀትሎት-	ተቃትሎ / ተቃትሎት-	አቅትሎ / አቅትሎት-	አስተቅትሎ / አስተቅትሎት-	አስተቃትሎ / አስተቃትሎት-

	D	Dt		CD	CDt	
PERF	ቀተለ	ተቀተለ		አቀተለ	አስተቀተለ	
IMPF	ይቄትል	ይትቄተል		ያቄትል	ያስተቄትል	
SUBJ	ይቀትል	ይትቀተል		ያቀትል	ያስተቀተል	
IMPV	ቀትል	ተቀተል		አቀትል	አስተቀትል	
INF	ቀትሎ / ቀትሎት-	ተቀትሎ / ተቀትሎት-		አቀትሎ / አቀትሎት-	አስተቀቴሎ / አስተቃትሎት-	

	L	Lt		CL	CLt	
PERF	ቃተለ	ተቃተለ		ኣቃተለ	አስተቃተለ	
IMPF	ይቃትል	ይትቃተል		ያቃትል	ያስተቃትል	
SUBJ	ይቃትል	ይትቃተል		ያቃትል	ያስተቃትል	
IMPV	ቃትል	ተቃተል		ኣቃትል	አስተቃትል	
INF	ቃትሎ / ቃትሎት-	ተቃትሎ / ተቃትሎት-		ኣቃትሎ / ኣቃትሎት-	አስተቃትሎ / አስተቃትሎት-	

	Q	Qt	Qlt	CQ	CQt	CQlt
PERF	ቀትለደ	ተቀትለደ	ተቀታለደ	አቀትለደ	አስተቀትለደ	አስተቀታለደ
IMPF	ይቀተልድ	ይትቀተልድ	ይትቀታልድ	ያቀተልድ	ያስተቀተልድ	ያስተቀታልድ
SUBJ	ይቀትልድ	ይትቀትለድ	ይትቀታለድ	ያቀትልድ	ያስተቀትልድ	ያስተቀታልድ
IMPV	ቀትለድ	ተቀትለድ	ተቀታለድ	አቀትልድ	አስተቀትልድ	አስተቀታለድ
INF	ቀትልዶ / ቀትልዶት-	ተቀትልዶ /ተቀትልዶት-	አስተቀትልዶ / ተቀታደት-	አቀትልዶ / አቀትልዶት-	አስተቀትልዶ / አስታቃትልዶት-	አስተቀታልዶ / አስተቀታልዶት-

2. Full Paradigm of the Perfect for G, D, L, Q Derivational Patterns

		G	D	L	Q
3MS	ውእቱ	ነገረ	ገበረ	ነጸረ	ባረከ	ደንገፀ
3FS	ይእቲ	ነገረት	ገበረት	ነጸረት	ባረከት	ደንገፀት
2MS	አንተ	ነገርከ	ገበርከ	ነጸርከ	ባረከ	ደንገፅከ
2FS	አንቲ	ነገርኪ	ገበርኪ	ነጸርኪ	ባረኪ	ደንገፅኪ
1CS	አነ	ነገርኩ	ገበርኩ	ነጸርኩ	ባረኩ	ደንገፅኩ
3MP	እሙንቱ	ነገሩ	ገበሩ	ነጸሩ	ባረኩ	ደንገፁ
3FP	እማንቱ	ነገራ	ገበራ	ነጸራ	ባረካ	ደንገፃ
2MP	አንትሙ	ነገርክሙ	ገበርክሙ	ነጸርክሙ	ባረክም	ደንገፅክሙ
2FP	አንትን	ነገርክን	ገበርክን	ነጸርክን	ባረክን	ደንገፅክን
1CP	ንሕነ	ነገርነ	ገበርነ	ነጸርነ	ባረክነ	ደንገፅነ

3. Full Paradigm of the Perfect for Gt, Glt, Dt, Lt, Qt, Qlt Derivational Patterns

		Gt	Glt	Dt	Lt	Qt	Qlt
3MS	ውእቱ	ተነግረ	ተናገረ	ተነጸረ	ተባረከ	ተደንገፀ	ተደናገፀ
3FS	ይእቲ	ተነግረት	ተናገረት	ተነጸረት	ተባረከት	ተደንገፀት	ተደናገፀት
2MS	አንተ	ተነገርከ	ተናገርከ	ተነጸርከ	ተባረከ	ተደንገፅከ	ተደናገፅከ
2FS	አንቲ	ተነገርኪ.	ተናገርኪ.	ተነጸርኪ.	ተባረኪ.	ተደንገፅኪ.	ተደናገፅኪ.
1CS	አነ	ተነገርኩ	ተናገርኩ	ተነጸርኩ	ተባረኩ	ተደንገፅኩ	ተደናገፅኩ
3MP	እሙንቱ	ተነግሩ	ተናገሩ	ተነጸሩ	ተባረኩ	ተደንገፁ	ተደናገፁ
3FP	እማንቱ	ተነግራ	ተናገራ	ተነጸራ	ተባረካ	ተደንገፃ	ተደናገፃ
2MP	አንትሙ·	ተነገርክሙ·	ተናገርክሙ·	ተነጸርክሙ·	ተባረክሙ·	ተደንገፅክሙ·	ተደናገፅክሙ·
2FP	አንትን	ተነገርክን	ተናገርክን	ተነጸርክን	ተባረክን	ተደንገፅክን	ተደናገፅክን
1CP	ንሕነ	ተነገርነ	ተናገርነ	ተነጸርነ	ተባረከነ	ተደንገፅነ	ተደናገፅነ

4. Full Paradigm of the Perfect for CG, CD, CL, CQ Derivational Patterns

		CG	CD	CL	CQ
3MS	ውእቱ	አንገረ	አነጸረ	አባረከ	አደንገፀ
3FS	ይእቲ	አንገረት	አነጸረት	አባረከት	አደንገፀት
2MS	አንተ	አንገርከ	አነጸርከ	አባረከ	አደንገፅከ
2FS	አንቲ	አንገርኪ.	አነጸርኪ.	አባረኪ.	አደንገፅኪ.
1CS	አነ	አንገርኩ	አነጸርኩ	አባረኩ	አደንገፅኩ
3MP	እሙንቱ	አንገሩ	አነጸሩ	አባረኩ	አደንገፁ
3FP	እማንቱ	አንገራ	አነጸራ	አባረካ	አደንገፃ
2MP	አንትሙ·	አንገርክሙ·	አነጸርክሙ·	አባረክሙ·	አደንገፅክሙ·
2FP	አንትን	አንገርክን	አነጸርክን	አባረክን	አደንገፅክን
1CP	ንሕነ	አንገርነ	አነጸርነ	አባረከነ	አደንገፅነ

5. Full Paradigm of the Perfect for CGt, CGlt, CDt, CLt, CQt Derivational Patterns

		CGt	CGlt	CDt	CLt	CQt
3MS	ውእቱ	አስተንገረ	አስተናገረ	አስተነጸረ	አስተባረከ	አስተደንገፀ
3FS	ይእቲ	አስተንገረት	አስተናገረት	አስተነጸረት	አስተባራከት	አስተደንገፀት
2MS	አንተ	አስተንገርከ	አስተናገርከ	አስተነጸርከ	አስተባራከ	አስተደንገፅከ
2FS	አንቲ	አስተንገርኪ.	አስተናገርኪ.	አስተነጸርኪ.	አስተባራኪ.	አስተደንገፅኪ.
1CS	አነ	አስተንገርኩ	አስተናገርኩ	አስተነጸርኩ	አስተባራኩ	አስተደንገፅኩ
3MP	እሙንቱ	አስተንገሩ	አስተናገሩ	አስተነጸሩ	አስተባራኩ	አስተደንገፁ
3FP	እማንቱ	አስተንገራ	አስተናገራ	አስተነጸራ	አስተባራካ	አስተደንገፃ
2MP	አንትሙ·	አስተንገርክሙ·	አስተናገርክሙ·	አስተነጸርክሙ·	አስተባራከሙ·	አስተደንገፅክሙ·
2FP	አንትን	አስተንገርክን	አስተናገርክን	አስተነጸርክን	አስተባራክን	አስተደንገፅክን
1CP	ንሕነ	አስተንገርነ	አስተናገርነ	አስተነጸርነ	አስተባራከነ	አስተደንገፅነ

6. Full Paradigm of the Imperfect for G, D, L, Q Patterns

		G	D	L	Q
3MS	ውእቱ	ይነግር	ይገብር	ይኔጽር	ይባርክ	ይደነግፅ
3FS	ይእቲ	ትነግር	ትገብር	ትኔጽር	ትባርክ	ትደነግፅ
2MS	አንተ	ትነግር	ትገብር	ትኔጽር	ትባርክ	ትደነግፅ
2FS	አንቲ	ትነግሪ	ትገብሪ	ትኔጽሪ	ትባርኪ	ትደነግፒ
1CS	አነ	እነግር	እገብር	እኔጽር	እባርክ	እደነግፅ
3MP	እሙንቱ	ይነግሩ	ይገብሩ	ይኔጽሩ	ይባርኩ	ይደነግዑ
3FP	እማንቱ	ይነግራ	ይገብራ	ይኔጽራ	ይባርካ	ይደነገፃ
2MP	አንትሙ	ትነግሩ	ትገብሩ	ትኔጽሩ	ትባርኩ	ትደነግዑ
2FP	አንትን	ትነግራ	ትገብራ	ትኔጽራ	ትባርካ	ትደነገፃ
1CP	ንሕነ	ንነግር	ንገብር	ንኔጽር	ንባርክ	ንደነግፅ

7. Full Paradigm of the Imperfect for Gt, Glt, Dt, Lt, Qt, Qlt Derivational Patterns

		Gt	Glt	Dt	Lt	Qt	Qlt
3MS	ውእቱ	ይትነገር	ይትጋበር	ይትኔጸር	ይትባረክ	ይትደነግፅ	ይትደናገፅ
3FS	ይእቲ	ትትነገር	ትትጋበር	ትትኔጸር	ትትባረክ	ትትደነግፅ	ትትደናገፅ
2MS	አንተ	ትትነገር	ትትጋበር	ትትኔጸር	ትትባረክ	ትትደነግፅ	ትትደናገፅ
2FS	አንቲ	ትትነገሪ	ትትጋበሪ	ትትኔጸሪ	ትትባረኪ	ትትደነግፒ	ይትደናገፒ
1CS	አነ	እትነገር	እትጋበር	እትኔጸር	እትባረክ	እትደነግፅ	እትደናገፅ
3MP	እሙንቱ	ይትነገሩ	ይትጋበሩ	ይትኔጸሩ	ይትባረኩ	ይትደነግዑ	ይትደናገዑ
3FP	እማንቱ	ይትነገራ	ይትጋበራ	ይትኔጸራ	ይትባረካ	ይትደነገፃ	ይትደናገፃ
2MP	አንትሙ	ትትነገሩ	ትትጋበሩ	ትትኔጸሩ	ትትባረኩ	ትትደነግዑ	ትትደናገዑ
2FP	አንትን	ትትነገራ	ትትጋበራ	ትትኔጸራ	ትትባረካ	ትትደነገፃ	ትትደናገፃ
1CP	ንሕነ	ንትነገር	ንትጋበር	ንትኔጸር	ንትባረክ	ንትደነግፅ	ንትደናገፅ

8. Full Paradigm of the Imperfect for CG, CD, CL, CQ Derivational Patterns

		CG	CD	CL	CQ
3MS	ውእቱ	ያነግር	ያኔጽር	ያባርክ	ያደነግፅ
3FS	ይእቲ	ታነግር	ታኔጽር	ታባርክ	ታደነግፅ
2MS	አንተ	ታነግር	ታኔጽር	ታባርክ	ታደነግፅ
2FS	አንቲ	ታነግሪ	ታኔጽሪ	ታባርኪ	ታደነግፒ
1CS	አነ	አነግር	አኔጽር	አባርክ	አደነግፅ
3MP	እሙንቱ	ያነግሩ	ያኔጽሩ	ያባርኩ	ያደነግዑ
3FP	እማንቱ	ያነግራ	ያኔጽራ	ያባርካ	ያደነገፃ
2MP	አንትሙ	ታነግሩ	ታኔጽሩ	ታባርኩ	ታደነግዑ
2FP	አንትን	ታነግራ	ታኔጽራ	ታባርካ	ታደነገፃ
1CP	ንሕነ	ናነግር	ናኔጽር	ናባርክ	ናደነግፅ

Appendix B—Strong Verb Paradigms

9. Full Paradigm of the Imperfect for CGt, CGlt, CDt, CLt, CQt Derivational Patterns

		CGt	CGlt	CDt	CLt	CQt
3MS	ውእቱ	ያስተነግር	ያስተናግር	ያስተኔጽር	ያስተባርክ	ያስተደነግፅ
3FS	ይእቲ	ታስተነግር	ታስተናግር	ታስተኔጽር	ታስተባርክ	ታስተደነግፅ
2MS	አንተ	ታስተነግር	ታስተናግር	ታስተኔጽር	ታስተባርክ	ታስተደነግፅ
2FS	አንቲ	ታስተነግሪ	ታስተናግሪ	ታስተኔጽሪ	ታስተባርኪ	ታስተደነግጊ
1CS	አነ	አስተነግር	አስተናግር	አስተኔጽር	አስተባርክ	አስተደነግፅ
3MP	እሙንቱ	ያስተነግሩ	ያስተናግሩ	ያስተኔጽሩ	ያስተባርኩ	ያስተደነግዉ
3FP	እማንቱ	ያስተነግራ	ያስተናግራ	ያስተኔጽራ	ያስተባርካ	ያስተደነግጋ
2MP	አንትሙ	ታስተነግሩ	ታስተናግሩ	ታስተኔጽሩ	ታስተባርኩ	ታስተደነግዉ
2FP	አንትን	ታስተነግራ	ታስተናግራ	ታስተኔጽራ	ታስተባርካ	ታስተደነግጋ
1CP	ንሕነ	ናስተነግር	ናስተናግር	ናስተኔጽር	ናስተባርክ	ናስተደነግፅ

10. Full Paradigm of the Subjunctive for G, D, L, Q Patterns

		G	D	L	Q
3MS	ውእቱ	ይንግር	ይነጽር	ይባርክ	ይደንግፅ
3FS	ይእቲ	ትንግር	ትነጽር	ትባርክ	ትደንግፅ
2MS	አንተ	ትንግር	ትነጽር	ትባርክ	ትደንግፅ
2FS	አንቲ	ትንግሪ	ትነጽሪ	ትባርኪ	ትደንግጊ
1CS	አነ	እንግር	እነጽር	አባርክ	እደንግፅ
3MP	እሙንቱ	ይንግሩ	ይነጽሩ	ይባርኩ	ይደንግዉ
3FP	እማንቱ	ይንግራ	ይነጽራ	ይባርካ	ይደንግጋ
2MP	አንትሙ	ትንግሩ	ትነጽሩ	ትባርኩ	ትደንግዉ
2FP	አንትን	ትንግራ	ትነጽራ	ትባርካ	ትደንግጋ
1CP	ንሕነ	ንንግር	ንነጽር	ንባርክ	ንደንግፅ

11. Full Paradigm of the Subjunctive for Gt, Glt, Dt, Lt, Qt, Qlt Derivational Patterns

		Gt	Glt	Dt	Lt	Qt	Qlt
3MS	ውእቱ	ይትነገር	ይትናገር	ይትነጸር	ይትባረክ	ይትደነገፅ	ይትደናገፅ
3FS	ይእቲ	ትትነገር	ትትናገር	ትትነጸር	ትትባረክ	ትትደነገፅ	ትትደናገፅ
2MS	አንተ	ትትነገር	ትትናገር	ትትነጸር	ትትባረክ	ትትደነገፅ	ትትደናገፅ
2FS	አንቲ	ትትነገሪ	ትትናገሪ	ትትነጸሪ	ትትባረኪ	ትትደነገጊ	ትትደናገጊ
1CS	አነ	እትነገር	እትናገር	እትነጸር	እትባረክ	እትደነገፅ	እትደናገፅ
3MP	እሙንቱ	ይትነገሩ	ይትናገሩ	ይትነጸሩ	ይትባረኩ	ይትደነገዉ	ይትደናገዉ
3FP	እማንቱ	ይትነገራ	ይትናገራ	ይትነጸራ	ይትባረካ	ይትደነገጋ	ይትደናገጋ
2MP	አንትሙ	ትትነገሩ	ትትናገሩ	ትትነጸሩ	ትትባረኩ	ትትደነገዉ	ትትደናገዉ
2FP	አንትን	ትትነገራ	ትትናገራ	ትትነጸራ	ትትባረካ	ትትደነገጋ	ትትደናገጋ
1CP	ንሕነ	ንትነገር	ንትናገር	ንትነጸር	ንትባረክ	ንትደነገፅ	ንትደናገፅ

12. Full Paradigm of the Subjunctive for CG, CD, CL, CQ Derivational Patterns

		CG	CD	CL	CQ
3MS	ውእቱ	ያንግር	ያነጽር	ያባርክ	ያደንግፅ
3FS	ይእቲ	ታንግር	ታነጽር	ታባርክ	ታደንግፅ
2MS	አንተ	ታንግር	ታነጽር	ታባርክ	ታደንግፅ
2FS	አንቲ	ታንግሪ	ታነጽሪ	ታባርኪ	ታደንግዒ
1CS	አነ	አንግር	አነጽር	አባርክ	አደንግፅ
3MP	እሙንቱ	ያንግሩ	ያነጽሩ	ያባርኩ	ያደንግዑ
3FP	እማንቱ	ያንግራ	ያነጽራ	ያባርካ	ያደንግፃ
2MP	አንትሙ	ታንግሩ	ታነጽሩ	ታባርኩ	ታደንግዑ
2FP	አንትን	ታንግራ	ታነጽራ	ታባርካ	ታደንግፃ
1CP	ንሕነ	ናንግር	ናነጽር	ናባርክ	ናደንግፅ

13. Full Subjunctive Paradigm for CGt, CGlt, CDt, CLt, CQt Derivational Patterns

		CGt	CGlt	CDt	CLt	CQlt
3MS	ውእቱ	ያስተንግር	ያስተናግር	ያስተነጽር	ያስተባርክ	ያስተደንግፅ
3FS	ይእቲ	ታስተንግር	ታስተናግር	ታስተነጽር	ታስተባርክ	ታስተደንግፅ
2MS	አንተ	ታስተንግር	ታስተናግር	ታስተነጽር	ታስተባርክ	ታስተደንግፅ
2FS	አንቲ	ታስተንግሪ	ታስተናግሪ	ታስተነጽሪ	ታስተባርኪ	ታስተደንግዒ
1CS	አነ	አስተንግር	አስተናግር	አስተነጽር	አስተባርክ	አስተደንግፅ
3MP	እሙንቱ	ያስተንግሩ	ያስተናግሩ	ያስተነጽሩ	ያስተባርኩ	ያስተደንግዑ
3FP	እማንቱ	ያስተንግራ	ያስተናግራ	ያስተነጽራ	ያስተባርካ	ያስተደንግፃ
2MP	አንትሙ	ታስተንግሩ	ታስተናግሩ	ታስተነጽሩ	ታስተባርኩ	ታስተደንግዑ
2FP	አንትን	ታስተንግራ	ታስተናግራ	ታስተነጽራ	ታስተባርካ	ታስተደንግፃ
1CP	ንሕነ	ናስተንግር	ናስተናግር	ናስተነጽር	ናስተባርክ	ናስተደንግፅ

14. Full Paradigm of the Imperatives

		G	D	L	Q
MS	አንተ	ንግር	ግብር	ነጽር	ባርክ	ደንግፅ
FS	አንቲ	ንግሪ	ግብሪ	ነጽሪ	ባርኪ	ደንግዒ
MP	አንትሙ	ንግሩ	ግብሩ	ነጽሩ	ባርኩ	ደንግዑ
FP	አንትን	ንግራ	ግብራ	ነጽራ	ባርካ	ደንግፃ

		Gt	Glt	Dt	Lt	Qt	Qlt
MS	አንተ	ተነገር	ተናገር	ተነጸር	ተባረክ	ተደንገፅ	ተደናገፅ
FS	አንቲ	ተነገሪ	ተናገሪ	ተነጸሪ	ተባረኪ	ተደንግዒ	ተደናገዒ
MP	አንትሙ	ተነገሩ	ተናገሩ	ተነጸሩ	ተባረኩ	ተደንግዑ	ተደናገዑ
FP	አንትን	ተነገራ	ተናገራ	ተነጸራ	ተባረካ	ተደንግፃ	ተደናገፃ

(Continued)

Appendix B—Strong Verb Paradigms

(Imperative Paradigms Continued)

		CG	CD	CL	CQ
MS	አንተ	አንግር	አነጽር	አባርክ	አደንግፅ
FS	አንቲ	አንግሪ	አነጽሪ	አባርኪ	አደንግኢ
MP	አንትሙ	አንግሩ	አነጽሩ	አባርኩ	አደንግፉ
FP	አንትን	አንግራ	አነጽራ	አባርካ	አደንግፋ

		CGt	CGlt	CDt	CLt	CQt
MS	አንተ	አስተንግር	አስተናግር	አስተነጽር	አስተባርክ	አስተደንግፅ
FS	አንቲ	አስተንግሪ	አስተናግሪ	አስተነጽሪ	አስተባርኪ	አስተደንግኢ
MP	አንትሙ	አስተንግሩ	አስተናግሩ	አስተነጽሩ	አስተባርኩ	አስተደንግፉ
FP	አንትን	አስተንግራ	አስተናግራ	አስተነጽራ	አስተባርካ	አስተደንግፋ

15. N Verbs

A special type of verb root derivational pattern is marked by the addition of -ን- to the front of the root (mostly quadraliteral roots). These forms occur rarely in AG III Mark. The root ኩ-ር-ኩ-ር N 'to roll', Nt 'to be rolled about' is one that appears and is used below in the chart for illustration, even though it does not appear in the Nt derivation.

	Perfect	Imperfect	Subjunctive	Imperative
N	አንኩርኩረ	ያንኩረኩር	ያንኩርኩር	አንኩርኩር
Nt	ተንኩርኩረ	ይትንኩረኩር	ይትንኩርኩር	ትንኩርኩር

Nt Imperfect and Subjunctive forms are very rare.

These verbs, as a semantic class, almost always refer to a process involving the constant repetition of a single action, e.g., rolling about, strolling about, shaking, dripping, flaming, raging, muttering, grumbling.

APPENDIX C

WEAK VERB PARADIGMS

The verbal paradigms in the lessons of this textbook use roots that have three regular consonants (i.e., no gutturals or glides). These are referred to as **strong verbs**. Gəʿəz, however, contains many more weak verbs than strong. **Weak verbs** have one or more "weak" (e.g., glide) consonants in the root that may either affect an adjacent vowel (e.g., causing a consonant in the 1° *a* to adjust to its 4° *ā* form) or combine with an adjacent vowel to create a new vowel.

Gəʿəz weak verbs fall into two main groups: those that have a guttural consonant (አ, ዐ, ህ, ሕ, ኀ) and those that have a glide (ው, ይ). And, of course, some roots fall into both categories. Taking each of the subtypes in both groups individually, Gəʿəz weak verbs are:

- I-Guttural—verbs with አ, ዐ, ህ, ሕ, ኀ as the first root consonant.
- II-Guttural—verbs with አ, ዐ, ህ, ሕ, ኀ as the second root consonant.
- III-Guttural—verbs with አ, ዐ, ህ, ሕ, ኀ as the third root consonant.
- I- ው
- II- ው/ይ
- III-ው/ይ

Each of these types is described in the following sections, with one addition: the final section provides the Imperfect, Subjunctive, and Imperative to fill out the paradigm for ብ-ህ-ል 'to say'.

Finally, note that, root with identical 2nd and 3rd consonant (C2=C3) typically show all three root consonants (ነበበ 'he spoke'); however, there are cases (especially in AG III Mark) in which the 3rd consonant is dropped. These are not presented in this Appendix.

1. I-Guttural Roots

A. Perfect

The Perfect is regular in verbs from I-guttural (አ, ዐ, ህ, ሕ, ኀ) roots.

B. Imperfect, Subjunctive, and Imperative

The Subjunctive and Imperative are regular. However, in the G Imperfect, the initial guttural of the verbal root influences the prefix resulting in an -*a*- prefix vowel the throughout the paradigm.

Full Paradigm for G Imperfect, Subjunctive, and Imperative: አ-ስ-ር 'to bind'

		Imperfect	Subjunctive	Imperative
3MS	ውእቱ	የአስር	ይእስር	
3FS	ይእቲ	ተአስር	ትእስር	
2MS	አንተ	ተአስር	ትእስር	አስር
2FS	አንቲ	ተአስሪ	ትእስሪ	አስሪ
1CS	አነ	አአስር	አእስር	
3MP	እሙንቱ	የአስሩ	ይእስሩ	
3FP	እማንቱ	የአስራ	ይእስራ	
2MP	አንትሙ	ተአስሩ	ትእስሩ	አስሩ
2FP	አንትን	ተአስራ	ትእስራ	አስራ
1CP	ንሕነ	ነአስር	ንእስር	

C. Other Forms

Converb and Infinitive

ኀሊፍ-	'[he] having passed by'
አሲር	'to bind'

Adjective/Passive Participle—ቅቱል

ዕጹብ	'harsh, difficult'
ኅቡእ	'hidden'

Noun Types

አማኒ	'one who believes'
ዐቃቢ (PL ዐቀብት)	'guard'
ኀላፊ (PL ኀለፍት)	'passer-by, one passing'
አማን	'truth'; ADJ 'true, faithful'
ማኀደር (PL መኃድር)	'dwelling-place, residence'

Note: Before the guttural in the first syllable the normal -a- vowel is lengthened to -ā-.

2. II-Guttural Roots

A. Perfect

Only one type of G verb requires special attention when the second root consonant is a guttural (እ, ዕ, ህ, ሕ, ኅ)—in the ገብረ type of G verb (e.g., ክሕደ 'to deny') the first vowel is -ə- rather than the expected -a-. D and L verbs are regular.

Full Paradigm for Perfect

		G ነበረ-type: ሰ-እ-ል 'to request'	G ገብረ-type: ከ-ሕ-ድ 'to deny'
3MS	ውእቱ	ሰአለ	ክሕደ
3FS	ይእቲ	ሰአለት	ክሕደት
2MS	አንተ	ሰአልከ	ክሕድከ
2FS	አንቲ	ሰአልኪ	ክሕድኪ
1CS	አነ	ሰአልኩ	ክሕድኩ
3MP	እሙንቱ	ሰአሉ	ክሕዱ
3FP	እማንቱ	ሰአላ	ክሕዳ
2MP	አንትሙ	ሰአልክሙ	ክሕድክሙ
2FP	አንትን	ሰአልክን	ክሕድክን
1CP	ንሕነ	ሰአልነ	ክሕድነ

Note: Some II-Guttural verbs exhibit a D derivational patterns (e.g., መሀረ 'to teach') that is synonymous with the corresponding G derivational pattern (መህረ). This suggests that the gemination of the guttural consonants was in the process of being lost (if not already lost) in the earliest attestation of the language.

B. Imperfect, Subjunctive, and Imperative

All II-Guttural verbs exhibit the same deviation from the strong verb paradigm: the imperfect shows vowel assimilation (*aGGə > əGGə); both the subjunctive and imperative contain -a- as the stem vowel (note also that the imperative also exhibits a vowel assimilation, *əGa > aGa).

Full Paradigm for Imperfect, Subjunctive, and Imperative

		Imperfect	Subjunctive	Imperative
3MS	ውእቱ	ይልእክ	ይልአክ	
3FS	ይእቲ	ትልእክ	ትልአክ	
2MS	አንተ	ትልእክ	ትልአክ	ለአክ
2FS	አንቲ	ትልእኪ	ትልአኪ	ለአኪ
1CS	አነ	እልእክ	እልአክ	
3MP	እሙንቱ	ይልእኩ	ይልአኩ	
3FP	እማንቱ	ይልእካ	ይልአካ	
2MP	አንትሙ	ትልእኩ	ትልአኩ	ለአኩ
2FP	አንትን	ትልእካ	ትልአካ	ለአካ
1CP	ንሕነ	ንልእክ	ንልአክ	

Note: A number of II-Guttural Imperfects have -e- instead of -ə- in the first stem syllable, especially ይሬኢ (for ይርኢ) 'he sees'. The reason (and origin) for the optional variation with the -e- vowel is not clear.

C. Other Forms

Converb and Infinitive

The G derivation infinitive may reflect a change of the first vowel: -a- > -ə-.

ስኢል-	'[he] having requested'
ብሂል	'to say'
ስሒት	'to err'

Adjective/Passive Participle—ቅቱል

| ጽሑፍ | 'written' |
| እኁዝ | 'captive, held'; 'possessed by' |

Noun Types

ጸሓፊ (PL ጸሓፍት)	'scribe'
ላእክ (PL ለአክ)	'servant'
መጽሐፍ (PL መጻሕፍት)	'book'

3. III-Guttural Roots

A. Perfect

Verbs from roots III-Guttural act differently in the G versus other derivational patterns. In the 3rd person forms, all G forms lack a vowel between C_2 and C_3, e.g., መጽአ, ወፅአ, whereas D, L, and Q verbs have -ə- between C_2 and C_3, e.g., D ከሐ, Q ተንሥአ. (Note that this is also the pattern for CG verbs, e.g., አምጽአ, አግብአ). In contrast, all the derivational patterns have an -ā- before the final root consonant when the inflectional affixes begin with a consonant (i.e., in the 1st and 2nd person forms).

Appendix C—Weak Verb Paradigms

Full Paradigm for Perfect

		G ም-ጽ-እ 'to come'	D ን-ስ-ሕ 'to repent'	Q/L ት-ን-ሥ-እ 'to rise, get up'
3MS	ውእቱ	መጽአ	ነስሐ	ተንሥአ
3FS	ይእቲ	መጽአት	ነስሐት	ተንሥአት
2MS	አንተ	መጻእከ	ነሳሕከ	ተንሥእከ
2FS	አንቲ	መጻእኪ	ነሳሕኪ	ተንሥእኪ
1CS	አነ	መጻእኩ	ነሳሕኩ	ተንሥእኩ
3MP	እሙንቱ	መጽኡ	ነስሑ	ተንሥኡ
3FP	እማንቱ	መጽአ	ነስሐ	ተንሥአ
2MP	አንትሙ	መጻእክሙ	ነሳሕክሙ	ተንሥእክሙ
2FP	አንትን	መጻእክን	ነሳሕክን	ተንሥእክን
1CP	ንሕነ	መጻእነ	ነሳሕነ	ተንሥእነ

B. Imperfect, Subjunctive, and Imperative

The imperfect for III-Guttural roots is regular. But the subjunctive and imperative have the vowel *-ā-* before the final root consonant (e.g., ይምጻእ), unless a vowel follows that consonant, whether an inflectional affix (e.g., ትምጽኢ) or a cliticized pronoun complement (e.g., ይምጽአከ 'it/he will come upon you'). In those cases, the *-ā-* becomes *-ə-*.

Full Paradigm for Imperfect, Subjunctive, and Imperative

		Imperfect	Subjunctive	Imperative
3MS	ውእቱ	ይመጽእ	ይምጻእ	
3FS	ይእቲ	ትመጽእ	ትምጻእ	
2MS	አንተ	ትመጽእ	ትምጻእ	ምጻእ
2FS	አንቲ	ትመጽኢ	ትምጽኢ	ምጽኢ
1CS	አነ	እመጽእ	እምጻእ	
3MP	እሙንቱ	ይመጽኡ	ትምጽኡ	
3FP	እማንቱ	ይመጽአ	ትምጽአ	
2MP	አንትሙ	ትመጽኡ	ትምጽኡ	ምጽኡ
2FP	አንትን	ትመጽአ	ትምጽአ	ምጽአ
1CP	ንሕነ	ንመጽእ	ንምጻእ	

C. Other Forms

Converb and Infinitive

ወፂአ-	'[he] having exited'
ሰሚዐ	'[he] having heard'
በሊዐ	'to eat'
በዊአ	'to enter'

Adjective/Passive Participle—ቅቱል

| ርቱዕ | 'righteous'; 'straight' |
| ብዙኅ | 'any, much' |

Noun Types

ሰማዒ (PL ሰማዕት)	'witness, martyr'
ስምዕ (PL ስምዓት)	'rumor, report'; 'testimony'; 'martyrdom, martyrs'
ግብአት	'return'; 'conversion'
ፍርሀት (PL ፍርሀታት)	'fear, terror, awe'

4. I-ወ Roots

A. Perfect

The Perfect is regular in verbs from I-ወ roots. There is only one I-ይ root used in AG III Mark (and only three listed in Leslau's *Dictionary*); all three behave as strong verbs.

B. Imperfect, Subjunctive, and Imperative

In the G Subjunctive and Imperative many of I-ወ verbs have forms in which the initial ወ- of the root is dropped. Note that the vowel between the remaining root consonants is typically *-a-*. Note also that some verbs have two or even three Subjunctive forms. Finally, the verb ወሀበ 'to give' has an irregular Imperfect, but since it is frequent, it is included below in the chart.

Full Paradigm for Imperfect

		G I-ወ typical ወ-ር-ድ 'to go down'	G I-ወ ወ-ህ-ብ 'to give'	G I-ወ ገብረ-type ወ-ድ-ቅ 'to fall'
3MS	ወእቱ	ይወርድ	ይሁብ	ይወድቅ
3FS	ይእቲ	ትወርድ	ትሁብ	ትወድቅ
2MS	አንተ	ትወርድ	ትሁብ	ትወድቅ
2FS	አንቲ	ትወርዲ	ትሁቢ	ትወድቂ
1CS	አነ	አወርድ	አሁብ	አወድቅ
3MP	እሙንቱ	ይወርዱ	ይሁቡ	ይወድቁ
3FP	እማንቱ	ይወርዳ	ይሁባ	ይወድቃ
2MP	አንትሙ	ትወርዱ	ትሁቡ	ትወድቁ
2FP	አንትን	ትወርዳ	ትሁባ	ትወድቃ
1CP	ንሕነ	ንወርድ	ንሁብ	ንወድቅ

Full Paradigm for Subjunctive

		G I-ወ ወ-ር-ድ 'to go down'	G I-ይ ወ-ህ-ብ 'to give'	G I-ወ ገብረ-type ወ-ድ-ቅ 'to fall'
3MS	ወእቱ	ይረድ	የሀብ	ይደቅ
3FS	ይእቲ	ትረድ	ተሀብ	ትደቅ
2MS	አንተ	ትረድ	ተሀብ	ትደቅ
2FS	አንቲ	ትረዲ	ተሀቢ	ትደቂ
1CS	አነ	እረድ	አሀብ	እደቅ
3MP	እሙንቱ	ይረዱ	የሀቡ	ይደቁ
3FP	እማንቱ	ይረዳ	የሀባ	ይደቃ
2MP	አንትሙ	ትረዱ	ተሀቡ	ትደቁ
2FP	አንትን	ትረዳ	ተሀባ	ተደቃ
1CP	ንሕነ	ንረድ	ንሀብ	ንደቅ

Full Paradigm for Imperative

		G I-ወ ወ-ር-ድ 'to go down'	G I-ይ ወ-ህ-ብ 'to give'	G I-ወ ገብረ-type ወ-ድ-ቅ 'to fall'
2MS	አንተ	ረድ	ሀብ	ደቅ
2FS	አንቲ	ረዲ	ሀቢ	ደቂ
2MP	አንትሙ	ረዱ	ሀቡ	ደቁ
2FP	አንትን	ረዳ	ሀባ	ደቃ

C. Other Forms

Converb and Infinitive

ወሪድ-	'[he] having gone down'
ወፂእ-	'[he] having exited'
ወዲቅ	'to fall'

Adjective/Passive Participle—ቅቱል

ውሉድ	(PL of ወልድ)

Noun Types

ትውልድ (PL ትውልዳት) 'a generation'; 'progeny, offspring'

5. II-ው/ይ Roots

A. Perfect

The Perfect of G verbs from roots II-ው and II-ይ is distinctive. From roots II-ው, e.g., ቅ-ው-ም 'to stand', the stem of the Perfect has -o- throughout; from roots II-ይ, e.g., ሥ-ይ-ም 'to appoint', the stem has -e- throughout.

Full Paradigm for Perfect

		G II-ው ቅ-ው-ም 'to stand'	G II-ይ ሥ-ይ-ም 'to appoint'
3MS	ውእቱ	ቆመ	ሤመ
3FS	ይእቲ	ቆመት	ሤመት
2MS	አንተ	ቆምከ	ሤምከ
2FS	አንቲ	ቆምኪ	ሤምኪ
1CS	አነ	ቆምኩ	ሤምኩ
3MP	እሙንቱ	ቆሙ	ሤሙ
3FP	እማንቱ	ቆማ	ሤማ
2MP	አንትሙ	ቆምክሙ	ሤምክሙ
2FP	አንትን	ቆምክን	ሤምክን
1CP	ንሕነ	ቆምነ	ሤምነ

A few verbs from roots which are also III-guttural or III-ው/ይ retain the second root consonant as "strong" and are inflected like the ordinary G verbs III-guttural or III-ው/ይ. For example:

ሠውዐ	'he sacrificed'	ሐይወ	'he lived, recovered'
ሠውዐት	'she sacrificed'	ሐይወት	'she lived, recovered'
ሠወዕከ	'you sacrificed'	ሐየውከ / ሐዮከ	'you lived, recovered'
ሠወዕኪ	etc.	ሐየውኪ / ሐዮኪ	etc.

BUT ሥ-ው-ዕ may also be inflected like ቅ-ው-ም, e.g., ሦዐ 'he sacrificed'

D verbs from roots II-ው/ይ are regular and offer no special problems: ፈወሰ 'to heal', ጠየቀ 'to examine'.

Causative-resultative derivational patterns of roots II-ው typically exhibit the loss of the second root consonant. For example, for the root ቅ-ው-ም, the CG is:

አቀመ
አቀመት
አቀምከ
አቀምኪ
አቀምኩ   etc.

The CG form አቆመ is also attested, inflected like the G ቆመ.

If the II-ው root is also III-Guttural, -a- is replaced by -ǝ-. For example, the CG for the root ብ-ው-አ is:

አብአ
አብአት
አብአከ. etc.

From roots II-ይ the CG form አኄደ (root ከ-ይ-ደ) is the normal one, with loss of the second radical ይ.

B. Imperfect

In the Imperfect, the II-ው/ይ is retained due to the gemination of the Imperfect pattern (i.e., ይቀትል = ይቀውም). However, in the Subjunctive and Imperative forms, the ው/ይ of the root combines with an adjacent vowel to produce -u- or -i- vowels, respectively.

Full Paradigm for Imperfect

		G II-ው ቀ-ው-ም 'to stand'	G II-ይ ሠ-ይ-ም 'to appoint'
3MS	ውእቱ	ይቀውም	ይሠይም
3FS	ይእቲ	ትቀውም	ትሠይም
2MS	አንተ	ትቀውም	ትሠይም
2FS	አንቲ	ትቀውሚ	ትሠይሚ
1CS	አነ	እቀውም	እሠይም
3MP	እሙንቱ	ይቀውሙ	ይሠይሙ
3FP	እማንቱ	ይቀውማ	ይሠይማ
2MP	አንትሙ	ትቀውሙ	ትሠይሙ
2FP	አንትን	ትቀውማ	ትሠይማ
1CP	ንሕነ	ንቀውም	ንሠይም

Full Paradigm for Subjunctive

		G II-ው ቀ-ው-ም 'to stand'	G II-ይ ሠ-ይ-ም 'to appoint'
3MS	ውእቱ	ይቁም	ይሢም
3FS	ይእቲ	ትቁም	ትሢም
2MS	አንተ	ትቁም	ትሢም
2FS	አንቲ	ይቁሚ	ትሢሚ
1CS	አነ	እቁም	እሢም
3MP	እሙንቱ	ይቁሙ	ይሢሙ
3FP	እማንቱ	ይቁማ	ይሢማ
2MP	አንትሙ	ትቁሙ	ትሢሙ
2FP	አንትን	ትቁማ	ትሢማ
1CP	ንሕነ	ንቁም	ንሢም

Full Paradigm for Imperative

		G II-ው ቀ-ው-ም 'to stand'	G II-ይ ሠ-ይ-ም 'to appoint'
2MS	አንተ	ቁም	ሢም
2FS	አንቲ	ቁሚ	ሢሚ
2MP	አንትሙ	ቁሙ	ሢሙ
2FP	አንትን	ቁማ	ሢማ

The above forms are typical for nearly all verbs of these two root types. A few verbs II-ው exhibit alternate forms with 7° -o- in the Subjunctive and Imperative:

| PERF ሐረ | IMPF የሐውር | SUBJ ይሕር / ይሑር | IMPV ሕር / ሑር |
| PERF ጸረ | IMPF ይጻውር | SUBJ ይጽር / ይጹር | IMPV ጽር / ጹር |

Two verbs, በአ and ሞአ, have a 4° -ā- in the Subjunctive and Imperative (the -ā- is typically retained through all forms):

| PERF በአ | IMPF ይበውእ | SUBJ ይባእ | IMPV ባእ |
| PERF ሞአ | IMPF ይመውእ | SUBJ ይማእ / ይሙእ | IMPV ማእ |

C. Other Forms

Converb and Infinitive

| በዊአ- | '[he] having entered' |
| ቀዊም- | '[he] having stood' |

The vowel of the second syllable may be replaced: -i- > by -ə-.

| ቀዊም or ቀውም | 'to stand' |
| ሠዪጥ or ሠይጥ | 'to sell' |

Adjective/Passive Participle—ቅቱል

ምዉት   'dead'

Noun Types

ዐዋዲ	'messenger, herald'; 'preacher'
ምሥያጥ (PL ምሥያጣት)	'marketplace, forum'
መባእ (PL መባኣት)	'offering'
መካን	'place, locale'
መሥዋዕት	'sacrifice'
መሣይምት	'container(s), basket(s)'

6. III-ው/ይ Roots

A. Perfect

G verbs from these roots exhibit both ነገረ and ገብረ types (examples below). When the final stem syllables -aw- and -ay- are closed (in the 1st and 2nd person forms), there is an optional contraction *aw > o*, which is quite common, and *ay > e*, which is less common. These same contractions occur in D, L, and Q verbs. Note that the 3s forms of ሀ-ል-ው often exhibit the contraction of the final syllable, e.g., ሀሎ.

A number of G verbs are both II-guttural and III-ይ. If such a verb follows the ነገረ pattern (e.g., ሰሐየ 'to be beautiful'), it is formed like በከየ. If such a verb follows the ገብረ pattern (cf. ከሕደ), there is a regular contraction -əy- > -i-:

| ርኢከ | (< *ርእይከ) | ርኢከሙ | (< *ርእይከሙ) |

etc.

The most frequent verbs of this type are ርእየ 'to see', ርዕየ 'to graze', ጥዕየ 'to get well', and ወዕየ 'to burn'.

Full Paradigm for Perfect

		G III-ዉ ድ-ል-ዉ 'to be fitting'	G III-ይ ብ-ክ-ይ 'to weep'	G ገብረ-type ር-እ-ይ 'to see'
3MS	ውእቱ	ደለወ	በከየ	ርእየ
3FS	ይእቲ	ደለወት	በከየት	ርእየት
2MS	አንተ	ደለውከ / ደሎከ	በከይከ / በኬከ	ርኢከ
2FS	አንቲ	ደለውኪ / ደሎኪ	በከይኪ / በኬኪ	ርኢኪ
1CS	አነ	ደለውኩ / ደሎኩ	በከይኩ / በኬኩ	ርኢኩ
3MP	እሙንቱ	ደለዉ	በከዩ	ርእዩ
3FP	እማንቱ	ደለዋ	በከያ	ርእያ
2MP	አንትሙ	ደለውክሙ / ደሎክሙ	በከይክሙ / በኬክሙ	ርኢክሙ
2FP	አንትን	ደለውክን / ደሎክን	በከይክን / በኬክን	ርኢክን
1CP	ንሕነ	ደለውነ / ደሎነ	በከይነ / በኬነ	ርኢነ

B. Imperfect, Subjunctive, and Imperative

The Imperfect, Subjunctive, and Imperative show the normal patterns: IMPF ይቀትል, SUBJ ይቅትል/ይቅተል, IMPV ቅትል/ቅተል. However, when the verb stem ends in -əy and -əw and are not followed by a vowel of the verb inflection (e.g., -u for 3mp), these changes typically occur: -əy > i and əw > u.

Full Paradigm for Imperfect

		G III-ዉ ድ-ል-ዉ 'to be fitting'	G III-ይ ብ-ክ-ይ 'to weep'	G ገብረ-type ር-እ-ይ 'to see'
3MS	ውእቱ	ይደሉ	ይበኪ	ይሬኢ
3FS	ይእቲ	ትደሉ	ትበኪ	ትሬኢ
2MS	አንተ	ትደሉ	ትበኪ	ትሬኢ
2FS	አንቲ	ትደልዊ	ትበክዪ	ትሬአዪ
1CS	አነ	እደሉ	እበኪ	እሬኢ
3MP	እሙንቱ	ይደልዉ	ይበክዩ	ይሬአዩ
3FP	እማንቱ	ይደልዋ	ይብክያ	ይሬአያ
2MP	አንትሙ	ትደልዉ	ትበክዩ	ትሬአዩ
2FP	አንትን	ትደልዋ	ትበክያ	ትሬአያ
1CP	ንሕነ	ንደሉ	ንበኪ	ንሬኢ

Full Paradigm for Subjunctive

		G III-ዉ ድ-ል-ዉ 'to be fitting'	G III-ይ ብ-ክ-ይ 'to weep'	G ገብረ-type ር-እ-ይ 'to see'
3MS	ውእቱ	ይድሉ / ይድለዉ	ይብኪ	ይርአይ
3FS	ይእቲ	ትድሉ	ትብኪ	ትርአይ
2MS	አንተ	ትድሉ	ትብኪ	ትርአይ
2FS	አንቲ	ትድለዊ	ትብክዪ	ትርአዪ
1CS	አነ	እድሉ	እብኪ	እርአይ
3MP	እሙንቱ	ይድለዉ	ይብክዩ	ይርአዩ
3FP	እማንቱ	ይድለዋ	ይብክያ	ይርአያ
2MP	አንትሙ	ትድለዉ	ትብክዩ	ትርአዩ
2FP	አንትን	ትድለዋ	ትብክያ	ትርአያ
1CP	ንሕነ	ንድሉ	ንብኪ	ንርአይ

Full Paradigm for Imperative

		G III-ው ድ-ል-ው 'to be fitting'	G III-ይ ብ-ከ-ይ 'to weep'	G ገብረ-type ር-እ-ይ 'to see'
2MS	አንተ	ደሉ	ብኪ	ርኢ
2FS	አንቲ	ደልዊ	ብከዪ	ረአዪ
2MP	አንትሙ	ደልዉ	ብከዩ	ረአዩ
2FP	አንትን	ደልዋ	ብከያ	ረአያ

C. Other Forms

Converb and Infinitive

ረኢይ-   '[he] having seen'

በኪይ-   '[he] having wept'

The vowel of the second syllable may be replaced: -i- > by -ə-.

ርኢይ and ርአይ   'to see'

በኪይ and በከይ   'to weep'

Adjective/Passive Participle—ቅፉል

ድልው   'fitting, proper'

ብኩይ   'mourner'

ርኡይ   'seen, regarded, noticed'

Noun Types

እትወት   'return (home); return, yield (of crops)'

እከይ (PL እከያት)   'evil, wickedness'

ጕያ   'flight'

ርእየት   'appearance, aspect, form'

ማዕዶት (PL ማዕዶታት) 'the opposite side' (of river, lake, mountains, etc.);

ሙዳይ (PL -āt ሙዳያት) 'a container of any sort; basket, hamper'

7. The Verb ብ-ህ-ል

Lesson 6 introduced the verb from the root ብ-ህ-ል 'to say'. There it was noted that it has been replaced by a unique but frequently occurring form. that is based on the Imperfect (note the inflectional affixes) but has a Preterite (simple past) meaning.

The "Preterite" paradigm for this verb is below:

3MS	ውእቱ	ይቤ	he said
3FS	ይእቲ	ትቤ	she said
2MS	አንተ	ትቤ	you said
2FS	አንቲ	ትቤሊ	you said
1CS	አነ	እቤ	I said
3MP	እሙንቱ	ይቤሉ	they said
3FP	እማንቱ	ይቤላ	they said
2MP	አንትሙ	ትቤሉ	you said
2FP	አንትን	ትቤላ	you said
1CP	ንሕነ	ንቤ	we said

The forms reflects two sound losses. First, note the loss of the second root consonant -ሀ- between vowels, which is a fairly common occurrence in Semitic languages. Second, note the loss of the final root consonant -ል when the paradigm form would have ended with a consonant (3ms, 3fs, 2ms, 1cs, 1cp). When the paradigm form ends with a vowel (2fs, 3mp, 3fp, 2mp, 2fp), the ል occurs and the form is regular.

When clitic pronouns are added to indicate the addressee of the speech, the final -ል of the root also occurs, even on the forms that otherwise drop it:

ወይቤሎሙ፡ኢየሱስ፡ንዑ፡   'and Jesus said (to) them, "Come ..."' (Mk 1:17)

The Imperfect, Subjunctive, and Imperative are also irregular, with uniform loss of the root's -ሀ-.

		Imperfect	Subjunctive	Imperative
3MS	ውእቱ	ይብል	ይበል	
3FS	ይአቲ	ትብል	ትበል	
2MS	አንተ	ትብል	ትበል	በል
2FS	አንቲ	ትብሊ	ትበሊ	በሊ
1CS	አነ	እብል	እበል	
3MP	እሙንቱ	ይብሉ	ይበሉ	
3FP	እማንቱ	ትብላ	ይበላ	
2MP	አንትሙ	ትብሉ	ትበሉ	በሉ
2FP	አንትን	ትብላ	ትበላ	በላ
1CP	ንሕነ	ንብል	ንበል	

The Imperfect following እንዘ may be used after any speech verb to introduce the direct speech. In many cases, it is best left untranslated for smooth English:

ወአፈድፊደ፡ትጋልፍተ፡ጴጥሮስ፡እንዘ፡ይብል፡እመውትሂ፡ምስሌከ፡
and Peter swore abundantly while saying, "I will die with you!"' (Mk 14:31)

Rarely other derivations are used and when they occur, they are regular (except the missing -ሀ- in the CG):

ተብህለ   Gt 'to be spoken, said, to be spoken of, mentioned'
ተባሀለ   Glt 'to speak/debate/argue (with one another/among themselves)'; ተባሉ፡በበይናቲሆሙ፡ (Mk 9:34)
አበለ   CG 'to cause to say'

APPENDIX D

THE VERB WITH ENCLITIC PRONOUNS

1. Perfect

	VerbBase	+me	+you(MS)	+you(FS)	+him	+her	+us	+you(MP)	+you(FP)	+them(M)	+them(F)
3MS	ቀተለ	ቀተለኒ	ቀተለከ	ቀተለኪ	ቀተሎ	ቀተላ	ቀተለነ	ቀተለክሙ	ቀተለክን	ቀተሎሙ	ቀተሎን
3FS	ቀተለት	ቀተለተኒ	ቀተለተከ	ቀተለተኪ	ቀተለቶ	ቀተለታ	ቀተለተነ	ቀተለተክሙ	ቀተለተክን	ቀተለቶሙ	ቀተለቶን
2MS	ቀተልከ	ቀተልከኒ			ቀተልኮ	ቀተልካ	ቀተልከነ			ቀተልከሙ	ቀተልከን
2FS	ቀተልኪ	ቀተልከኒ			ቀተልኮ	ቀተልኪያ	ቀተልክነ			ቀተልኮሙ	ቀተልኮን
1CS	ቀተልኩ		ቀተልኩከ	ቀተልኩኪ	ቀተልኮ	ቀተልኳ		ቀተልኩክሙ	ቀተልኩክን	ቀተልኳሙ	ቀተልኳን
3MP	ቀተሉ	ቀተሉኒ	ቀተሉከ	ቀተሉኪ	ቀተልዎ	ቀተልዋ	ቀተሉነ	ቀተሉክሙ	ቀተሉክን	ቀተልዎሙ	ቀተልዎን
3FP	ቀተላ	ቀተላኒ	ቀተላከ	ቀተላኪ	ቀተላሁ	ቀተላሃ	ቀተላነ	ቀተላክሙ	ቀተላክን	ቀተላሆሙ	ቀተላሆን
2MP	ቀተልክሙ	ቀተልክሙኒ			ቀተልክምዎ	ቀተልክምዋ	ቀተልክሙነ			ቀተልክምዎሙ	ቀተልክምዎን
2FP	ቀተልክን	ቀተልክናኒ			ቀተልክናሁ	ቀተልክናሃ	ቀተልክናነ			ቀተልክናሆሙ	ቀተልክናሆን
1CP	ቀተልነ		ቀተልናከ	ቀተልናኪ	ቀተልናሁ	ቀተልናሃ		ቀተልናክሙ	ቀተልናክን	ቀተልናሆሙ	ቀተልናሆን

2. Imperfect

	VerbBase	+me	+you(MS)	+you(FS)	+him	+her	+us	+you(MP)	+you(FP)	+them(M)	+them(F)
3MS	ይቀትል	ይቀትለኒ	ይቀትለከ	ይቀትለኪ	ይቀትሎ	ይቀትላ	ይቀትለነ	ይቀትለክሙ	ይቀትለክን	ይቀትሎሙ	ይቀትሎን
3FS	ትቀትል	ትቀትለኒ	ትቀትለከ	ትቀትለኪ	ትቀትሎ	ትቀትላ	ትቀትለነ	ትቀትለክሙ	ትቀትለክን	ትቀትሎሙ	ትቀትሎን
2MS	ትቀትል	ትቀትለኒ			ትቀትሎ	ትቀትላ	ትቀትለነ			ትቀትሎሙ	ትቀትሎን
2FS	ትቀትሊ	ትቀትልኒ			ትቀትልዮ	ትቀትልያ	ትቀትልነ			ትቀትልዮሙ	ትቀትልዮን
1CS	እቀትል		እቀትለከ	እቀትለኪ	እቀትሎ	እቀትላ		እቀትለክሙ	እቀትለክን	እቀትሎሙ	እቀትሎን
3MP	ይቀትሉ	ይቀትሉኒ	ይቀትሉከ	ይቀትሉኪ	ይቀትልዎ	ይቀትልዋ	ይቀትሉነ	ይቀትሉክሙ	ይቀትሉክን	ይቀትልዎሙ	ይቀትልዎን
3FP	ይቀትላ	ይቀትላኒ	ይቀትላከ	ይቀትላኪ	ይቀትላሁ	ይቀትላሃ	ይቀትላነ	ይቀትላክሙ	ይቀትላክን	ይቀትላሆሙ	ይቀትላሆን
2MP	ትቀትሉ	ትቀትሉኒ			ትቀትልዎ	ትቀትልዋ	ትቀትሉነ			ትቀትልዎሙ	ትቀትልዎን
2FP	ትቀትላ	ትቀትላኒ			ትቀትላሁ	ትቀትላሃ	ትቀትላነ			ትቀትላሆሙ	ትቀትላሆን
1CP	ንቀትል		ንቀትለከ	ንቀትለኪ	ንቀትሎ	ንቀትላ		ንቀትለክሙ	ንቀትለክን	ንቀትሎሙ	ንቀትሎን

APPENDIX E

NUMERALS

1. Cardinal Numerals

A. Numeral Forms

	Masculine		Feminine	
one	አሐዱ COMP አሐደ		አሐቲ COMP አሐተ	
two	ክልኤቱ	ክልኤተ	ክልኤቲ	ክልኤተ
three	ሠለስቱ	ሠለስተ	ሠላስ	ሠላስ
four	አርባዕቱ	አርባዕተ	አርባዕ	አርባዕ
five	ኃምስቱ	ኃምስተ	ኃምስ	ኃምስ
six	ስድስቱ	ስድስተ	ስሱ	ስሱ
seven	ሰብዐቱ	ሰብዐተ	ሰብዑ	ሰብዑ
eight	ሰማንቱ	ሰማንተ	ሰማኒ	ሰማኒ
nine	ትስዐቱ	ትስዐተ	ትስዑ	ትስዑ
ten	ዐሠርቱ	ዐሠርተ	ዐሡሩ	ዐሡሩ

Note: common variant forms: masculine (7) ሰባዕቱ, (8) ሰማኒቱ, (9) ተስዐቱ, ተሳዕቱ; feminine (10) ዐሡር.

Note: the masculine numerals in -ቱ have complement form with -ተ but the feminines in -ú (and ሰማኒ) have no distinct complement form.

Note: the form ክልኤ is used for both masculine and feminine 'two'.

B. Numeral Syntax

Cardinal numerals normally precede the counted noun.

Other than with አሐዱ 'one', agreement in gender does not always occur, even with nouns referring to humans. Indeed, the numerals in -ቱ are often used regardless of the gender of the noun.

Numerals agree with the counted noun concerning whether the it has the complement -*a*. The counted noun may be either singular or plural, with a preference for the former:

አሐዱ፡ብእሲ	'one man'
አሐቲ፡ብእሲት	'one woman'
ክልኤቱ፡አብያት	'two houses'
ክልኤቲ፡ሀገር	'two cities'
ክልኤ፡ደመና	'two clouds'
ሠለስቱ፡ወርኅ	'three months'
ኃምስ፡ዕለት	'five days'
ስሱ፡አንስት	'six women'
ሰብዐቱ፡ሰብእ	'seven men', 'seven people'

The numeral አሐዱ 'one' frequently has a semantic role similar to a definite article:

| አሐዱ፡ብእሲ | 'the man', 'a certain man' |

Numbers rarely stand in construct; the partitive is expressed by እም-:

| ሠለስቱ፡እምአርዳኢሁ | 'three of his disciples' |

2. Ordinal Numbers

From three onward the ordinal numbers are based on the same roots as the cardinals, with the pattern ቃትል (F ቃትልት); the complement form is simply in -a.

	Masculine	Feminine
third	ሣልስ	ሣልስት
fourth	ራብዕ	ራብዕት
fifth	ኃምስ	ኃምስት
sixth	ሳድስ	ሳድስት
seventh	ሳብዕ	ሳብዕት
eighth	ሳምን	ሳምንት
ninth	ታስዕ	ታስዕት
tenth	ዓሥር	ዓሥርት

For 'first' ቀዳሚ (F ቀዳሚት) is used. 'Second' may be expressed in several ways:

ካልእ (F -t ካልእት), usually, but not exclusively, when only two items are involved

ዳግም (F -t ዳግምት)

ካዕብ (F -t ካዕብት), which is rare

ባዕድ (F ባዕድ), which has also the additional meaning 'other, strange, foreign'

All of the ordinals except ካልእ appear also with the adjectival suffixes -āwi and -āy. The ordinal adjectives normally precede their noun:

ሣልስ፡አንቀጽ	'the third gate'
ራብዓዊ፡ብእሲ	'the fourth man'
ሳብዓዊት፡ሀገር	'the seventh city'

Note: The feminine form for ordinals in -āy is -it: ሣልሲት፡ብእሲት 'the third woman'.

A further derivative from the ordinal stem is ዓሥራት 'a tenth, tithe'.

There is a second series of ordinals based on the pattern ቀቱል and used almost exclusively to designate days of the week or month or hours of the day:

በዐሥር፡ዕለት	'on the tenth day' (of the month)
ሠሉስ፡ሌሊት	'the third night' (of the week or of the particular time period in question)
ረቡዕ፡ለወርኅ	'the fourth day of the month'

They also occur in place of the regular cardinals when days, hours, or months are counted:

ነበረ፡ህየ፡ሠሉስ፡ዕለተ   'He stayed there three days'

Note in particular that 'second' is ሰኑይ (F ሰኒት), based on a root not used in the other number series. When the context is clear, the nouns for day and hour are omitted:

በሰኑይ   'on the second (day)' or 'at the second (hour)'

3. Cardinal Adverbs

From three to ten the pattern ቅትል with the complement -a (ቅትለ) denotes 'X times', etc.

ሥልስ	'three times, thrice'
ርብዐ	'four times'
ኀምስ	'five times'
ስድስ	'six times'
ስብዐ	'seven times'

ስምነ	'eight times'
ትስዐ	'nine times'
ዐሥረ	'ten times'

These forms of the numbers are also used occasionally as feminine cardinals:

| ሥልስ፡ሀገር | 'three cities' |

'Once' may be expressed by ኣሐተ or ምዕረ.

'Twice' is expressed by ካዕበ or ዳግመ, both of which are frequent in the sense 'again, a second time'.

4. Numbers Above Ten

11-19. The gender distinctions noted with the units are preserved in the teens. Thus,

Masculine	Feminine	
ዐሠርቱ፡ወአሐዱ	ዐሥሩ፡ወአሐቲ	11
ዐሠርቱ፡ወክልኤቱ	ዐሥሩ፡ወክልኤ	12
ዐሠርቱ፡ወሠለስቱ	ዐሥሩ፡ወሠላስ	13
etc.		

When days of the month are enumerated (ordinal or cardinal), the forms ዐሡር፡ወሰኑይ, ዐሡር፡ወሡሉስ, etc. are used.

20-90. The tens are based on the corresponding units with the ending -ā, excepting 20, where the base of 10 is used:

ዕሥራ	'20'
ሠላሳ	'30'
ኣርብዓ	'40'
ኀምሳ	'50'
ስሳ	'60'
ሰብዓ	'70'
ሰማንያ	'80'
ተስዓ, ትስዓ	'90'

These are unmodified for case or gender. Units are simply added, but the normal gender distinctions are retained.

ዕሥራ፡ ወአሐዱ / አሐትቲ	'21'
ዕሥራ፡ወክልኤቱ / ክልኤ	'22'
etc.	

5. Hundreds and Thousands

'100' is ምእት (PL አምኣት).

'1000' is normally expressed as '10 hundred': ዐሠርቱ፡ምእት.

'2000' is '20 hundred', ዕሥራ፡ምእት

etc.

Ordinals above ten may be expressed by cardinals. There are, however, separate ordinal forms of the tens: ዕሥራዊ '20th', ሠላሳዊ '30th', etc.

In Ethiopic texts the numbers are frequently represented by figures (see Lesson 1.4); these must, of course, be read with the appropriate cardinal or ordinal form.

APPENDIX F
MANUSCRIPT IMAGES WITH TEXT

1. The Gospel of Mark, Chapters 1-3 (Abba Garima III)
Page 1 Facsimile

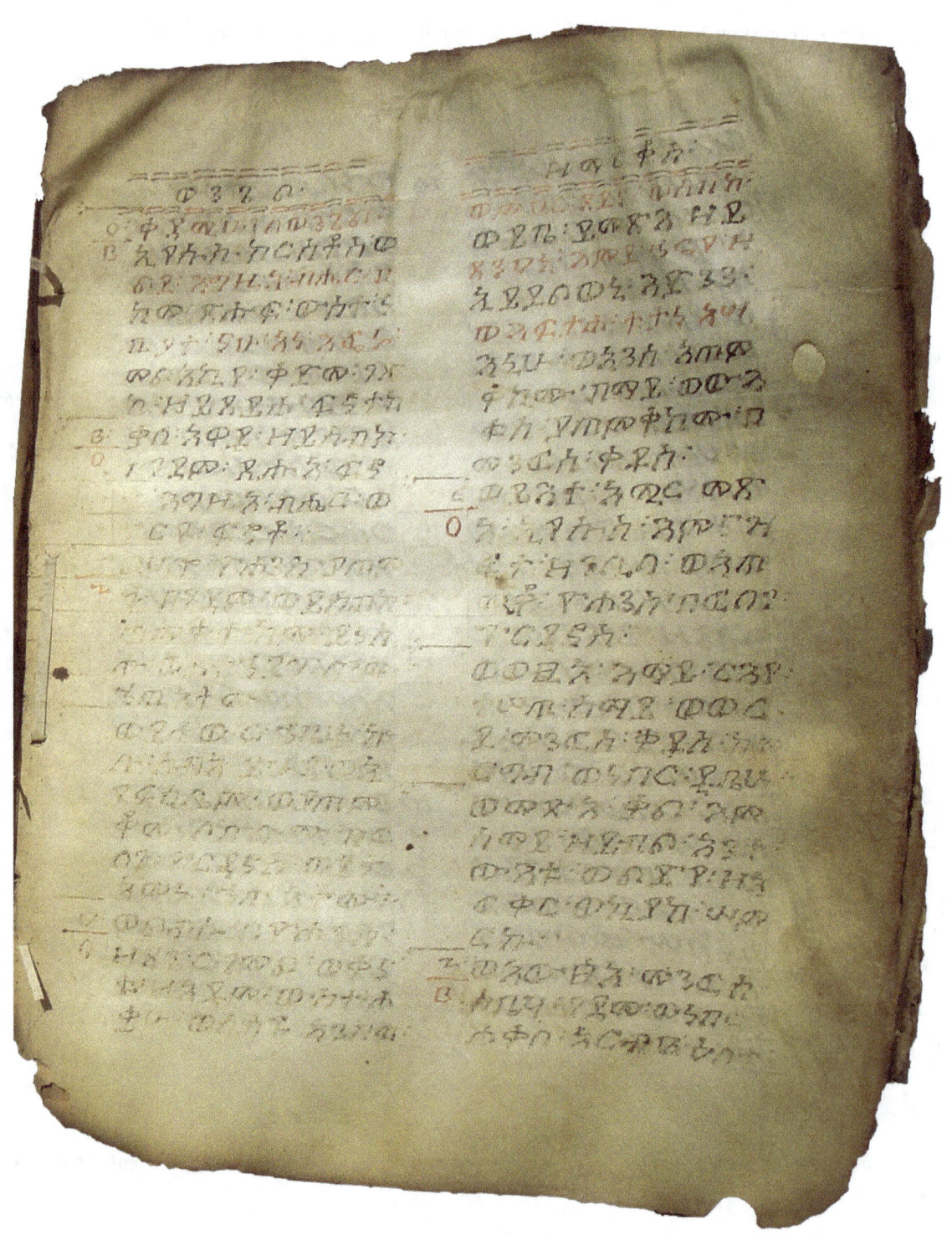

Page 1 Layout

ዉ ን ጌ ል፡	ዘማርቆስ፡
ቀዳሚሁ፡ለወንጌል፡ ኢየሱስ፡ክርስቶስ፡ወ ልደ፡እግዚአ፡ብሔር፡በ ከመ፡ጽሐፍ፡ውስተ፡ነ ቢያት፡ናሁ፡አነ፡እፌኑ፡ መልአኪየ፡ቅድመ፡ገጽ ከ፡ዘይጻይሕ፡ፍኖተከ፡ ቃለ፡አዋዲ፡ዘይሰብክ፡ በገዳም፡ጺሑአ፡ፍኖ ተ፡እግዚአ፡ብሔር፡ወ ዐርዩ፡ፍኖቶ። ወሀሎ፡ዮሐንስ፡ያጠም ቅ፡በገዳም፡ወይሰብክ፡ ጥምቀተ፡ከመ፡ይነስ ሑ፡ወይትኅደግ፡ሎሙ፡ ኃጢአቶሙ። ወይሐውሩ፡ኃቤሁ፡ኵ ሉ፡ሰብአ፡ይሁዳ፡ወኢ የሩሳሌም፡ወያጠም ቆሙ፡ለኵሎሙ፡በፈ ለገ፡ዮርዳኖስ፡ወይት አመኑ፡ኃጢአቶሙ። ወልብሱ፡ለዮሐንስ፡ ዘጸጉረ፡ገመል፡ወቅና ቱ፡ዘአዲም፡ውስተ፡ሐ ቊሁ፡ወሲሳዩ፡አንበጣ፡	ወምዐረ፡ጸደና፡ወሰበከ፡ ወይቤ፡ይመጽእ፡ዘይ ጸንዐኒ፡እምድኅሬየ፡ዘ ኢይደልወኒ፡እድንን፡ ወእፍታሕ፡ቲታነ፡አሣ እኒሁ፡ወአንሰ፡አጠም ቀክሙ፡በማይ፡ወውእ ቱሰ፡ያጠምቀክሙ፡በ መንፈስ፡ቅዱስ፡ ወይእተ፡አሚረ፡መጽ አ፡ኢየሱስ፡እምናዘ ሬት፡ዘገሊላ፡ወአጥ መቆ፡ዮሐንስ፡በፈለገ፡ ዮርዳኖስ፡ ወወዪአ፡እማይ፡ርእየ፡ ተኃጠ፡ሰማይ፡ወወረ ደ፡መንፈስ፡ቅዱስ፡ከመ፡ ርግብ፡ወነበረ፡ዲቤሁ። ወመጽአ፡ቃል፡እም ሰማይ፡ዘይብል፡አንተ፡ ውእቱ፡ወልድየ፡ዘአ ፈቅር፡ወኪያከ፡ሠመ ርኩ። ወአውፅአ፡መንፈስ፡ ሶቤሃ፡ገዳም፡ወነበረ፡ ሐቅለ፡አርብዐ፡ዕለተ፡

173

Page 2 Facsimile

Appendix F—Manuscript Images with Text

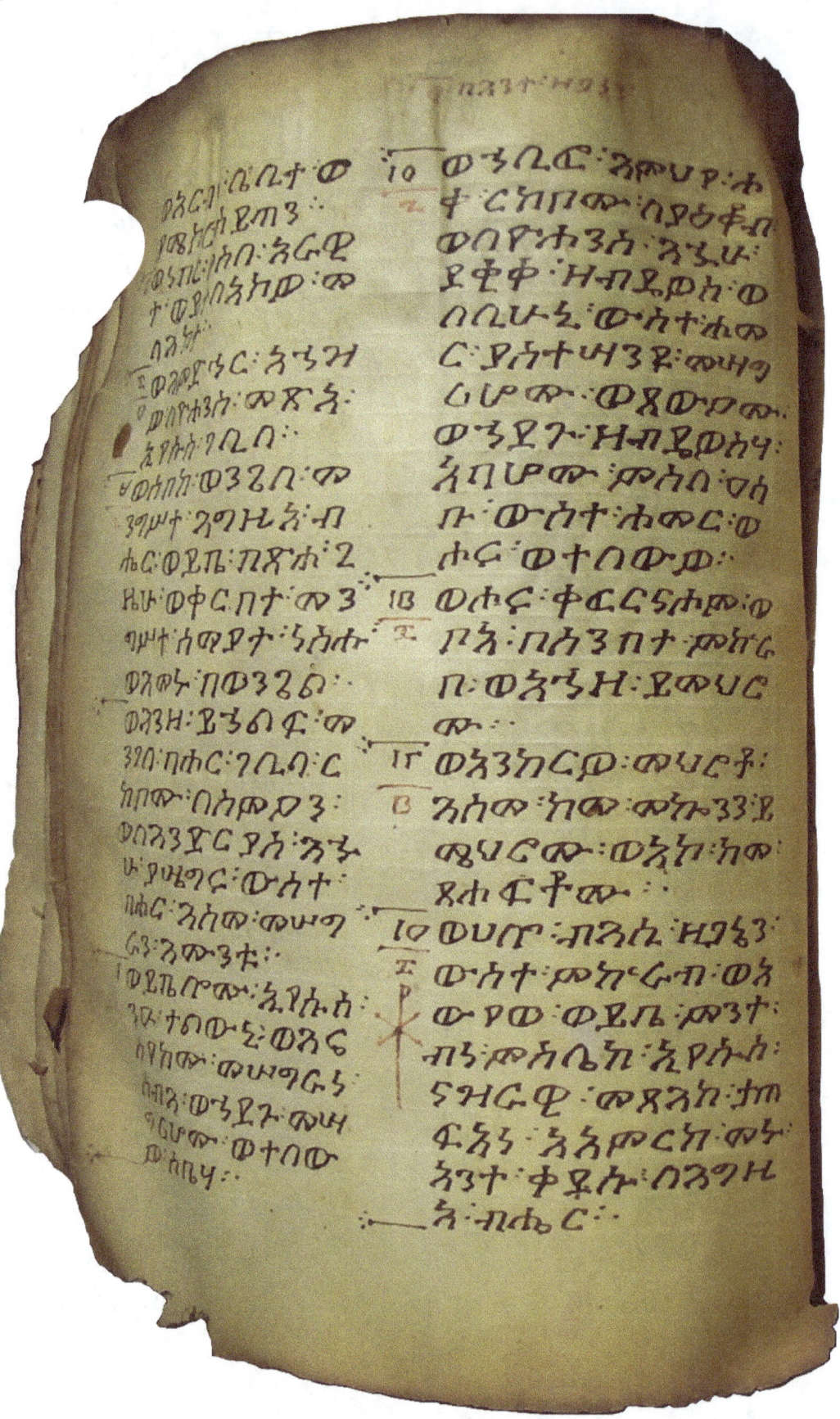

Page 2 Layout

ወአርብዓ፡ሌሊተ፡ወያሜክሮ፡ሰይጣን፡ወነበረ፡ምስለ፡አራዊት፡ወይትለአክዎ፡መላእክት።
ወእምድኅረ፡አኀዞ፡ለዮሐንስ፡መጽአ፡ኢየሱስ፡ገሊላ።
ወሰበከ፡ወንጌለ፡መንግሥተ፡እግዚአብሔር፡ወይቤ፡በጽሐጊዜሁ፡ወቀርበት፡መንግሥተ፡ሰማያት፡ነስሑ፡ወእመኑ፡በወንጌል።
ወእንዘ፡ይኈልፍ፡መንገለ፡ባሕረ፡ገሊላ፡ረከቦሙ፡ለስምዖን፡ወለእንድርያስ፡እኍሁ፡ያሤግሩ፡ውስተ፡ባሕር፡እስመ፡መሥገራን፡እሙንቱ።
ወይቤሎሙ፡ኢየሱስ፡ንዑ፡ትልውኒ፡ወእሬስየክሙ፡መሥግራነ፡ሰብእ፡ወንደቱ፡መሥገሪሆሙ፡ወተለውዎ፡ሶቤሃ።

ወንሊፎ፡እምህየ፡ሐቀ፡ረከቦሙ፡ለያዕቆብ፡ወለዮሐንስ፡እኍሁ፡ደቂቀ፡ዘብዴዎስ፡ወሊሁኒ፡ውስተ፡ሐመር፡ያስተሣንዩ፡መሣገሪሆሙ፡ወጸውዖሙ፡ወንደቱ፡ዘብዴዎስሃ፡አባሆሙ፡ምስለ፡ዐሳቡ፡ውስተ፡ሐመር፡ወሐሩ፡ወተለውዎ።
ወሐሩ፡ቅፍርናሐም፡ወቦአ፡በሰንበት፡ምኵራበ፡ወእንዘ፡ይመህሮሙ።
ወአንከርዎ፡መህሮቶ፡እስመ፡ከመ፡መኰንን፡ይሜህሮሙ፡ወአኮ፡ከመ፡ጸሐፍቶሙ።
ወሀሎ፡ብእሲ፡ዘጋኔን፡ውስተ፡ምኵራብ፡ወአውየወ፡ወይቤ፡ምንተ፡ብነ፡ምስሌከ፡ኢየሱስ፡ናዝራዊ፡መጻእከ፡ታጠፍአነ፡አአምረከ፡መኑ፡አንተ፡ቅዱሱ፡ለእግዚአ፡ብሔር።

Page 3 Facsimile

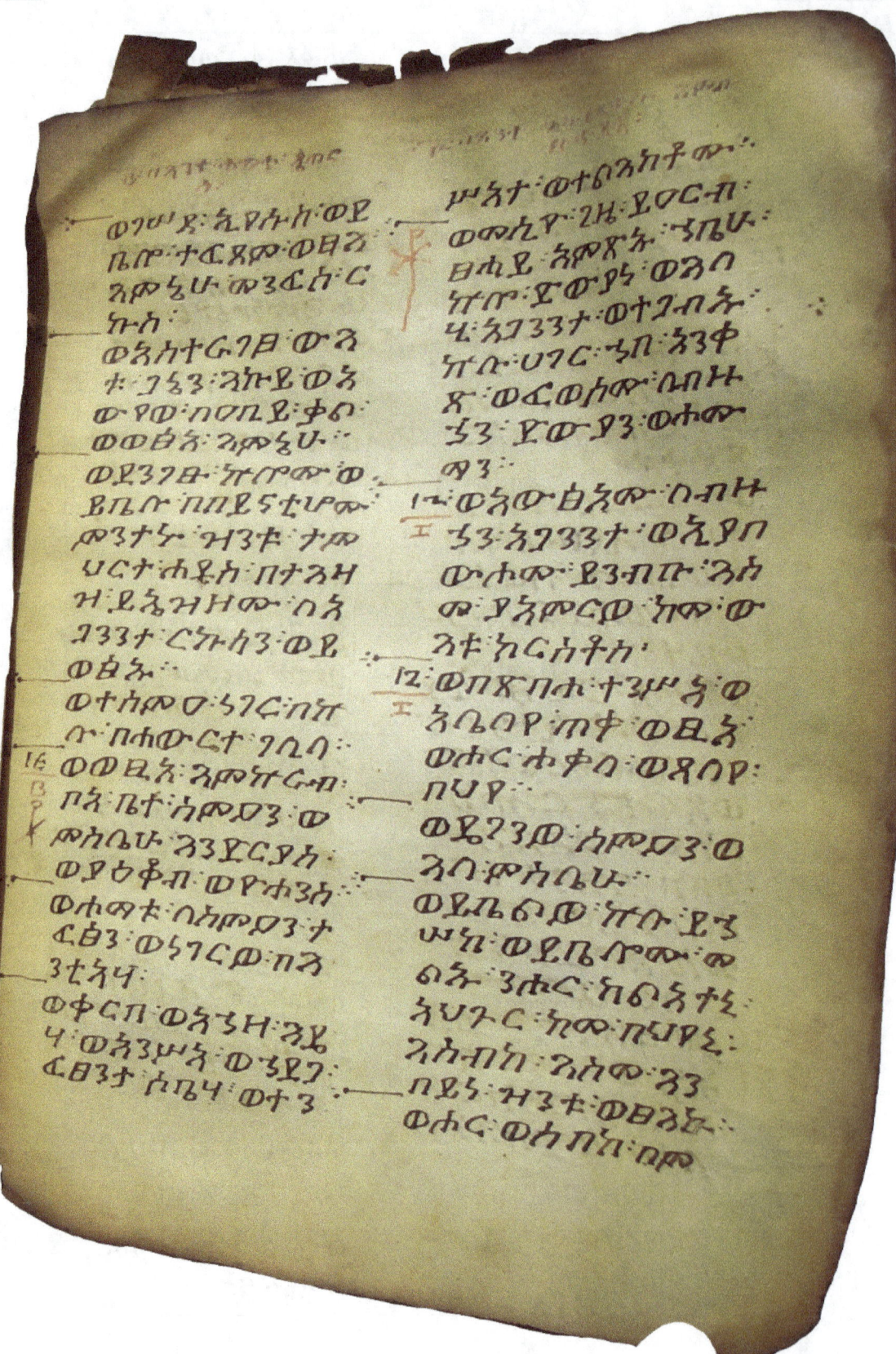

Page 3 Layout

ወገሠጸ፡ኢየሱስ፡ወይ
ቤሎ፡ተፈጸም፡ወፃእ
እምኔሁ፡መንፈስ፡ር
ኩስ፡
ወአስተራገፆ፡ውእ
ቱ፡ጋኔን፡እኩይ፡ወአ
ውየወ፡በዐቢይ፡ቃል፡
ወወፅአ፡እምኔሁ።
ወደንገፁ፡ኵሎሙ፡ወ
ይቤሉ፡በበይናቲሆሙ፡
ምንትኑ፡ዝንቱ፡ትም
ህርት፡ሐዲስ፡በትእዛ
ዝ፡ይኤዝዘሙ፡ለአ
ጋንንት፡ርኩሳን፡ወይ
ወፅኡ።
ወተሰምዐ፡ነገሩ፡በኵ
ሉ፡በሐውርተ፡ገሊላ።
ወወኢአ፡እምኵራብ፡
ቦአ፡ቤተ፡ስምዖን፡ወ
ምስሌሁ፡እንድርያስ፡
ወያዕቆብ፡ወዮሐንስ።
ወሐማቱ፡ለስምዖን፡ት
ፈፅን፡ወነገርዎ፡በእ
ንቲአሃ፡
ወቀርበ፡ወአንዛእዬ
ሃ፡ወአንሥአ፡ወንደጋ
ፈፀንታ፡ሰቤሃ፡ወተን

ሥእት፡ወተልእከቶሙ።
ወመሲዮ፡ጊዜ፡የዐርብ፡
ፀሓይ፡አምጽኡ፡ኀቤሁ፡
ኵሎ፡ድውያን፡ወአለ
ሂ፡አጋንንት፡ወተጋብኡ።
ኵሉ፡ሀገር፡ኀበ፡እንቀ
ጽ፡ወፈወሶሙ፡ለብዙ
ኃን፡ድውያን፡ወሕሙ
ማን።
ወአውፅአሙ፡ለብዙ
ኃን፡አጋንንት፡ወኢያበ
ውሐሙ፡ይንብቡ፡እስ
ም፡ያአምርዎ፡ከመ፡ው
እቱ፡ክርስቶስ፡
ወበጽባሕ፡ተንሥአ፡ወ
አሌለየ፡ጥቀ፡ወሢአ፡
ወሓረ፡ሐቅለ፡ወጸለየ፡
በህየ።
ወዴገንዎ፡ስምዖን፡ወ
እለ፡ምስሌሁ።
ወይቤልዎ፡ኵሉ፡ይኅ
ሢከ፡ወይቤሎሙ፡መ
ልኡ፡ንሓር፡ካልአተኒ፡
አህጉር፡ከመ፡በህየኒ፡
እስብክ፡እስመ፡እን
በይነ፡ዝንቱ፡ወፃእኩ፡
ወሓረ፡ወሰበከ፡በም

Page 4 Facsimile

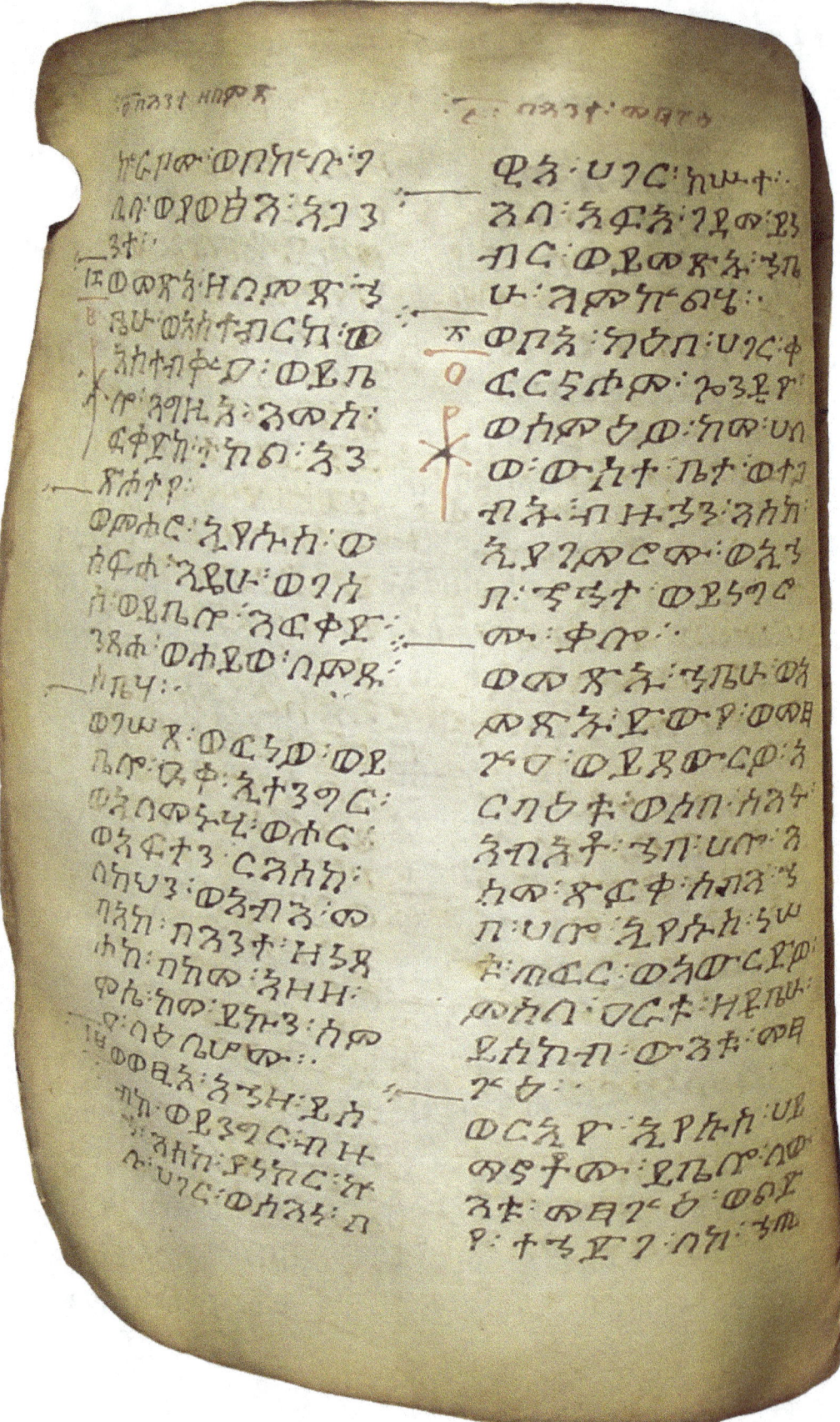

Page 4 Layout

ኩራበሙ፡ወበኵሉ፡ገሊላ፡ወያወፅእ፡አጋንንተ። ወመጽአ፡ዘለምጽ፡ኃቤሁ፡ወአስተብረከ፡ወአስተብቍዖ፡ወይቤሎ፡እግዚእ፡እመሰ፡ፈቀድከ፡ትክል፡አንጽሖትየ። ወምሕሮ፡ኢየሱስ፡ወሰፍሐ፡እዴሁ፡ወገሰሶ፡ወይቤሎ፡እፈቅድ፡ንጻሕ፡ወሐይወ፡ለምጹ፡ሶቤሃ። ወገሠጾ፡ወፈነዎ፡ወይቤሎ፡ዑቅ፡ኢትንግር፡ወኢለመኑሂ፡ወሐር፡ወአፍትን፡ርእሰከ፡ለካህን፡ወአብእ፡መባአከ፡በእንተ፡ዘነጻሕከ፡በከመ፡አዘዘ፡ሞሴ፡ከመ፡ይኩን፡ስምዐ፡ላዕሌሆሙ። ወወፊአ፡አንዘ፡ይስብክ፡ወይንግር፡ብዙኃ፡እስከ፡ያነክር፡ኰሉ፡ሀገር፡ወስእነ፡በ	ዊአ፡ሀገር፡ክሡተ። እላ፡አፍአ፡ገዳም፡ይነብር፡ወይመጽኡ፡ኃቤሁ፡እምኵልሄ። ወቦአ፡ካዕበ፡ሀገረ፡ቅፍርናሖም፡ጐንዲዮ፡ወሰምዕዋ፡ከመ፡ሀለወ፡ውስተ፡ቤት፡ወተጋብኡ፡ብዙኃን፡እስከ፡ኢያገምሮሙ፡ወኢን፡በኖት፡ወይነግሮሙ፡ቃሎ። ወመጽኡ፡ኃቤሁ፡ወአምጽኡ፡ድውየ፡ወመጋዕዎ፡ወይጸውርዎ፡አርባዕቱ፡ወሶበ፡ስእኑ፡አብአቶ፡ኃበ፡ሀሎ፡እስመ፡ጽፉቅ፡ሰብእ፡ኃበ፡ሀሎ፡ኢየሱስ፡ነሡቱ፡ጠፈረ፡ወአውረድዎ፡ምስለ፡ዐራቱ፡ዘዲቤሁ፡ይሰክብ፡ውእቱ፡መጋጉዕ። ወርኢዮ፡ኢየሱስ፡ሀይማኖቶሙ፡ይቤሎ፡ለውእቱ፡መፃጉዕ፡ወልድየ፡ተኀድገ፡ለከ፡ኃጢ

179

Page 5 Facsimile

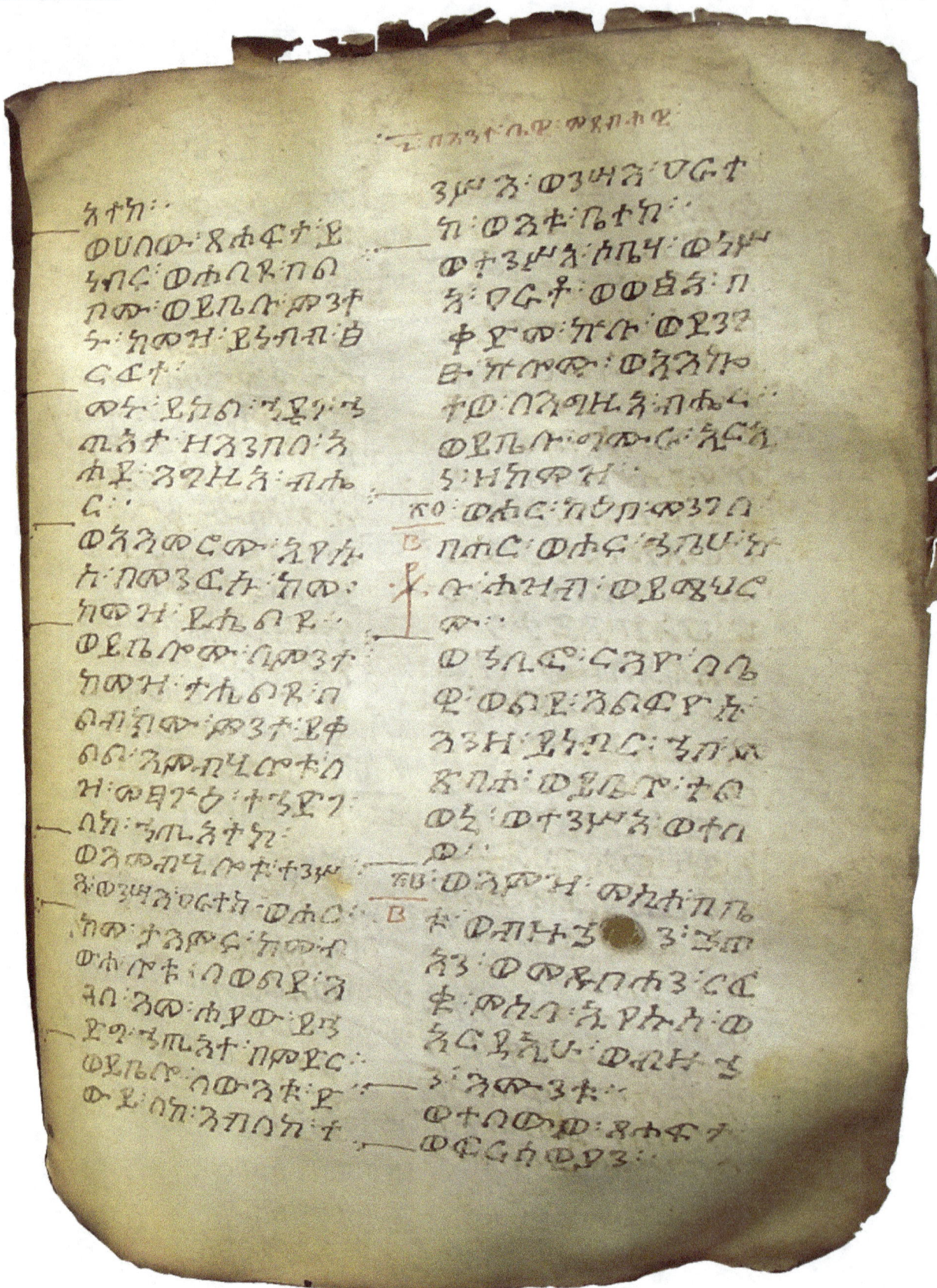

Page 5 Layout

አትከ።
ወሀለው፡ጸሐፍት፡ይ
ነብሩ፡ወሐለዩ፡በል
ቦሙ፡ወይቤሉ፡ምንተ
ኑ፡ከመዝ፡ይነብብ፡ፅ
ርፈት፡
መኑ፡ይክል፡ኅዲገ፡ኃ
ጢአተ፡ዘእንበለ፡አ
ሐዱ፡እግዚአ፡ብሔ
ር።
ወአእመሮሙ፡ኢየሱ
ስ፡በመንፈሱ፡ከመ፡
ከመዝ፡ይሔልዩ።
ወይቤሎሙ፡ለምንት፡
ከመዝ፡ትሔልዩ፡በ
ልብከሙ፡ምንት፡ይቀ
ልል፡እምብሂሎቱ፡ለ
ዝ፡መፃጉዕ፡ተንድገ፡
ለከ፡ኃጢአተከ፡
ወእምብሂሎቱ፡ተንሥ
እ፡ወንሣእ፡ዐራተከ፡ወሐር።
ከመ፡ታእምሩ፡ከመ፡ብ
ውሕ፡ሎቱ፡ለወልደ፡እ
ጓለ፡እመ፡ሕያው፡ይኃ
ድግ፡ኃጢአተ፡በምድር።
ወይቤሎ፡ለውእቱ፡ድ
ው፡ይ፡ለከ፡እብለከ፡ተ
ንሥእ፡ወንሣእ፡ዐራተ
ከ፡ወእቱ፡ቤተከ።
ወተንሥእ፡ሶቤሃ፡ወነሥ
አ፡ዐራቶ፡ወወፅአ፡በ
ቅድመ፡ኵሉ፡ወደንገ
ፁ፡ኵሎሙ፡ወአእኰ
ትዎ፡ለእግዚአ፡ብሔር፡
ወይቤሉ፡ግሙራ፡ኢርኢ
ነ፡ዘከመዝ።
ወሐረ፡ካዕበ፡መንገለ፡
ባሕር፡ወሐሩ፡ኀቤሁ፡ኲ
ሉ፡ሕዝብ፡ወይሜህሮ
ሙ።
ወንሊፎ፡ርእዮ፡ለሌ
ዊ፡ወልደ፡እልፍዮስ፡
እንዘ፡ይነብር፡ኀበ፡ም
ጽባሕ፡ወይቤሎ፡ትል
ወኒ፡ወተንሥእ፡ወተለ
ዎ።
ወእምዝ፡መስሐ፡በቤ
ቱ፡ወብዙኃን፡ኃጥ
አን፡ወመጸብሓን፡ረፈ
ቁ፡ምስለ፡ኢየሱስ፡ወ
አርዳኢሁ፡ወብዙኃ
ን፡እሙንቱ።
ወተለውዎ፡ጸሐፍት፡
ወፈሪሳዊያን፡

Page 6 Facsimile

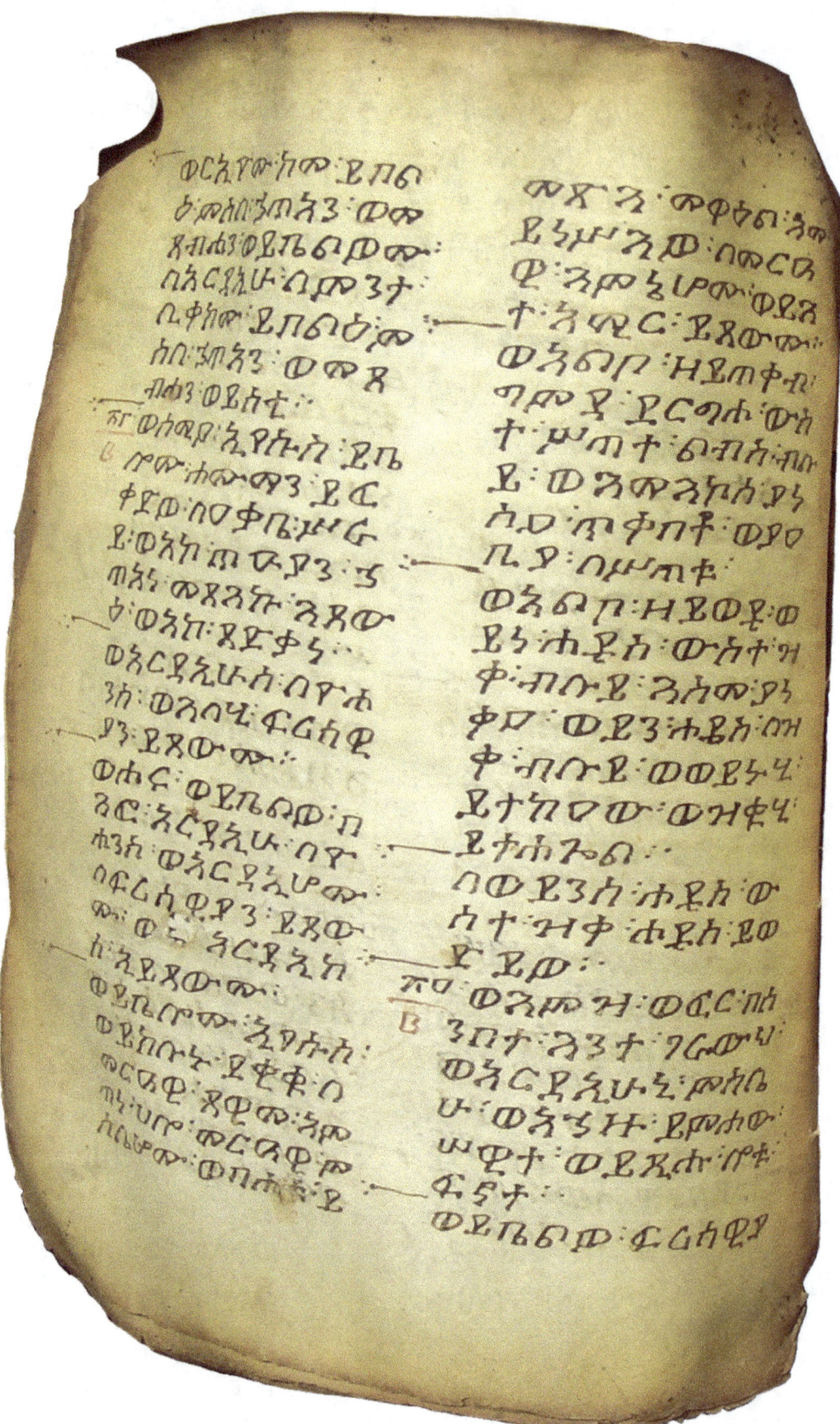

Page 6 Layout

ወርኢዮሙ፡ከመ፡ይበል ዕ፡ምስለ፡ኃጥኣን፡ወመ ጸብሓን፡ወይቤልዎሙ፡ ለአርዳኢሁ፡ለምንት፡ ሊቅክሙ፡ይበልዕ፡ም ስለ፡ኃጥኣን፡ወመጸ ብሓን፡ወይሰቲ። ወሰሚዖ፡ኢየሱስ፡ይቤ ሎሙ፡ሕሙማን፡ይፈ ቅድዎ፡ለዐቃቤ፡ሥራ ይ፡ወአኮ፡ጡያን፡ኃ ጥኣነ፡መጻእኩ፡እጸው ዕ፡ወአኮ፡ጻድቃነ። ወአርዳኢሁስ፡ለዮሐ ንስ፡ወእለሂ፡ፈሪሳዊ ያን፡ይጸውሙ። ወሐሩ፡ወይቤልዎ፡በ እፎ፡አርዳኢሁ፡ለዮ ሐንስ፡ወአርዳኢሆሙ፡ ለፈሪሳዊያን፡ይጸው ሙ፡ወአርዳኢከ ሰ፡ኢይጸውሙ። ወይቤሎሙ፡ኢየሱስ፡ ወይክሉኑ፡ደቂቁ፡ለ መርዓዊ፡ጸዊም፡አም ጣነ፡ሀሎ፡መርዓዊ፡ም ስሌሆሙ፡ወባሕቱ፡ይ	መጽእ፡መዋዕል፡አመ፡ ይነሥእዎ፡ለመርዓ ዊ፡እምኔሆም፡ወእ ተ፡አሚረ፡ይጸውሙ። ወአልቦ፡ዘይጠቅብ፡ ግምደ፡ደርግሐ፡ውስ ተ፡ሥጠተ፡ልብስ፡ብሉ ይ፡ወእ<ሙ>አኮሰ፡ያነ ስዖ፡ጥቅበቶ፡ወያዐ ቢያ፡ለሥጠቱ። ወአልቦ፡ዘይወዲ፡ወ ይነ፡ሐዲሰ፡ውስተ፡ዝ ቅ፡ብሉይ፡እስመ፡ያነ ቅዖ፡ወይን፡ሐዲስ፡ለዝ ቅ፡ብሉይ፡ወወይኑሂ፡ ይትከዐው፡ወዝቁኒ፡ ይትሐጎል። ለወይንስ፡ሐዲስ፡ው ስተ፡ዝቅ፡ሐዲስ፡ይወ ድይዎ። ወእምዝ፡ወፈረ፡በሰ ንበት፡እንተ፡ገራውህ፡ ወአርዳኢሁኒ፡ምስሌ ሁ፡ወአንዙ፡ይምሐው፡ ሥዊተ፡ወይጺሑ፡ሎቱ፡ ፍኖተ። ወይቤልዎ፡ፈሪሳዊያ

Page 7 Facsimile

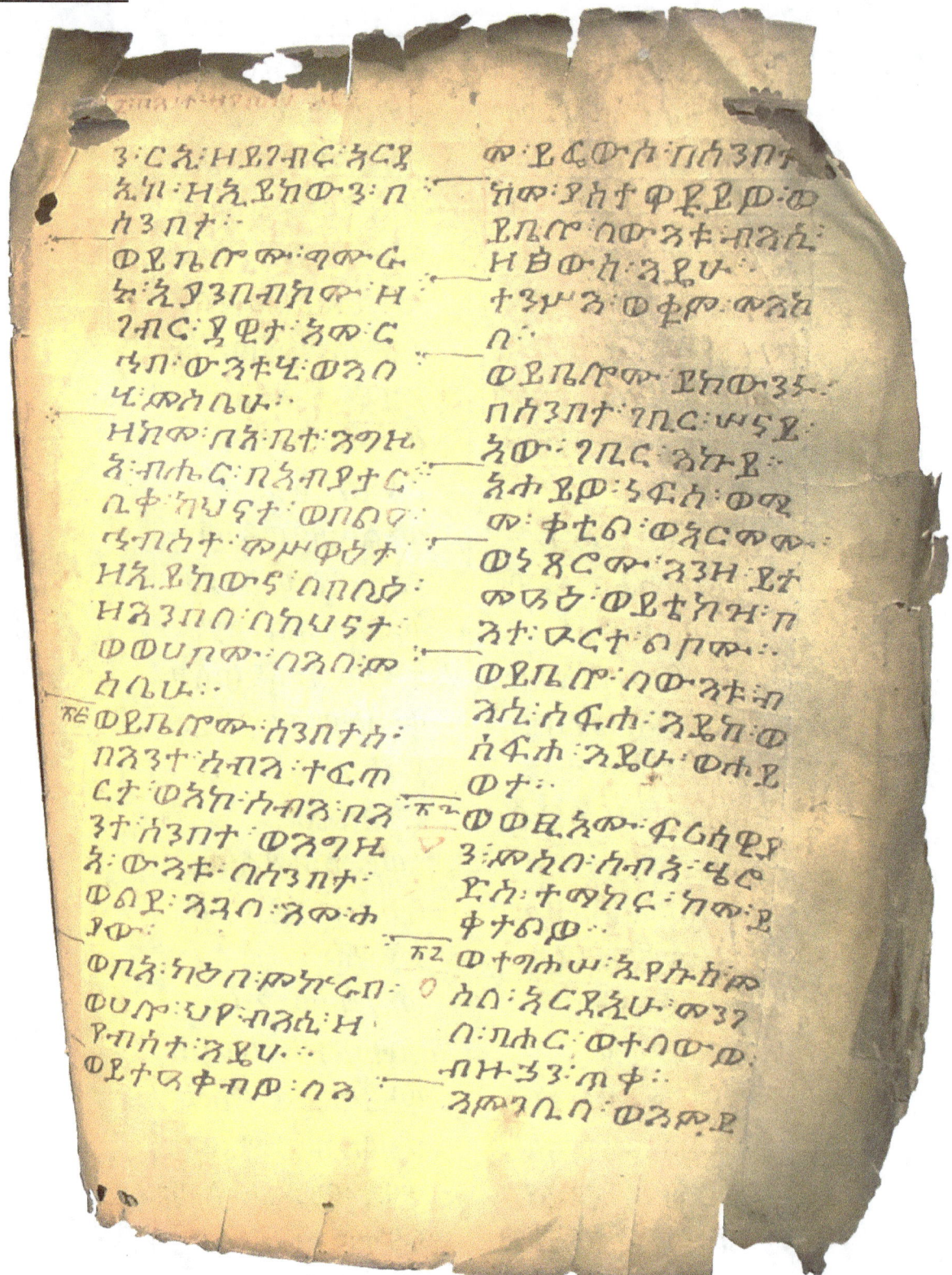

Page 7 Layout

ን፡ርኢ፡ዘይገብሩ፡እርዳ
ኢከ፡ዘኢይከውን፡በ
ሰንበት።
ወይቤሎሙ፡ግሙራ
ኑ፡ኢያንበብክሙ፡ዘ
ገብረ፡ዳዊት፡አመ፡ር
ኅበ፡ውእቱሂ፡ወእለ
ሂ፡ምስሌሁ።
ዘከመ፡ቦአ፡ቤተ፡እግዚ
አ፡ብሔር፡በአብያታር፡
ሊቀ፡ካህናት፡ወበልዐ፡
ኅብስተ፡መሥዋዕት፡
ዘኢይከውኖ፡ለበሊዐ፡
ለዘእንበለ፡ለካህናት፡
ወወሀቦሙ፡ለእለ፡ም
ስሌሁ።
ወይቤሎሙ፡ሰንበትሰ፡
በእንተ፡ሰብእ፡ተፈጥ
ረት፡ወአኮ፡ሰብእ፡በእ
ንተ፡ሰንበት፡ወእግዚ
አ፡ውእቱ፡ለሰንበት፡
ወልደ፡እጓለ፡እመ፡ሕ
ያው።
ወቦአ፡ካዕበ፡ምኩራብ፡
ወሀሎ፡ህየ፡ብእሲ፡ዘ
የብስት፡እዴሁ።
ወይትዐቀብዎ፡ለእ

ሙ፡ይፌውሶ፡በሰንበት፡
ከመ፡ያስተዋድይዎ፡ወ
ይቤሎ፡ለውእቱ፡ብእሲ፡
ዘፅውስ፡እዴሁ።
ተንሥእ፡ወቁም፡ማእከ
ሉ።
ወይቤሎሙ፡ይከውኑ፡
በሰንበት፡ገቢረ፡ሠናይ፡
አው፡ገቢረ፡እኩይ።
አሕይዎ፡ነፍስ፡ወሚ
ሙ፡ቀቲል፡ወአርመሙ፡
ወነጸሮሙ፡እንዘ፡ይት
መዓዕ፡ወይቴክዝ፡በ
እ‹ን›ተ፡ዑረተ፡ልቦሙ፡
ወይቤሎ፡ለውእቱ፡ብ
እሲ፡ስፋሕ፡እዴከ፡ወ
ሰፍሐ፡እዴሁ፡ወሐይ
ወት።
ወወፂአሙ፡ፈሪሳዊያ
ን፡ምስለ፡ሰብአ፡ሄሮ
ድስ፡ተማከሩ፡ከመ፡ይ
ቅትልዎ።
ወተግሕሠ፡ኢየሱስ፡ም
ስለ፡አርዳኢሁ፡መንገ
ለ፡ባሕር፡ወተለውዎ፡
ብዙኃን፡ጥቀ።
እምገሊላ፡ወእእምይ

185

Page 8 Facsimile

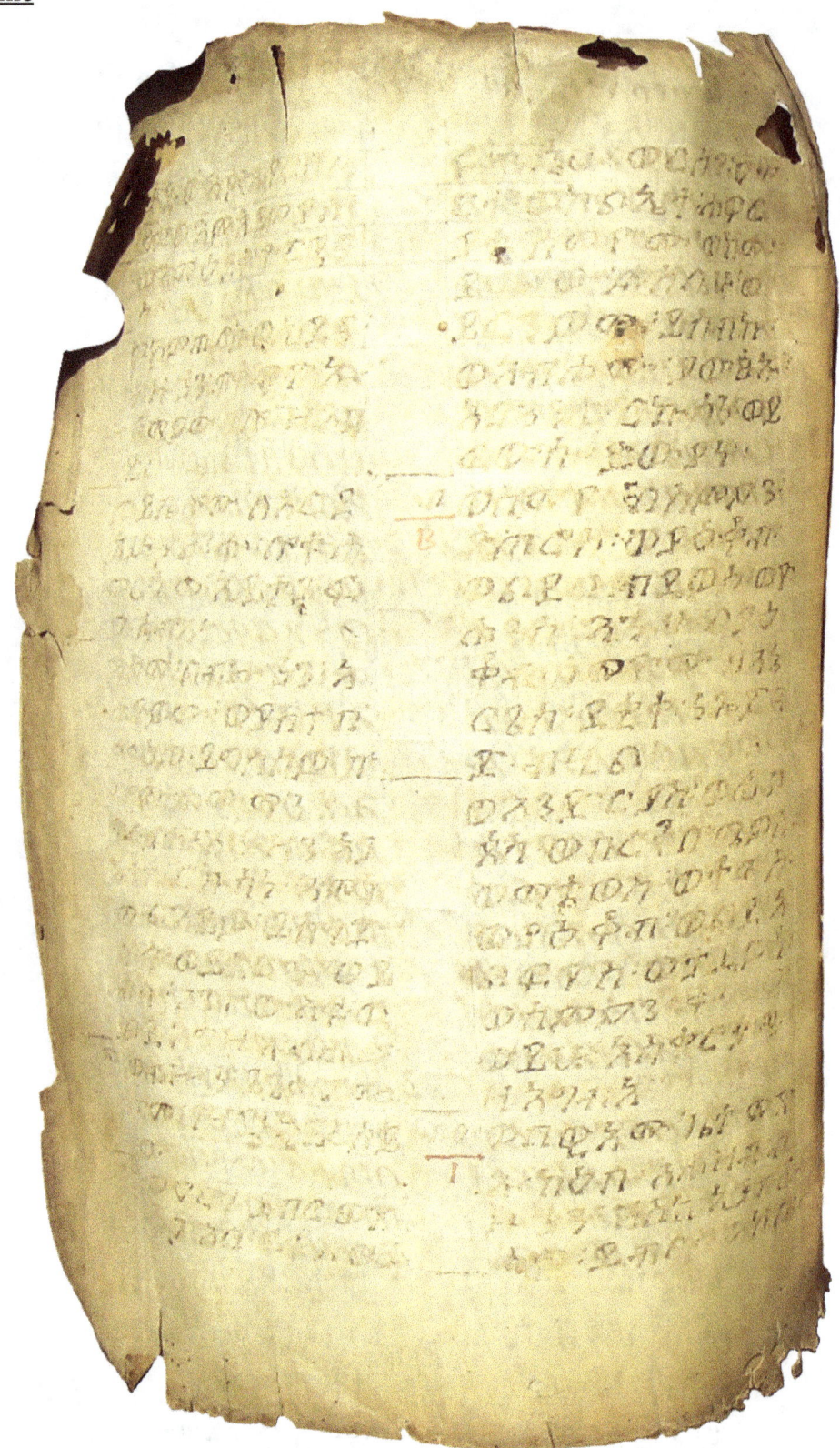

Page 8 Layout

ሁዳ፡ወእምኢየሩሳሌም፡ወእምኢዶምያስ፡ወእመዕዶተ፡ዮርዳኖስ፨ ወእምጢሮስ፡ወሲዶና፡ወብዙኃን፡ጥቀ፡መጽኡ፡ሰሚዖሙ፡ኩሎ፡ዘገብረ፨ ወይቤሎሙ፡ለአርዳኢሁ፡ያፅንሑ፡ሎቱ፡ሐመረ፡ከመ፡ኢይትጋፍዖ፡ሰብእ፨ እስመ፡ለብዙኃን፡አሕየዎሙ፡ወያስተበቍዕዎ፡ይግስስዎ፡ኩሎሙ፡ሕሙማን፨ ወእለሂ፡እኑዛነ፡አጋንንት፡ርኩሳን፡እምከመ፡ርእይዎ፡ይሰግዱ፡ሎቱ፡ወይጸርኁ፡ወይብሉ፡አንተ፡ውእቱ፡ወልደ፡እግዚአ፡ብሔር፨ ወብዙኅ፡ይጌሥጾሙ፡ከመ፡ገሀደ፡ኢይሬስይዎ፨ ወዐርገ፡ደብረ፡ወጸውዐ፡እለ፡ፈቀደ፡ወሐ

ሩ፡ኃቤሁ፡ወረሰየ፡ዐሠርተ፡ወክልኤተ፡ሐዋርያተ፡ሰመዮሙ፡ወከሙ፡የሀልዉ፡ምስሌሁ፡ወይፈንዎሙ፡ይስብኩ፡ወአብሐሙ፡ያውፅኡ፡አጋንንተ፡ርኩሳነ፡ወይፈውሱ፡ድውያነ፨ ወሰመዮ፡ለስምዖን፡ጴጥሮስ፡ወያዕቆብ፡ወልደ፡ዘብዴዎስ፡ወዮሐንስ፡እኁሁ፡ለያዕቆብ፡ወሰመዮሙ፡ባአኔርጌስ፡ደቂቀ፡ነጐድጓድ፡ብሂል፨ ወእንድርያስ፡ወፊልጶስ፡ወበርቶሎሜዎስ፡ወማቴዎስ፡ወቶማስ፡ወያዕቆብ፡ወልደ፡እልፍዮስ፡ወታዴዎስ፡ወስምዖን፡ቀነናዊ፡ወይሁዳ፡አስቆሮታዊ፡ዘአግብአ፨ ወበዊአሙ፡ቤተ፡መጽኡ፡ካዕበ፡አሕዛብ፡ብዙኃን፡እስከ፡ኢያበውሕዎም፡ይብላዕ፡እክለ፡

Page 9 Facsimile

Appendix F—Manuscript Images with Text

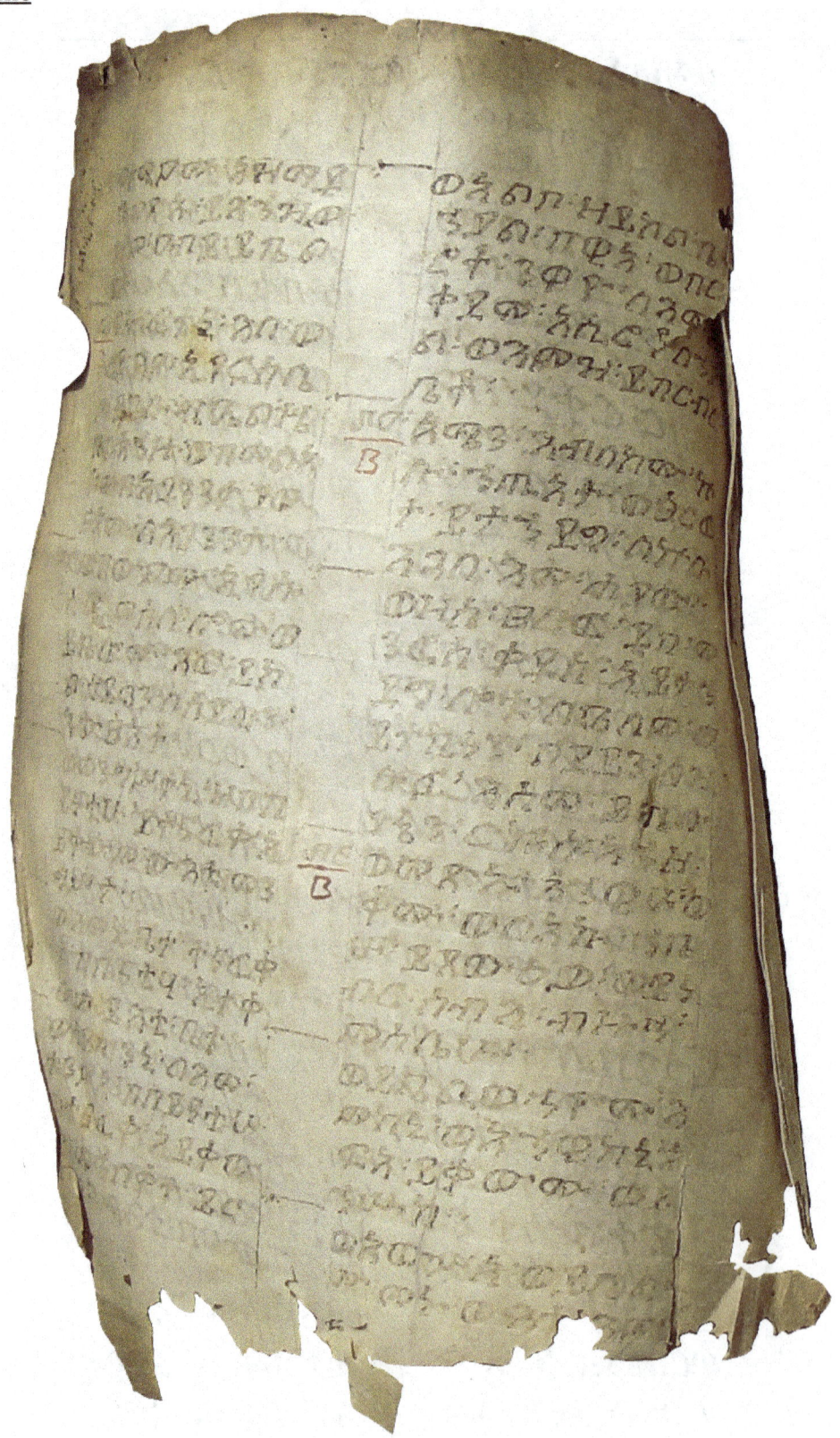

Page 9 Layout

ወሰሚያሙ፡አዝማዲሁ፡መጽኡ፡ይአነዝዎ፡እስመ፡ዐብደ፡ይቤልዎ፡፡
ወጸሐፍትኒ፡እለ፡ወረዱ፡እምኢየሩሳሌም፡ይቤሉ፡ብዔል፡ዜቡል፡አንዞ፡ወበመልአኮሙ፡ለአጋንንት፡ያወፅአሙ፡ለአጋንንት፡፡
ወጸውዖሙ፡ኢየሱስ፡ወመሰሎሙ፡ወይቤሎሙ፡እፎ፡ይክል፡ሰይጣን፡ለሰይጣን፡አውፅአቶ፡፡
ወመንግሥትኒ፡ዘበይናቲሁ፡ይትናፈቅ፡ኢይቀውም፡ውእቱ፡መንግሥት፡፡
ወእመኒ፡ቤት፡ተናፈቀት፡በበይናቲሃ፡ኢትቀውም፡ይእቲ፡ቤት፡፡
ወሰይጣንኒ፡ለእመ፡ተንሥአ፡በበይናቲሁ፡ወተናፈቀ፡ኢይቀውም፡ማኅለቅተ፡ይረክብ፡

ወአልቦ፡ዘይክል፡ቤተ፡ኃያል፡በዊአ፡ወበርሮተ፡ንዋዮ፡ለእመ፡ኢቀደም፡አሲሮቶ፡ለኃያል፡ወእምዝ፡ይበረብር፡ቤቶ፡፡
አሜን፡እብለክሙ፡ኮሉ፡ኃጢአት፡ወፅርፈት፡ይትኀደግ፡ለኮሉ፡እጓለ፡እመ፡ሕያው፡፡
ወዘሰ፡ፀረፈ፡ዲበ፡መንፈስ፡ቅዱስ፡ኢይትኀደግ፡ሎቱ፡ለዓለም፡ወይትኴነን፡በደይን፡ለዘሉፉ፡እስመ፡ይቤሉ፡ጋኔን፡ርኩስ፡አንዞ፡ወመጽኡ፡አኀዊሁ፡ወቆሙ፡ወለአኩ፡ኀቤሁ፡ይጸውዕዎ፡ወይነብር፡ሰብእ፡ብዙኅ፡ምስሌሁ፡፡
ወይቤልዎ፡ነዮሙ፡እምከኒ፡ወአኀዊከኒ፡አፍአ፡ይቀውሙ፡ወየኀሥኩ፡፡
ወአውሥአ፡ወይቤሎሙ፡መኑ፡ውእቱ፡እምየ፡

Page 10 Facsimile

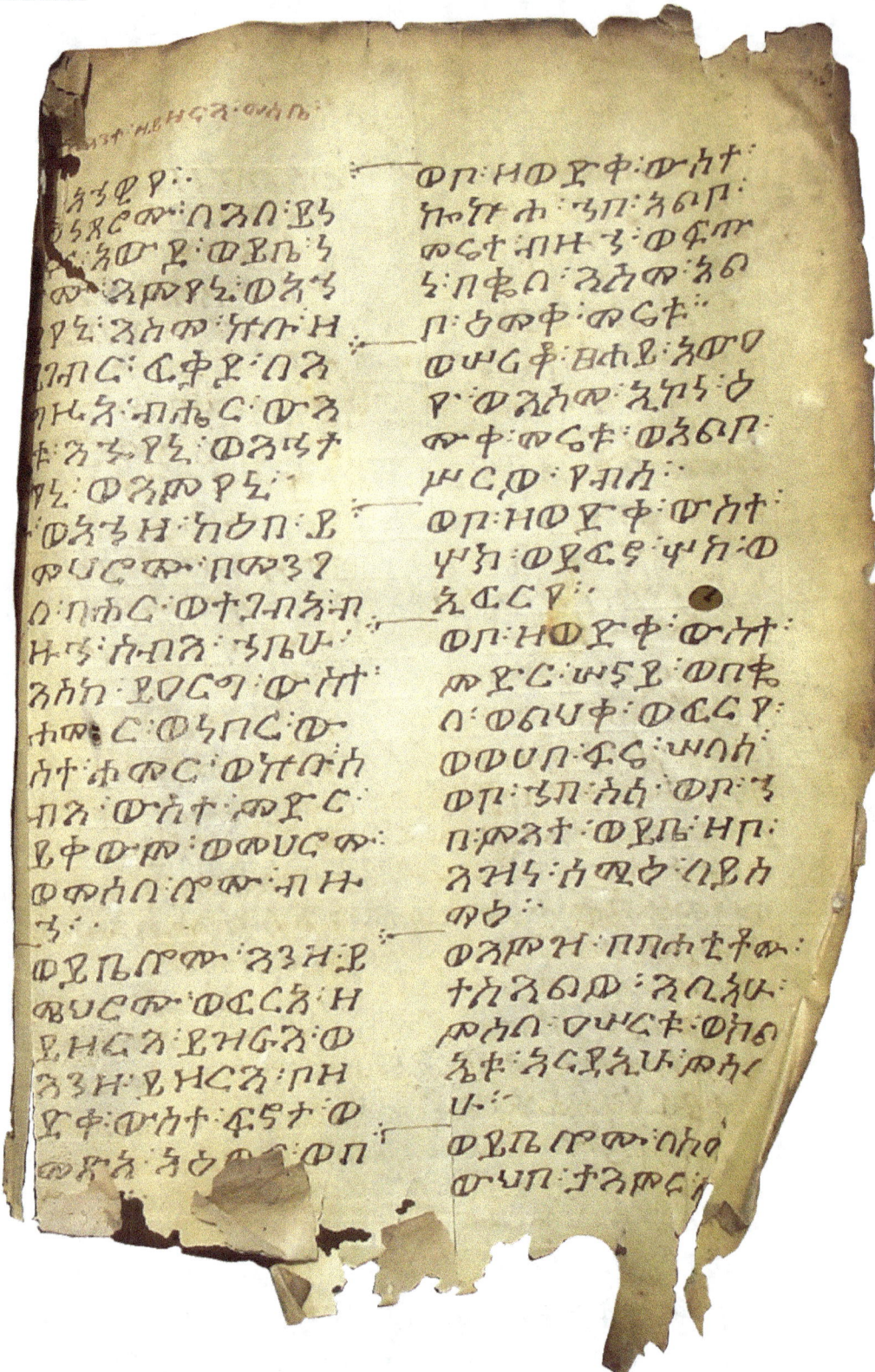

Page 10 Layout

ወአጎዊየ።
ወነጻሮሙ፡ለእለ፡ይነ
ብሩ፡አውዶ፡ወይቤ፡ነ
ዮሙ፡እምየኒ፡ወአጎ
ዊየኒ፡እስሙ፡ኵሉ፡ዘ
ይገብር፡ፈቃዶ፡ለእ
ግዚእ፡ብሔር፡ውእ
ቱ፡እጉየኒ፡ወእጎት
የኒ፡ወእምየኒ።
ወእጎዘ፡ካዕበ፡ይ
መህሮሙ፡በመንገ
ለ፡ባሕር፡ወተጋብአ፡ብ
ዙን፡ሰብእ፡ጎቤሁ፡
እስከ፡ይዐርግ፡ውስተ
ሐመር፡ወነበረ፡ው
ስተ፡ሐመር፡ወኵሉ፡ሰ
ብእ፡ውስተ፡ምድር፡
ይቀውም፡ወመህሮሙ።
ወመሰለ፡ሎሙ፡ብዙ
ጎ።
ወይቤሎሙ፡እንዘ፡ይ
ሜህሮሙ፡ወፈረአ፡ዘ
ይዘርእ፡ይዝራእ፡ወ
እንዘ፡ይዘርእ፡ቦዘ
ወድቀ፡ውስተ፡ፍኖት፡ወ
መጽአ፡አዕዋፍ፡ወበ
ልዕዎ፡

ወቦ፡ዘወድቀ፡ውስተ፡
ኵኵሕ፡ጎበ፡አልቦ፡
መሬት፡ብዙጎ፡ወፍጡ
ነ፡በቀለ፡እስሙ፡አል
ቦ፡ዕመቅ፡መሬቱ።
ወሠረቆ፡ፀሐይ፡አውዐ
ዮ፡ወእስሙ፡ኢኮነ፡ዕ
ሙቀ፡መሬቱ፡ወአልቦ፡
ሥርዎ፡የብሰ።
ወቦ፡ዘወድቀ፡ውስተ፡
ሦክ፡ወደፈኖ፡ሦክ፡ወ
ኢፈርየ።
ወቦ፡ዘወድቀ፡ውስተ፡
ምድር፡ሠናይ፡ወበቀ
ለ፡ወልህቀ፡ወፈርየ፡
ወወሀበ፡ፍሬ፡ሠላሳ፡
ወቦ፡ጎበ፡ስሳ፡ወቦ፡ጎ
በ፡ምእት፡ወይቤ፡ዘቦ፡
እዝን፡ሰሚዐ፡ለይስ
ማዕ።
ወእምዝ፡በባሕቲቶሙ፡
ተስእልዎ፡እሊአሁ፡
ምስለ፡ዐሥርቱ፡ወክል
ኤቱ፡አርዳኢሁ፡ምሳሌ
ሁ።
ይቤሎሙ፡ለክሙ፡ተ
ውህበ፡ታእምሩ፡ምስ

2. The Gospel of Luke (Abba Garima III)
Page 1 Facsimile

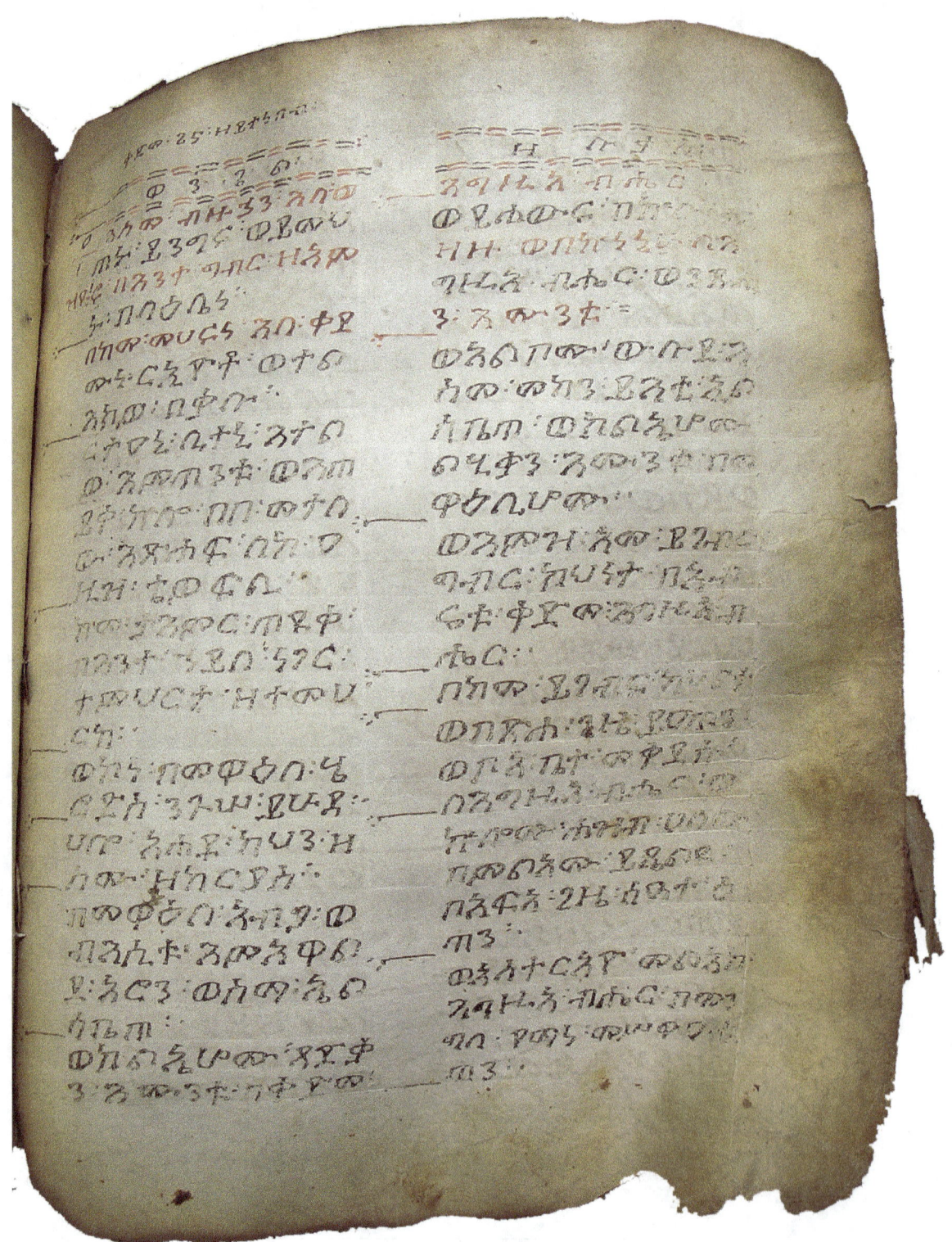

Page 1 Layout

ወ፡ን፡ጌ፡ል፡	ዘ፡ሉ፡ቃ፡ስ፡
እስመ፡ብዙኃን፡እለ፡ወጠኑ፡ይንግሩ፡ወይመህሩ፡በእንተ፡ግብር፡ዘአምኑ፡በላዕሴነ። በከመ፡መሀሩነ፡እለ፡ቀደሙ፡ርኢዮቶ፡ወተልእክዎ፡ቢቃሉ። ረትዐኒ፡ሊተኒ፡እትልዎ፡እምጥንቱ፡ወእጠይቅ፡ኩሎ፡በበ፡መተሉው፡እጽሐፍ፡ለከ፡ዐዚዝ፡ቴዎፍሊ። ከመ፡ታእምር፡ጥየቀ፡በእንተ፡ኂለ፡ነገር፡ትምህርተ፡ዘተመህርከ። ወኮነ፡በመዋዕለ፡ሄሮድስ፡ንጉሠ፡ይሁደ። ሀሎ፡አሐዱ፡ካህን፡ዘስሙ፡ዘከርያስ። በመዋዕለ፡አብያ፡ወብእሲቱ፡እምአዋለደ፡አሮን፡ወስማ፡ኤልሳቤጥ። ወክልኤሆሙ፡ጻድቃን፡እሙንቱ፡በቅድመ፡	እግዚአ፡ብሔር፡ወይሐውሩ፡በኩሉ፡ትእዛዙ፡ወኮነኑ፡ለእግዚአ፡ብሔር፡ወንጹሐን፡እሙንቱ። ወአልበሙ፡ውሉደ፡እስመ፡መካን፡ይእቲ፡ኤልሳቤጥ፡ወክልኤሆሙ፡ልሂቃን፡እሙንቱ፡በመዋዕሊሆሙ። ወእምዝ፡አመ፡ይገብር፡ግብረ፡ክህነት፡በአብሬቱ፡ቅድመ፡እግዚአ፡ብሔር። በከመ፡ይገብሩ፡ካህናት፡ወበጽሐ፡ጊዜ፡ይዕጥን። ወቦአ፡ቤተ፡መቅደሱ፡ለእግዚአ፡ብሔር፡ወኩሎሙ፡ሕዝብ፡ሀለው፡በምልአሙ፡ይጼልዮ፡በአፍአ፡ጊዜ፡ሰዓተ፡ዕጣን። ወአስተርአዮ፡መልአከ፡እግዚአ፡ብሔር፡በመንግለ፡የማነ፡መሥዋዕ፡ዕጣን።

193

3. 1513 Psalter (KCL)
Psalm 1 Facsimile

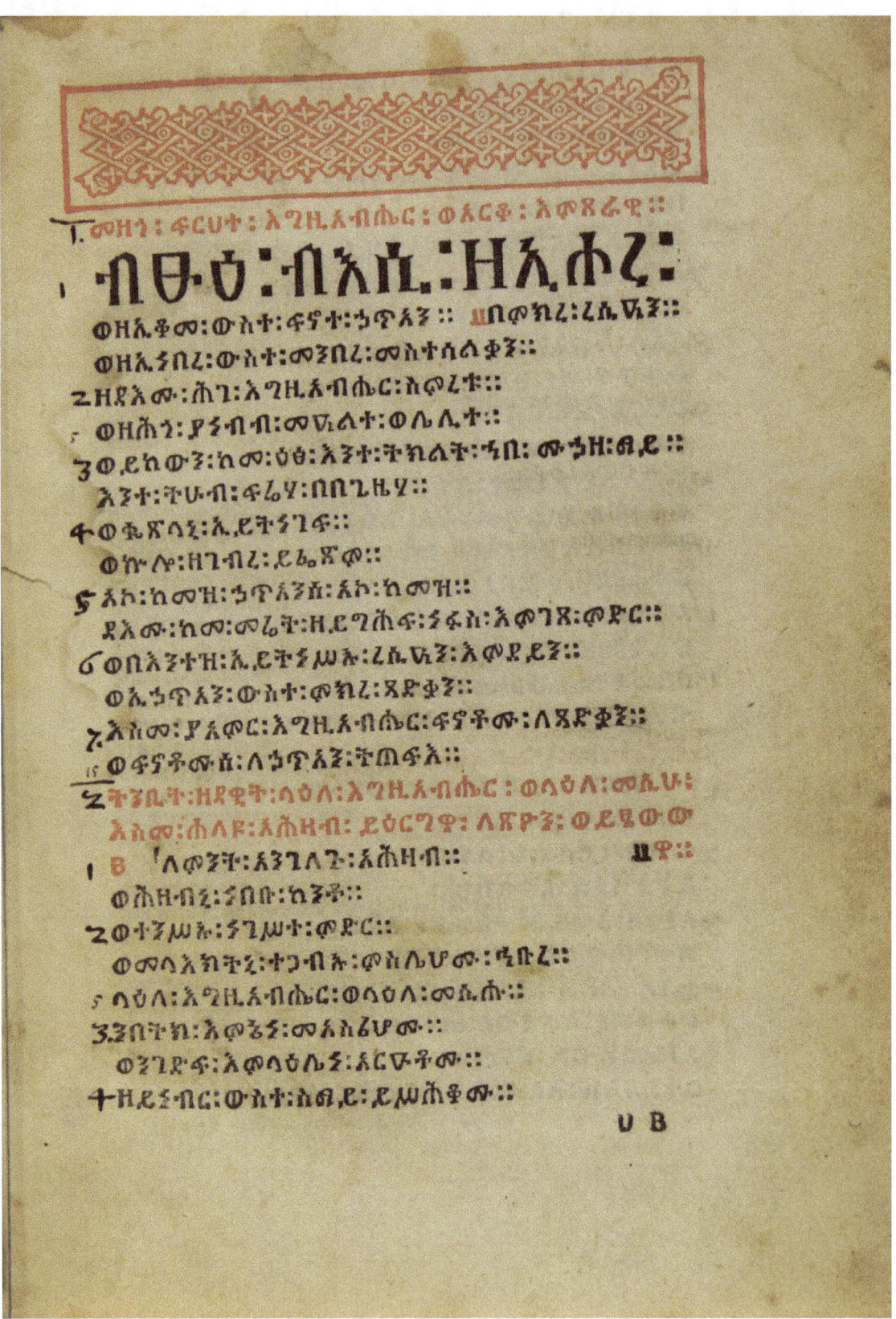

Psalm 23 (22) Facsimile

፳፪ መዝሙር፡ ዘዳዊት፡፡

1. ፳፪ እግዚአብሔር፡ ይሬእየኒ፡ ወአልቦ፡ ዘየኃጥአኒ፡፡
   ወስተ፡ ብሔር፡ ሠዓር፡ ህየ፡ የኃድረኒ፡፡
2. ወኅበ፡ ጻየ፡ ዕረፍት፡ ሐፀነኒ፡፡
3. ወዜጠ፡ ለነፍስየ፡ ወመርሐኒ፡ ፍናተ፡ ጽድቅ፡
   በእንተ፡ ስመ፡ ዚአሁ፡፡
4. እመኒ፡ ሐርኩ፡ ጻእከለ፡ ጽላሎተ፡ ሞት፡፡
   ኢይፈርህ፡ ለእኩይ፡ እስመ፡ አንተ፡ ወስሌየ፡፡
5. በትርከ፡ ወከስታውከ፡ እሙንቱ፡ ነወጻኒ፡፡
6. ወሠሩዕከ፡ ጸደ፡ በቅድምየ፡፡
   በአንጻሬሆሙ፡ ለአለ፡ ይሣቅየኒ፡፡
7. ወአጽሐድከ፡ በቅብእ፡ ርእስየ፡፡
   ጽዋዕከኒ፡ ጽኁዕ፡ ወያረዊ፡፡
8. ከመ፡ ታንበረኒ፡ ቤት፡ ለእግዚአብሔር፡ ለነዋኅ፡ መዋዕል፡፡

4. Gunda Gunde Jubilees (GG-101)
Page 1 Facsimile

Page 2 Facsimile

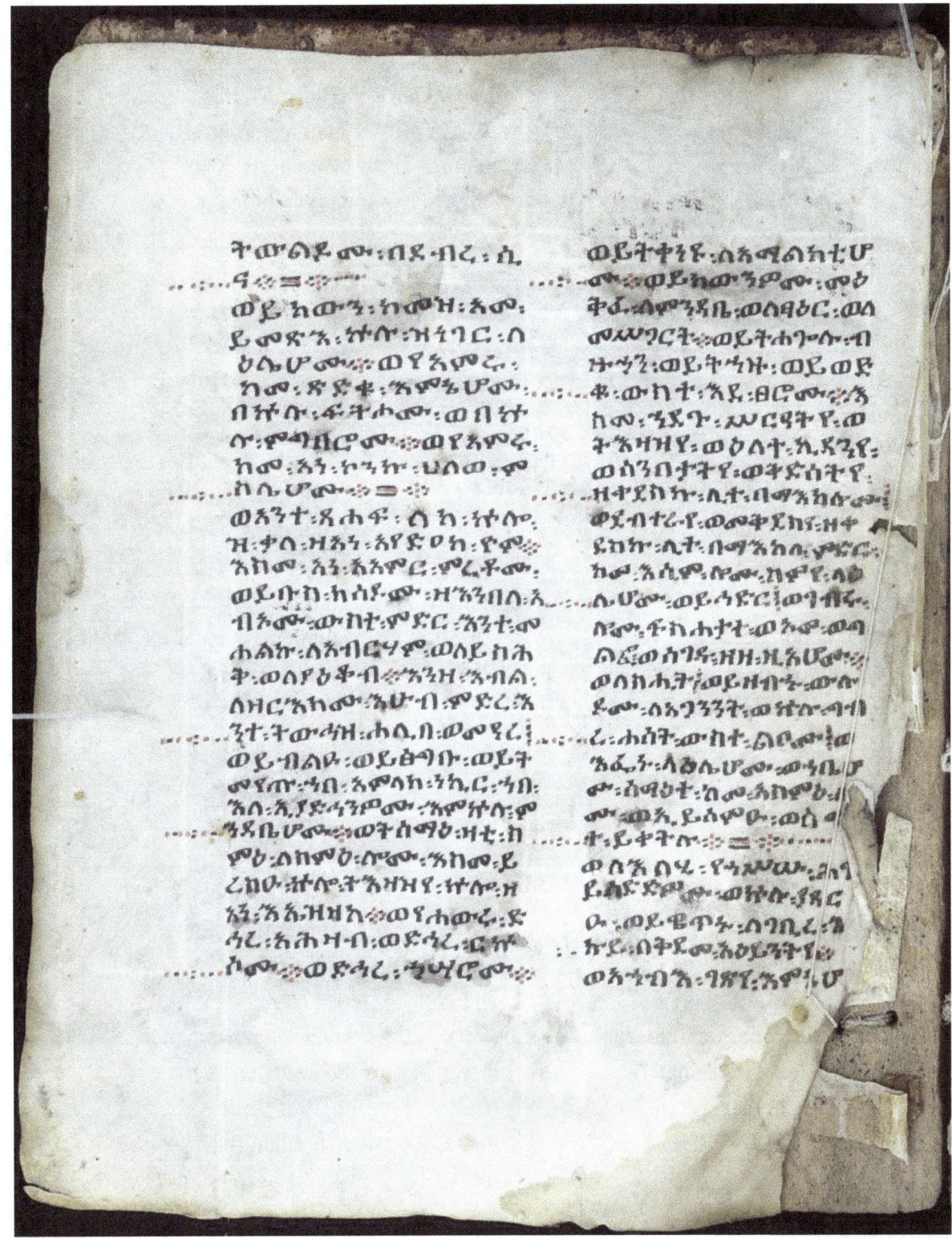

APPENDIX G
VOCABULARY LISTS BY CHAPTER

Vocabulary 2

በ	in	እግዚአ፡ብሔር	God	
ድኅረ	behind, after	ብእሲ	man, person (PL ሰብእ)	
ኀበ	to, by, near	ብእሲት	woman (PL አንስት)	
ከመ	like, that	ኀጢአት	sin (PL ኀጣውእ)	
ለ	to	ልብስ	clothes, garment (PL አልባስ)	
ቅድመ	before	ማይ	water (PL ማያት)	
ውስተ	in, into	መንፈስ	spirit (PL መንፈሳት)	
		ወልድ	son (PL ውሉድ)	
		ወንጌል	gospel	

Vocabulary 3

እም	from, (more) than	ፍኖት	path, road (PL ፍናው)	
አመ	at the time of	ገዳም	wilderness (PL ገዳማት)	
እንበለ	without, except	ገመል	camel (PL አግማል)	
እንተ	through, via, to	ክርስቶስ	Christ	
በእንተ	about, because	መልአክ	angel, messenger (PL መላእክት)	
ዲበ	upon, over, against	ነቢይ	prophet (PL ነቢያት)	
ላዕለ	on, above, against	ሲሳይ	food	
ምስለ	with	ቃል	voice, sound (PL ቃላት)	
ወ-	and			

Vocabulary 4

እንዘ	while, as	አብ	father (PL አበው)	
እስመ	because, that	እኁ	brother (PL አኀው)	
ህየ	there	አሚር	day, time	
መንገለ	to, toward	ዕለት	day (PL ዕለታት)	
-ኒ	also, too; even, indeed	ፈለግ	river (PL አፍላግ)	
ሶበ	if, then, immediately	ሐመር	boat (PL አሕማር)	
ዘ-	which, that	ሌሊት	night (PL ለያልይ)	
		መሠግር	fisherman (PL መሠግራን)	
		ሰማይ	sky, heaven (PL ሰማያት)	

Vocabulary 5

አኀዘ	he took, seized (G)	ተለወ	he followed (G)	
በጽሐ	he arrived (G)	ወረደ	he went down (G)	
ኀደገ	he left; he forgave (G)	አርዌ	animal, wild beast (PL አራዊት)	
		ባሕር	sea (PL ባሕራት)	

መጽአ[1]	he came, it occurred (G)	ጊዜ	time, season, hour (PL ጊዜያት)
ነበረ	he sat, dwelt (G)	ሐቅል	plain, wilderness (PL አሕቃል)
ሰበከ	he preached (G)	መንግሥት	kingdom (PL መንግሥታት)
ቀርበ	he approached, was near (G)	ርግብ	dove (PL አርጋብ)
ርእየ[2]	he saw (G)		
ረከበ	he found (G)		
ሠመረ	he delighted in, approved of (G)		

Vocabulary 6

ቦአ [ብ-ው-እ][3]	he came, entered (G)	ብሔር	region, district (PL ብሔውርት)
ሐረ [ሐ-ው-ር]	he went (G)	ጋኔን	demon (PL አጋንንት)
ወፅአ	he left, exited (G)	መህርት	teaching
ይቤ [ብ-ህ-ል]	he said	መኰንን	judge (PL መኳንንት)
		ምኵራብ	synagogue, temple (PL ምኵራባት)
በበይናቲ	between	ነገር	speech, thing (PL ነገራት)
መኑ	who	ሰንበት	sabbath (PL ሰናብት)
ምንት	what, why	ጸሐፊ	scribe (PL ጸሐፍት)
		ትእዛዝ	commandment, law (PL ትእዛዛት)

Vocabulary 7

አዘዘ	he ordered, commanded (D)	አኮ	no, not
ገሠጸ	he rebuked, chastised (D)	-ሂ	also, too; even, indeed
ሀለወ[4]	he existed, was (D)	ኵል	all, every, each
መህረ	he taught (D)	-ኑ	[interrogative marker]
		-ስ	but, however; indeed

Vocabulary 8

ፈፀነ	he had a fever (G)	እድ	hand (PL እደው)
ፈወሰ	he cured, he healed (D)	አንቀጽ	door, gate (PL አናቅጽ)
ነገረ	he said, told (G)	ቤት	house (PL አብያት)
		ፀሐይ	sun (PL ፀሐያት)
ኢ-	not	ፈፀንት	fever
ጥቀ	very, extremely	ሀገር	city (PL አህጉር)
		ሐማት	mother-in-law (PL ሐማታት)
ብዙኅ	many, much (F ብዝኅት, MP ብዙኃን, FP ብዙኃት)	ጽባሕ	morning (PL ጽባሓት)

---

[1] On verbs whose third root consonant is a guttural, see the Appendix, §C.3.

[2] On verbs whose third root consonant is ው or ይ, see the Appendix, §C.6.

[3] On verbs whose second root consonant is ው or ይ, see the Appendix, §C.5. On verbs that end in a guttural, see Appendix §C.3.

[4] On verbs whose third root consonant is ው or ይ, see the Appendix, §C.6. Note that the third singular forms of ሀ-ል-ው often exhibit the contraction of the final syllable, e.g., ሀሎ.

Vocabulary 9 N/A

Vocabulary 10

ፈነወ[5]	he sent (D)	እግዚእ	lord, master (PL አጋእዝት)
ፈቀደ	he desired, wanted (G)	ገብር	servant, slave (PL አግብርት)
ገሰሰ	he touched (G)	ካህን	priest (PL ካህናት)
ሐይወ	he lived, recovered (G)	ለምጽ	leprosy
ክህለ	he was able (G)	መባእ	offering (PL መባአት)
ኮነ [ከ-ው-ን][6]	he/it was, became (G)	ርእስ	head; self (PL አርእስት)
ምሕረ	he had mercy on, pity for (G)		
መልአ[7,8]	he set out, hurried (D)	አላ	but, except
ስእነ	he was unable (G)	እመ	if
ሰፍሐ	he extended, expanded (G)	እንበይነ	because
		እስከ	up to, until
		ኩልሄ	everywhere, wherever

Vocabulary 11

አጥመቀ	he baptized (CG)	አዲም	skin, leather
ደለወ[9]	he was suitable, fitting (G)	ዐዋዲ	messenger (PL ዐዋድያት)
ፈትሐ[10]	he opened, loosed (G)	ገጽ	face (PL ገጻት)
ነስሐ	he repented (D)	ሐቅ	hip, loin (PL ሐቁያት)
ጼሐ [ጽ-ይ-ሕ][11]	he leveled, paved (G)	ቅናት	belt, girdle (PL ቅናውት)
ጸሐፈ	he wrote (G)	ጸጉር	hair
ጸንዐ	he was strong, firm, powerful (G)	ጥምቀት	baptism (PL ጥምቀታት)
ተአምነ	he believed, confessed (Gt)		
		ቀዳሚ	beginning, first (ADJ)

Vocabulary 12

አፍቀረ	he loved, cherished (CG)	ዐሳብ	hireling
አመከረ	he tempted, tested (CD)	ደቂቅ	children
አምነ[12]	he believed, trusted, confessed (G)	መሥገርት	snare, net (PL መሣግር)
አስተሣነየ [ሥ-ን-ይ][13]	he beautified, restored (CGlt)		
አሠገረ	he fished, cast (nets) (CD)	አርብዓ	forty (NUM)

---

[5] On verbs whose third root consonant is ው or ይ, see the Appendix, §C.6.
[6] On verbs whose second root consonant is ው or ይ, see the Appendix, §C.5.
[7] On verbs whose third root consonant is a guttural, see the Appendix, §C.3.
[8] Note that in most later mss, this verb is from the root ም-ል-ዕ (see Leslau 2006).
[9] On verbs whose third root consonant is ው or ይ, see the Appendix, §C.6.
[10] On verbs whose third root consonant is a guttural, see the Appendix, §C.5.
[11] On verbs whose second root consonant is ው or ይ, see the Appendix, §C.5.
[12] On verbs whose first root consonant is a guttural, see the Appendix, §C.1.
[13] On verbs whose third root consonant is ው or ይ, see the Appendix, §C.6.

አውፅአ[14]	he took out, expelled (CG)	ሕቀ	little (ADV)
ኀለፈ	he passed by (G)	ቅዱስ	holy (ADJ)
ረሰየ	he put, set, made (D)		
ጸውዐ	he summoned, proclaimed (D)	-ሃ	used to mark some proper nouns as complement
ተሠጠ [ሠ-ጥ-ጥ]	he was torn, split (Gt)		
ተልአከ[15]	he was sent; he served (Gt)		

Vocabulary 13

አአመረ[16]	he knew, understood (CG)	ትምህርት	teaching (PL ትምህርታት)
አንከረ	he marvelled, was amazed (CG)		
አስተራገፀ	he made kick, convulse (CGlt)	እኩይ	evil, wicked (ADJ)
አውየወ[17]	he wailed, lamented (Q)	ዐቢይ	big (ADJ)
ደንገፀ	he was terrified, astonished (Q)	ሐዲስ	new (ADJ)
		ናዝራዊ	Nazarite (ADJ)
		ርኩስ	unclean, bad (ADJ)

Vocabulary 14

አብሐ [ብ-ው-ሕ][18]	he permitted, authorized (CG)	ድዉይ	sick, ill (ADJ)
አሌለየ[19]	he rose in dark (CL)	ሕሙም	ill, distressed (ADJ)
አንሥአ	he lifted, received (CG)		
ዐረበ[20]	(sun) set, it became evening (G)		
ዴገነ	he chased (L)		
ኀሠሠ	he sought, demanded (G)		
ጸለየ	he prayed (D)		
ተጋብአ[21]	it was gathered together (Glt)		
ተንሥአ	he rose, got up (Q)		

Vocabulary 15

አንጽሐ[22]	he purified, cleansed (CG)	ስምዕ	report, testimony (PL ስምዓት)
አስተብቍዐ	he implored (CGt)		
አስተብረከ	he knelt (CGt)	አፍአ/አፍአ	outside (ADV)
ነጽሐ	he was pure, clean (G)	ክሡት	revealed, uncovered (ADJ)

---

[14] On verbs whose third root consonant is a guttural, see the Appendix, §C.3.
[15] On verbs whose second root consonant is a guttural, see the Appendix, §C.2.
[16] On verbs whose first root consonant is a guttural, see the Appendix, §C.1.
[17] On verbs whose third root consonant is ው or ይ, see the Appendix, §C.6.
[18] On verbs whose second root consonant is ው or ይ, see the Appendix, §C.5. For third guttural verbs, see Appendix, §C.3.
[19] On verbs whose third root consonant is ው or ይ, see the Appendix, §C.6.
[20] On verbs whose first root consonant is a guttural, see the Appendix, §C.5.
[21] On verbs whose third root consonant is a guttural, see the Appendix, §C.3.
[22] On verbs whose third root consonant is a guttural, see the Appendix, §C.3.

Appendix G—Vocabulary Lists by Chapter

Vocabulary 16

አግመረ	he completed, held (CG)	እም	mother (PL እማት)
ሐለየ	he thought, devised (D)	ልብ	heart, mind (PL አልባብ)
ሰምዐ	he heard, listened (G)	ምድር	earth, ground (PL አምዳር)
ጾረ [ጽ-ው-ር]	he bore, carried (G)	መዓጉዕ	paralytic
ጐንዲዮ	after a time (ADV)	ሕያው	alive (ADJ)
ካዕበ	secondly, again (ADV)	ጽፉቅ	crowded, frequent, abundant (ADJ)

Vocabulary 17

ነበበ	he spoke, told (G)	እጓል	progeny, human (PL እጓላት)
ነሠተ	he destroyed, overturned (G)	እጓለ፡እመ፡ሕያው፡	human, mankind
ሰከበ	he lay down (G)	ዐራት	bed (PL ዐራታት)
ቀለለ	it was light, easy (G)	ፅርፈት	blasphemy (PL ፅርፈታት)
		ሀይማኖት	faith
አሐዱ	one (ADJ)	ኆኅት	door (PL ኆኃት)
አርባዕቱ	four (ADJ)	ጠፈር	roof, ceiling

Vocabulary 18

አአኰተ[23]	he praised (CG)	ምጽባሕ	tax office
በልዐ[24]	he ate (G)	መጸብሕ	tax collector (PL መጸብሓን)
መሰሐ	he dined, supped (G)	ረድእ	disciple (PL አርዳእ)
ረፈቀ	he reclined at meal (G)		
ሰትየ[25]	he drank (G)	ኃጥእ	sinner (ADJ)
ግሙራ	always, completely (ADV)		

Vocabulary 19

አዕበየ[26]	he increased (CG)	ዐቃቢ	guard, official (PL ዐቃብያን);
አንቅዐ[27]	he split, burst (CG)	ዐቃቤ፡ሥራይ	doctor, physician
ጸመ [ጽ-ው-ም][28]	he fasted (G)	ደርግሐ	patch, rag
ተሐጒለ[29] (Gt)	he perished, was destroyed	ግምድ	cut piece, slice (PL ግምዳት)
ተክዕወ[30]	it was poured out (Gt)	መዐልት	day, daytime, noontime (PL መዋዕል)
		መርዓዊ	groom, son-in-law (PL መርዓዊያን)

---

[23] On verbs whose first root consonant is a guttural, see the Appendix, §C.1.
[24] On verbs whose third root consonant is a guttural, see the Appendix, §C.3.
[25] On verbs whose third root consonant is ው or ይ, see the Appendix, §C.6.
[26] On verbs whose third root consonant is ው or ይ, see the Appendix, §C.6.
[27] On verbs whose third root consonant is a guttural, see the Appendix, §C.3.
[28] On verbs whose second root consonant is ው or ይ, see the Appendix, §C.5.
[29] On verbs whose first root consonant is a guttural, see the Appendix, §C.1.
[30] On verbs whose second root consonant is a guttural, see the Appendix, §C.2.

ጠቀበ	he sewed (G)	ሥራይ	medicine (PL ሥራያት)
ወደየ	he put, placed, set (G)	ሥጠት	tearing, fragment
		ጥቅበት	sewing, stitch
እፎ	why?	ወይን	vine, wine (PL አውያን)
አልቦ	there is not	ዝቅ	wineskin (PL ዝቃት)
አምጣነ	as long as		
ባሕቱ	but, however	ብሉይ	old, worn out (ADJ)
		ፈሪሳዊ	Pharisee (ADJ)
		ጻድቅ	righteous (ADJ)
		ጥዑይ	healthy (ADJ)

Vocabulary 20

አርመመ	he kept silent, was at rest (CG)	ገራህት	field, arable land (PL ገራውህ)
ገብረ	he did, worked (G)		
ርኅበ[31]	he was hungry (G)	ኅብስት	bread (PL ኅባውዝ)
ተዐቀበ[32]	he was watched; he was watchful (Gt)	ሊቅ	elder, chief (PL ሊቃን)
ተፈጥረ	it was created, produced (Gt)	መሥዋዕት	sacrifice (PL መሥዋዕታት)
ወፈረ[33]	he went out to the countryside (G)	ሠዊት	ear(s) of grain
ወሀበ	he gave (G)[34]		
የብሰ	it withered, dried up (G)	ፃውስ	crippled, lame (ADJ)
እለ	which, that (PLURAL)	ማእከለ	between; in the middle

Vocabulary 21

አንበበ	he read, recited (CG)	መሐወ	he uprooted, plucked out (G)
አስተዋደየ[35]	he accused, slandered (CGlt)	ቆመ [ቅ-ው-ም][36]	he arose, stood (G)

Vocabulary 22

አፅንሐ[37]	he prepared, kept ready (CG)	ዑረት	blindness
አሕየወ	he restored to life, healed, cured (CG)	ማዕዶት	opposite side (PL ማዕዶታት)
ገሀደ	be revealed, become visible (G)	ነፍስ	soul (PL ነፍሳት)
ነጸረ	he looked at (G)		
ሰፍሐ	he stretched forth, widened (G)	እኁዝ	seized, possessed (ADJ)
ሰገደ	he bowed down, prostrated himself (G)	ሠናይ	beautiful, proper, good (ADJ)
ቀተለ	he killed (G)		

---

[31] On verbs whose second root consonant is a guttural, see the Appendix, §C.2.

[32] On verbs whose first root consonant is a guttural, see the Appendix, §C.1.

[33] On verbs whose first root consonant is ው or ይ, see the Appendix, §C.4.

[34] On the irregular Imperfect of ወሀበ, see Appendix, §C.4.

[35] On verbs whose third root consonant is ው or ይ, see the Appendix, §C.6.

[36] On verbs whose second root consonant is ው or ይ, see the Appendix, §C.5.

[37] On verbs whose third root consonant is a guttural, see the Appendix, §C.3.

Appendix G—Vocabulary Lists by Chapter

ጸርኀ	he cried out, shouted (G)	አው·	or
ተጋፍዐ	oppressed one another, pressed upon (Glt)	ሚመ	or
ተግሕሠ[38]	he withdrew, retreated, avoided (Gt)		
ተከዘ	he was sad, distressed (D)		
ተምዕዐ	he was angry, indignant (Gt)		
ተማከረ	he counseled together, conspired (Glt)		

Vocabulary 23

አግብአ[39]	he took back; betrayed (CG)	እክል	food
ዐርገ[40]	he ascended, went up (G)	ደብር	mountain (PL አድባር)
ሰመየ[41]	he named, called (G)	ሐዋርያ	apostle (PL ሐዋርያት)
		ዘመድ	kin, family (PL አዝማድ)
ብሂለ	that is to say		
		አስቆሮታዊ	Iscariot (ADJ)
		ዐብድ	foolish, insane (ADJ)
		ዐሠርቱ	ten
		ክልኤቱ	two
		ቀናናዊ	Canaanite (ADJ)

Vocabulary 24

አሰረ[42]	he bound, imprisoned (G)	እኅት	sister (PL አኅات)
አውሥአ[43]	he answered, responded (CG)	ዓለም	world, eternity (PL ዓለማት)
በርበረ	he plundered (Q)	ደይን	judgment
ፀረፈ	he blasphemed (G)	ፈቃድ	desire, wish (PL ፈቃዳት)
ለአከ[44]	he sent a message, messenger (G)	ማኅለቅት	cessation, end
መሰለ	he spoke in parables (D)	ንዋይ	vessel, possessions (PL ንዋያት)
ቀደመ	he preceded (G)		
ተኰነነ	he was judged, condemned (Dt)	ኀያል	strong, valiant (ADJ)
ተናፈቀ	he was torn, divided (Glt)		
		አው·ደ	around
አሜን	truly, Amen	ነ-	behold!
ዝሉፉ	continuously, forever (ADV)		

---

[38] On verbs whose second root consonant is a guttural, see the Appendix, §C.2.
[39] On verbs whose third root consonant is a guttural, see the Appendix, §C.3.
[40] On verbs whose first root consonant is a guttural, see the Appendix, §C.1.
[41] On verbs whose third root consonant is ው or ይ, see the Appendix, §C.6.
[42] On verbs whose first root consonant is a guttural, see the Appendix, §C.1.
[43] On verbs whose third root consonant is a guttural, see the Appendix, §C.3.
[44] On verbs whose second root consonant is a guttural, see the Appendix, §C.2.

Appendix G—Vocabulary Lists by Chapter

Vocabulary 25

አፍተነ	he handed over for examination (CG)	አንበጠ	locust, grasshopper (PL አናብጥ)
አስተብረከ	he knelt, fell on his knees (CGt)	ሕዝብ	people, nation; crowd (PL አሕዛብ, ሕዘብ)
አተወ	he went home, departed (for home) (G)	መዐር	honey; honeycomb
ዐረየ	it was level; he was equal to (D)	ሠእን	shoe, sandal (PL አሣእን)
ዴገነ	he pursued, persecuted, tracked (Q/L)	ጸደና	wild bee, bee living underground
ፈጸመ	he completed; accomplished (D)	ቴታን	lace, thong, lace (PL ቶታናት)
ኪያ-	emphatic complement pronoun base	ናሁ	behold!, now!
ለሊ-	-self	ካልእ	(F ካልእት) other, another, second (ADJ)

Vocabulary 26

አስተርአየ (CGt)	it became visible; he made visible	አብሬት	alternation; turn of office
ዐጠነ	he burned incense (G)	ዕጣን	incense (PL ዕጣናት)
ረትዐ	it was straight; he was righteous (G)	መቅደስ	temple, sanctuary
ተመህረ	he was taught; he learned (Dt)	መሥዋዕ	altar (PL ምሥዋዓት)
ጠየቀ	he examined, investigated (D)	ስም	name; fame, reputation (PL አስማት)
ወጠነ	he began (G=D)	ጥንት	beginning
በበ	reduplication = distributive	ወለት	daughter, girl, maidservant (PL አዋልድ)
በምልኡ-	fully, completely, all together	የማን	the right (side or hand)
ጥዩቀ	precisely, accurately, certainly (ADV)	ዐዚዝ	powerful, strong, excellent (ADJ)
		ልሂቅ	old, grown-up, adult (ADJ)
		መካን	sterile, childless, barren (ADJ)
		መትለው	following; successive (ADJ)
		ንጹሕ	pure, clean; innocent (ADJ)

Vocabulary 27

ገሐፈ	he removed; he swept away (G)	ዕፅ	tree, shrub; wood (PL ዕፀው)
ተነግፈ	it was knocked off; it lost leaves (Gt)	ፍሬ	fruit (PL ፍሬያት, ፍርያት)
ጠፍአ	it was extinguished; he perished, was lost (G)	ሕግ	law, statute; custom
		ሙሓዝ	aqueduct, channel; river, brook
ዳእሙ	just, merely, only (ADV); furthermore, moreover; rather, but, on the contrary (CONJ)	ምክር	plan, counsel, advice
		መንበር	throne, seat, chair (PL መናብርት)
		መሬት	dirt, dust
		መስተሳልቅ	mocker, scorner (PL መስተሳልቃን)
		ቄጽል	leaf, foliage (PL አቍጽል)
		ብፁዕ	fortunate, blessed; dedicated (ADJ)
		ረሲዕ	godless, impious, sinful (ADJ)
		ትኩል	planted (ADJ)

Vocabulary 28

አጽሐድ	he caused to be tender; he anointed (CG)	ዕረፍት	rest, peace, quiet, repose
ፈርሀ	he was afraid; he feared, revered (G)	በትር	staff, branch, scepter; tribe (PL አብትር)
ሐፀነ	he nursed, reared, trained (G)	ሕይወት	life, lifetime
ኃደረ	he resided, dwelt, inhabited (G)	ማእድ	table, banquet, meal (PL ማእዳት)
ኀጥአ	he lacked, missed, sinned (G)	ምሕረት	mercy, pity (PL ምሥረታት)
መርሐ	he led, guided (G)	ሞት	death
ሜጠ [ም-ይ-ጥ]⁴⁵	he turned aside; he returned, restored (G)	ቅብእ	(olive) oil, ointment, butter
ሣቀየ	he afflicted, tormented (L)	ቀስታም	bow, shepherd's crook, rod
ሠርዐ	he arranged; he established; he made a covenant (G)	ሥዑር	grassy, covered with vegetation (ADJ)
		ጽድቅ	justice; truth; righteousness (PL ጽድቃት)
		ጽላሎት	shade, shadow(s), darkness
		ጽዋዕ	cup, goblet, chalice (PL ጽዋዓት)
አንጻረ	opposite, toward, in front of (ADV)	ነዋኅ	high (ADJ)
		ጽኑዕ	strong (ADJ)

Vocabulary 29

አንበረ	he set, placed; he settled (CG)	እብን	stone (PL እብን, አእባን)
አስሐተ	he led astray, into sin; he corrupted (CG)	እሳት	fire
ነደደ / ነደ	it burned (G)	ኢዮቤል	trumpet, jubilee (pl ኢዮቤላውሳት)
ጸለለ	it shaded, covered	ዓለም	world; eternity (PL ዓለማት)
አለበወ	he instructed (CD)	ዓም	year (PL ዓመታት)
ተናገረ	he spoke to, with (Glt)	ዐሡር	tenth day (of month); ten days
ተሰብዐ	it was made seven (times) (Gt)	ደመና	cloud(s) (PL ደመናት)
		ፀአት	exit, departure; exodus
መጠነ	during, according to, about, as long as	ግብር	deed, act; work, task (PL ግብራት, ግበር)
		ግብጽ	Egypt
		ኩፋሌ	partition, division, distribution
ሳብዕ	seventh (ADJ)	መጽሐፍ	writing; book, document (PL መጻሕፍት)
ሣልስ	third (ADJ)	ስብሐት	praise, glory, majesty (PL ስብሐታት)
		ሰዱስ	sixth day (of week, month); six days
		ሥርዐት	order; statue; testament (PL ሥርዐታት)
		ጽሌ / ጽላ	tablet (PL ጽላት)
		ወርኅ	moon, month (PL አውራኅ)

---

⁴⁵ On verbs whose second root consonant is ው or ይ, see the Appendix, §C.5.

Vocabulary 30

አስምዐ	he made summon; he summoned as a witness (CG)
ድኅነ	he was saved; he escaped safely (G)
ፀግበ /ጸግበ	he was sated, filled (G)
ኀብአ	he hid, concealed (G)
መሐለ	he swore, took an oath (G)
ቀደሰ	he sanctified, consecrated (D)
ረስዐ	he forgot; he was negligent, impious, godless (G)
ሰደደ	he persecuted; he drove out, banished (G)
ሰገደ	he bowed down; he worshipped (G)
ሤመ [ሥ-ይ-ም][46]	he appointed; he put, placed (G)
አዕረፈ /አጽረዐ	he ceased; he brought to a stop; he neglected (CG)
ተአኀዘ	he was seized, held (Gt)
ትሐጕለ / ተህጕለ	he was lost, destroyed (Gt)
ተመይጠ	he faced about, returned, turned away; he was converted (Gt)
ተቀንየ	he served, ministered (Gt)
ወድቀ	he fell (G)
ዉኅዘ/ዉሕዘ	it flowed (G)
ዘብሐ	he slaughtered, sacrificed (G)
ዚአ-	form of ዘ, relative before pronouns
ዘዘ	reduplication used for distributive
ሰማዒ	hearing, listening to, obedient (ADJ); noun: witness, martyr (PL ሰማዕት)
ነኪር	strange, foreign, different; marvelous (ADJ)
ይቡስ	dry, arid; paralyzed, stiff (ADJ)
ዓም/ኦም	tree(s), dense grove, woods (PL ዓጣት)
አምላክ	the Lord, god; (false) gods (PL አማልክት)
ዐይን	eye (PL አዕይንት)
ደብተራ	tabernacle;, sanctuary (PL ደባትር)
ዓዕር / ጻዕር	pain, torment; grief, sorrow
ፀር	enemy, adversary (PL አፀራር)
ፍሥሐት	narrow passage, ravine; elevated shrine (PL ፍሥሓታት)
ፍትሕ	precept, law; judgment, decision
ግልፎ	carved idol, statue (PL ግልፋት, አግልእት)
ሐሊብ	milk
ሒስት	reviling, blaming
ኀሳር / ኀሣር	dishonor, abominable thing, humiliation (PL ኀሳራት)
ኪዳን	pact, covenant; will, testament (PL ኪዳናት)
ክሳድ	neck (PL ክሰዳት, ክሳውድ)
ማዕቀፍ	obstacle, stumbling block (PL ማዕቀፋት)
መዓር	honey; honeycomb
ምግባር	action, behavior; workmanship (PL ምግባራት)
ምንዳቤ	affliction, torment
ምረት	bitterness, anger, rancor; rebellion
ቅድሳት	holiness, sanctity, sanctuary
ርኵስ	uncleanness; abomination
ስሕት	error, deceit (PL ስሕታት)
ዘርእ	seed; progeny, offspring (pl አዝርእት)

---

[46] On verbs whose second root consonant is ዉ or ይ, see the Appendix, §C.5.

GLOSS LEXICON

Although the student should also be able to look up words within the *Halḥam* order (which some lexica use), the words in this lexicon are arranged according to the order used in Wolf Leslau's *Comparative Dictionary of Ge'ez* (Harrassowitz, 2006):

አ	ዐ	በ	ደ	ጸ	ፈ	ገ	ሀ	ሐ	ኅ	ከ	ለ	መ	ነ	ፐ	ጰ	ቀ	ረ	ሰ	ሠ	ጸ	ተ	ጠ	ወ	የ	ዘ
ʾ	ʿ	b	d	ḍ	f	g	h	ḥ	ḫ	k	l	m	n	p	ṗ	q	r	s	ś	ṣ	t	ṭ	w	y	z

Note that the labiovelars (ጕ g^w, ኁ $ḫ^w$, ኵ k^w, and ቈ q^w) are not distinguished in this order but are included as simple variants within their non-labialized versions.

All words are listed according to their consonantal **root**, if it is obvious, otherwise the word is listed simply by its consonants. For example, both ንጉሥ *naguś* king and መንግሥት *mangəśt* kingdom will both be found under ነግሠ *nagśa* to become king, ruler. Even verbs with a ወ *w* or ይ *y* as the second or middle consonants, which do not exhibit the middle consonant in the 3MS Perfect form, are listed by their root, like so: [ቅ-ወ-ም] ቆመ. However, ቤት house is listed simply as ቤት, even though its likely root is ብይት *b-y-t*.

Verbs are listed first, followed by other items (e.g., nouns, adjectives) from the same root in successive and indented entries. Nouns and verbs are signaled by the specification of gender (M and/or F) and derivational class (e.g., CG). Other word classes are indicated by simple abbreviations: **PRON**(oun), **DEM**(onstrative), **ADJ**(ective), **ADV**(erb), **PREP**(osition), **CONJ**(unction), **REL**(ative), **INTER**(rogative), **INT**(erjection), **COMP**(lement).

For nouns that differ in form when a clitic pronoun is added, this bound form is provided. For most nouns only the most common plural form is given; for some, multiple plurals are listed. Thus,

ትእምርት (PL ትእምርታት, ተአምር, ተአምራት) sign, omen; miracle

Verbs are listed by the 3MS Perfect form, followed by an indication of the verbal root-related derivation (e.g., G). For verbs in G, the Imperfect and Subjunctive forms are also given in parentheses. The valency of verbs is not specified, leaving the English gloss to indicate the semantics; when the English gloss is ambiguous (monovalent versus bivalent), the specification COMP is listed for bivalent verbs. When the complement is a prepositional phrase, the preposition is listed. For verbs that may take different types of complements, both types are specified. Thus,

አምነ G (IMPF የአምን, SUBJ ይአምን) to be true; to believe, to profess, confess (COMP or ለ-); to believe, have faith in (በ-)

Any conjunctions that are *proclitic* (attached to the <u>front</u> of another word) or *enclitic* (attached to the <u>end</u> of another word) are noted as such using a hyphen before or after the item, e.g.,

-ሂ CONJ even, the very, ወ- CONJ and

እ '

-አ suffix denoting direct quotation; added to the first few words of a quotation and to the last, or, more rarely, to every single word of the text

ኢ- NEG not (prefixed directly to element negated), both verbal and nominal, e.g., ኢአሚን un-belief, disbelief.

ኦ VOC PART O!, Oh! Usually prefixed, as in ኦንጉሥ, O king, but with እግዚአ, it is regularly suffixed: እግዚኦ O Lord!

አብ (w/ CLIT PRON: አቡ-, COMP አባ; PL አበው) father (sometimes an honorific title applied to religious leaders); ancestor

    ቤተ፡አብ family

    አባ an honorific title applied to venerated men of any station in religious life

አብደ G (IMPF የአብድ, SUBJ ይአብድ) to be mad, to rage

    አብድ (F አብድ; PL አብዳን, አብዳት) ADJ foolish, stupid, ignorant, imprudent; mad, insane, enraged; NOUN fool

አብሐ see ብ-ው-ሐ

አብን (PL እበን, አእባን) stone

    እብነ፡በረድ hailstone(s)

አብያታር PN Abiathar

እድ (w/ CLIT PRON: እዴ-; PL እደው) hand

አዳም skin, hide, leather (of reddish color), red

ኢዶምያስ PN Idumea

አፍ (w/ CLIT PRON: አፉ-; PL አፈው) mouth

እፎ INTERROG ADV How? In what way? Why? How! How great! What!

አፍአ/ አፍኣ ADV out, outside, on or to the outside, beyond, outside part

    አፍአ፡እም- PREP on or to the outside of

እጓል (PL እጓላት) COLL and SING: the young of any animal or fowl, including humans; እጓለ፡እመሕያው mankind, man

እግር (PL እገር) foot; measure; ray (of sunlight)

እግዚአ፡ብሔር God; see ገዝአ

አሐዱ (COMP አሐደ) M one, a certain (one); አሐቲ (COMP አሐተ) F IDEM አሐተ ADV once, one time; አሑድ the first day of the week or month

እጉ / እጓው (COMP እጓወ or እጉወ; w/ CLIT PRON: እጉ-, COMP እኀor እጓዎ; PL እጓው) brother, blood relation, kinsman, friend

እኅት (PL አኃት) sister

እጓው see እጉ

አኀዘ G (IMPF የአኀዝ, SUBJ ይአኀዝ) to seize, grasp, hold, comprehend, restrain, make prisoner (COMP ለ-, or በ-); to take captive; to possess, control, occupy

    ተአኀዘ GT PASSIVE; also: to be taken as a pledge

    እኁዝ (F እኍዝት) PASS PTCP captive, held; possessed by (e.g., demons); joined, continuous

    አኃዚ owner, possessor; master, lord

አኮ NEG no, not, it is not

አክለ G (IMPF የአክል, SUBJ ይአክል/ይእክል) to be sufficient for, to satisfy (CLIT PRON or ለ-); to be approximately

    GT ተአክለ = CG አእከለto be satisfied, have enough

    እኩል (F እክልት) PASS PTCP sufficient, enough

    ማእከለ middle, centre; PREP (w/ CLIT PRON: ማእከሌ-) among, in the midst of; በማእከለ IDEM; እምማእከለ from among

እክል food, bread, grain, fodder, bait, produce of the field

አአኮተ CG to praise, give glory, glorify, thank, give thanks, be thankful, bless

አከየ G (IMPF የአኪ, SUBJ ይአከይ) to be evil, bad, wicked

    እኩይ (F እኪት) PASS PTCP evil, bad, wicked, noxious, vile

    እከይ (PL እከያት) evil, misfortune, viciousness, vice, wrongdoing, wickedness, iniquity, malice, calamity

አላ CONJ but, rather, on the contrary; except, unless

እለ REL CP which, that; see H

እላ DEM PRON FP these

እሉ DEM PRON MP these

አሌ፡ለ- EXCLAM: Woe unto

አልቦ NEG of ቦ; there is/ are not

አልፍ (PL አእላፋ) myriad, ten thousand

እለንቱ (COMP እለንተ) DEM PRON FP these

እሎንቱ (COMP እሎንተ) DEM PRON MP these

እም-/እምነ PREP (w/ CLIT PRON እምኔ-) from; more than; because of; rather than

    እምዝ ADV then, next, thereupon

    እምከመ CONJ as soon as

    እምዘ CONJ when

አመ (1) PREP at the time of, during; (2) CONJ when; (3) ADV when

    አሜሃ ADV at that time, then, next

    እምአሜሃ from that time onward

እመ / እም / ለእመ CONJ if, suppose that, whether

    እመበ:ከመ perhaps

    እመሂ ... እመሂ either ... or

    እመአኮ ADV otherwise, if that were not so

    ወእምአኮ ADV otherwise, if that were not so

እም (PL እማት) mother

    እመሕያው the mother of the living (Eve)

እምአርማትያስ PN Arimathea

አምኀ D kiss, embrace; greet, salute; worship, revere; offer a gift out of respect

    አምኃ kiss, salute, greetings; gift offered out of respect, present

እምላክ see መለክ

አምነ G (IMPF የአምን, SUBJ ይእመን) to be true; to believe, to profess, confess (COMP or ለ-); to believe, have faith in (በ-)

    ተአምነ / ተአምነ GT PASS; also: to believe in (COMP or በ-); to confess sins (COMP); to be confident, sure

    አአመነ CG to convert (COMP); to profess, assert, confirm as a fact

    አሙን (F እምንት) PASS PTCP faithful, trustworthy, true

    አሙነ ADV truly, in truth

    አሜን ADV truly; Amen

    አማኒ believer; ADJ faithful, true

    እምነት faith, belief, trust

    አሚን (PL አሚኖት) IDEM

    አማን ADJ true, faithful

    አማና ADV truly, surely, rightly, really

    በአማን ADV IDEM

    ማእመን, ምእመን, ማአሜን (F -ት) ADJ faithful, believing; true, trustworthy; NOUN a believer

እማንቱ PRON FP they

እሙንቱ MP they

አመረ D to tell, show, indicate, make (COMP1) known to (COMP2)

    አእመረ CG to know, understand, comprehend, realize, learn, be skilled in, recognize, acknowledge

    አሙር (F እምርት) PASS PTCP known, recognized

    አእምሮ knowledge

    ኢየአምሮ ignorance

    ማእምር ADJ skilled, knowing; NOUN soothsayer

    ትእምርት (PL ትእምርታት, ተአምር, ተአምራት) sign, omen; miracle

አሚር sun; day, time [only in fixed expressions, as below]

    እምውእቱ:አሚር from that day (past or future)

    እስከ:ውእቱ:አሚር until that day (past or future)

    ውእተ:አሚራ on that day

    ኵሎ:አሚረ every day, all day

እመት (PL እመታት) cubit, forearm

አነ PRON I

አንበጣ (PL አናብጥ) locust, grasshopper

እንበለ PREP (w/ CLIT PRON: እንበሌ-) without, except for, excepting, before, unless, regardless of; CONJ same meaning

    ዘእንበለ same

እንብየ INTERJ No, I refuse

እንበይነ / እምበይነ PREP because, on account, for the sake, concerning

አነዳ skin, hide, leather; ሐብለ:አነዳ thong

እንከ, እንከሙ PART so, then, therefore, now then, forthwith, yet, and so

አንቀጽ (PL አናቅጽ) door, vestibule, gate

አንስት (PL of ብእሲት) women, female, wife
    አንስቲያ (COLL) the women, the women folk

አንተ PRON MS you

አንቲ PRON FS you

አንትሙ PRON MP you

አንትን PRON FP you

እንተ (1) REL FS (or poetic for MS); (2) PREP via, by way of, in the direction of, because of

እንዘ CONJ while, when, as, even though, since

አርዑት yoke

ኦሪት the Mosaic Law, the Pentateuch

አርዌ (PL አራዊት) animal, wild beast

እስከ PREP up to, until, as far as, even also; CONJ until; with the result that

እስመ CONJ, (1) because, since, for; (2) that, the fact that (+ NOUN clause); (3) quotation introduction; (4) indeed (asseverative use)

እስክንድርያ PN Alexandria

አስቆሮታዊ ADJ Iscariot

አሰረ G (IMPF የአስር; SUBJ ይእር) to tie up, bind, imprison, fasten, fetter (COMP); to tie something (COMP) to: በ-/ውስተ)
    እሱር (F እስርት) PASS PTCP bound, tied, captive, restricted
    እስረት NOUN binding, tying
    ማእሰር, ማእስር, ማእሰርት (PL መአስር, መአስርት) bond, fetter; vow

እሳት fire

አተወ G (IMPF የአቱ, SUBJ ይእቱ/ ይአተዉ) to go home, come home; to depart (for home)

ኢትዮጵያ Ethiopia

አው CONJ or

እወ ADV surely, indeed, even; yes

እዋዲ see ዐዋዲ

አውደ see ዐውደ

አውየወ Q to wail, wail in mourning
    አውያት NOUN wailing

አይ (PL አያት) INTERR ADJ which?

ኢዮቤል (PL ኢዮቤላውሳት) trumpet, jubilee

ኢየሩሳሌም PN Jerusalem

አይቴ ADV where?; በአይቴ IDEM; እመአይቴ whence? from where?

አዜብ south, sound wind
    ንግሥተ፡አዜብ Queen of Sheba/Saba

እዝን (PL እዘን, አእዛን) ear

አዘዘ D to order, command (COMP) to do (SUBJ); to exercise dominion; to make a will, bequeath
    ተአዘዘ DT PASS; also: to obey (ለ-)
    እዙዝ (F እዝዝት) PASS PTCP commanded, ordered
    እዙዝ፡ውእቱ፡ከመ + SUBJ it has been commanded that [verb]
    በከመ፡አዘዘ፡በገብ as has been commanded by
    ትእዛዝ (PL ትእዛዛት) commandment, decree, command, edict, law, ordinance, order, will, provision

ዐ ʿ

ዐብድ see አብድ

ዐብየ G (IMPF የዐቢ, SUBJ ይዕቢ) to be big, large, great, important, famous, powerful, promoted, prevail
    አዕበየ CG to make (COMP) great, increase; to extol, exalt (COMP)
    ተዐበየ DT to be boastful, arrogant
    ዐቢይ (F ዐባይ; PL ዐበይት) ADJ big, great, large, important, old, notable; በዐቢይ፡ቃል in a loud voice
    ዕቢይ (PL ዕቢያት) greatness, size; magnificence, majesty

ዕድ (PL ዕደው) COLL, men, male, husband; also sometimes used as PL of ብእሲ

ዓዲ ADV still, yet, again, moreover, still more; with CLIT PRON = to still be, as inእንዘ ዓዲነ ዝየ while we are still here

ዕድሜ (PL ዕድሜያት) time, set time, proper time, opportune time, season, period

ዐደወ G (IMPF የዐዱ, SUBJ ይዕዱ, ይዐደዉ) to cross (COMP or COMP of goal or PREP phrase)

ተዐድወ GT to transgress (a law: እም-; against a person: ላዕለ); also = G

ተዐደወ DT IDEM

አዐደወ CG to bring/lead/ take across

ማዕዶት (PL መዓድው, ማዕዶታት) the opposite side, passage, bank (of river, mountain etc.), ford, ferry, boat

ማዕዶተ PREP across, to the opposite side of, beyond

ዕዳ debt, guilt

ዕድው (PL ዕድዋን) enemy, adversary

ዕፅ (PL ዕፀው) tree, shrub, brush; grove, woods; wood (material); a club, staff (of a spear)

ዕፄ (PL ዕፄያት) worm, moth; vermin

ዓለም (PL ዓለማት) world, this world, the secular world; the universe, all creation; eternity; all time past, present, and future.

ለዓለም ADV forever; IDEM እስከ፡ለዓለም፤ ለዓለመ፡ዓለም

ዓለማዊ (F ዓለማዊት) ADJ worldly, of this world

ዕለት see ወዐለ

ዓም, ዓመት (PL ዓመታት) year

ለለዓሙ ADV yearly, every year

ዖም (PL አዕዋም, ዖማት) tree(s), dense grove, woods

ዐመፀ D to do wrong, act unjustly, wickedly; to harm, injure

ዐመቀ G (IMPF ይዐምቅ, SUBJ ይዕመቅ) to be deep; to submerge

ዕሙቅ (F ዕምቅት) PASS PTCP deep, secret

ዐቀበ G (IMPF ይዐቅብ, SUBJ ይዕቀብ) to guard, keep watch on; to take care of, preserve, keep safe, handle with care; to observe, keep (e.g., the law)

ዐቃቢ (PL ዐቀብት) guard, guardian, keeper, watchman, official; often combined: ዐቃቢ፡ሥራይ doctor, physician, magician

ማዕቀፍ / ማዕቀፍ (PL ማዕቀፋት) impediment, obstacle, hindrance, stumbling block, cause of offense

ዐርበ/ዕርበ (IMPF ይዐርብ, SUBJ ይዕረብ/ ይዕርብ) to set, go down (of heavenly bodies); become evening

ዐረብ west; Arabia

ዐረባዊ / ዓረባዊ western

ዐርብ Friday

ምዕራብ the west

አዕረፈ CG to rest, find rest, be at ease, find relief; die

ዕረፍት rest, peace, quiet, repose

ዐርገ G (IMPF ይዐርግ, SUBJ ይዕርግ) to ascend, come/go up, climb

ዑረት blindness; see [ዕ-ው-ር] ዖረ

ዐረየ D to be level, smooth; to be equal to (ለ-, ምስለ, ከመ); to make (COMP) equal, level; to share (COMP) equally

ዐሰበ G (IMPF ይዐስብ, SUBJ ይዕስብ) to hire for wages

ዐስብ wages, hire, pay, reward

ዐሳቢ hireling, day-laborer, mercenary

ዐሰየ G (IMPF ይዐሲ, SUBJ ይዕሲ) to repay

ዕስት payment, reward

ዓሣ (PL ዓሣት) fish

ዐሥሩ (COMP IDEM) M; ዓዐሥርቱ (COMP ዐሥርቱ) F ten

ዓሥር (F ዓሥርት) ADJ tenth

ዐሡር the tenth day (of the month); ten days

ዐሥር/ ዕሥር F ten; ADV ten times

ዕሥራ twenty

ዐጽበ G (IMPF ይዐጽብ, SUBJ ይዕጽብ) to be difficult, hard; to be extraordinary, astonishing

አስተዐጸበ CDT to harass; to consider difficult; to admire, wonder, marvel

ዐጸወ G (IMPF ይዐጹ, SUBJ ይዕጹ) to close, shut, bolt, lock

ዐጠነ G (IMPF ይዐጥን; SUBJ ይዕጥን) to burn incense, offer incense, fumigate with incense

ዕጣን (PL ዕጣናት) incense

[ዕ-ው-ድ] ዖደ G (IMPF ይዐዱ, SUBJ ይዑድ) to go around, circulate, tour; to go around, surround (COMP); to avoid, circumvent (COMP)

ዐዋዲ/አዋዲ (PL አዋድያት) messenger, herald, preacher, crier

ዐውደ PREP around, surrounding

[ዕ-ው-ቅ] ዖቀ (IMPF ይዐውቅ, SUBJ ይዑቅ) G to know, understand, take heed

[ዕ-ው-ር] ዖረ G (IMPF ይዐውር; SUBJ ይዑር) to be blind

ዐወረ DT to neglect, overlook, let pass unnoticed; to despise

ዕዉር blind

ዑረት blindness

ዐይን (PL አዕይንት) eye

ሰብአ ዐይን spies, scouts

ተዐየነ DT to set up camp, to camp; with ላዕለ: to besiege

ዐዘዘ D to be strong, steadfast, vigorous, firm

ዐዚዝ ADJ powerful, mighty, strong, vigorous, excellent

ብ B

ብ- PREP in, into, on, with, by, by means of, by reason of, because of, according to, concerning, against (contiguity), out of, and with a suffixed pronoun may indicate possession (ብከ you have)

በበ Reduplication of the preposition gives it a distributive sense: በበ፡ምድሮሙ according to their (several) kinds; በበዘመዶሙ after their (several) kinds; በበ፡ዲናር፡ለዕለት for a penny each day

በእንተ PREP (w/ CLIT PRON: በእንቲአ-) about, concerning, regarding, with regard to, on account of, because of, for, for the sake of

በእንተ፡ምንት why?

በእንተ፡ዝ- thus, therefore, for the reason that

በእንተ፡ዘ- because

ብእሲ (PL ሰብአ) man, husband, person

ብእሲት (PL አንስት) woman, female, wife

በዐደ G (IMPF ይበዕድ, SUBJ ይባዕድ) to change, alter

ተበዐደ GT = ተባዐደGLT to move away, emigrate; to be changed, altered, alien, unfamiliar

ብዑድ (F በዕድት) PASS PTCP different, alien, strange

ባዕድ (F ባዕዳን) other, different; strange, alien

በዕድና change, difference

ብዕለ G (IMPF ይበዕል, SUBJ ይብዐል) to be rich, wealthy

ባዕል (F ባዕልት; PL አብዕልት) rich, wealthy, owner, possessor, master

በዐል IDEM

ብዑል (F ብዕልት) PASS PTCP rich, wealthy

ብዕል wealth, riches

ብዓል (PL ብዓላት) feast, festival, feast day, banquet

በበይናቲ- (CLIT PRON required) PREP among, between

ቢድበ Q to die

ብድብድ plague, fatal illness

በድን (PL አብድንት) corpse

በደረ G (IMPF ይበድር, SUBJ ይብድር) to hurry, precede, arrive first

አብደረ CG to prefer, choose, select, favor; with INF: to do something eagerly, willingly, with undivided attention

ተበድረ GT PASS of CG

ተባደረ GLT to compete with (in running), to race

ቢድር contest, race

በደወ G (IMPF ይበዱ, SUBJ ይብዱ) to be desert, wasteland

በድው desert wasteland, uncultivated area

በዳ IDEM

በፅዐ / በጽዐ G (IMPF ይበፅዕ, SUBJ ይብፃዕ) to vow

አብፅዐ CG to make or declare blessed; to obtain a vow; to become happy, blessed

ብፁዕ (F ብፅዕት) PASS PTCP fortunate, blessed; vowed, dedicated

ብፅዐት vow

ብፁዓዊ beatific, blessed

ብፅዓን beatification, blessedness

በግዕ (PL አባግዕ) sheep, ram

ብህለ G (IMPF ይብል, SUBJ ይበል; PAST ይቤ፡ለ-) to say, speak; to call someone (COMP) something (COMP); እንዘ፡ይብል frozen phrase introducing quotation

ተብህለ GT to be spoken, said; to be mentioned, named, spoken of

ተባህለ GLT to speak (debate, discuss, argue) with one another (ምስለ, በበይናት-, COMP)

ብሂል saying, statement, word; word, statement (marks the end of an appositive phrase)

ብህመ G (IMPF ይብህም, SUBJ ይብህም) to be mute

በሀም mute, dumb, speechless, one who speaks with difficulty

ብህመት muteness

ባህ/ ባሐ (w/ or w/o CLIT PRON 2ND PERS) EXCLAM Greetings!

ብሕአ G (IMPF ይብሕእ, SUBJ ይብላእ) to ferment

   CG አብሕአ to ferment (COMP)

   ተብሕአ GT = G

   ብሑእ (F ብሕእት) PASS PTCP fermented; leaven, yeast

   ብሒአ vinegar

   ብሕአት fermentation

ብሔር (PL ብሐውርት/ብሐዋርት) region, province, district; people of a district

ባሕር (PL አብሕርት) sea, ocean, lake, large river, west, northwest, north

ባሕርይ (PL ባሕርያት) pearl

በሐተ G (IMPF ይበሕት, SUBJ ይበሐት) to be alone

   ብሕትው ADJ alone, solitary

   ባሕቲት- ADJ/ADV alone, sole, only; used appositionally, always w/ CLIT PRON, e.g., አነ ባሕቲትየ I alone

   ባሕቱ ADV but, however; may occur first in the clause as ወባሕቱ or be placed after the first main element of the clause, *esp.* if this is an element preposed for emphasis

በይናቲ- see በበይናቲ-

ተበከረ GT to be the firstborn; to give birth for the first time

   በኩር firstborn

በከየ G (IMPF ይበኪ, SUBJይብኪ) to weep, mourn, bewail over (ዲበ, ላዕለ, በእንተ)

   ብካይ weeping, lamentation

በልዐ G (IMPF ይበልዕ, SUBJ ይብላዕ) to eat, consume, devour; accuse, slander

   ብላዕ food

   ምብልዕ (PL መባልዕት) food, dish, provisions

ባልሐ L to rescue, save, liberate

   ባለሒ liberator, protector

በልኀ G (IMPF ይብልኅ, SUBJ ይብላኅ) to be sharp

አብልኀ CG to sharpen

በሊኅ sharp

ብልኅ sharp point or edge

መበለት (PL መበለታት) widow, widowhood, poor

በለስ / በለሳ (PL በለስት, አብላስ) fig(s), fig-tree, sycamore

በልየ G (IMPF ይበሊ, SUBJ ይብሊ) to be old, worn out, decrepit, obsolete

   ብሉይ (F ብሊት) old, ancient, worn out, decrepit

   ሕፍ፡ብሊት the Old Testament

   በላዬ old, wearing out

በቍዐ G (IMPF የብቍዕ, SUBJ ይብቁዕ) to be useful, of benefit, profitable, suitable, gratifying; have an advantage

   ብቍዐኒ Please!

   አስተብቍዐ CGT to request, intercede, plead, implore, pray, exhort

   ባቍዕ useful, beneficial

በርበረ Q to pillage, plunder, ravage, search carefully, rummage, confiscate

በረድ hail

ብርሀ G (IMPF ይብርህ, SUBJ ይብረህ) to shine, be bright, be light

   አብርሀ CG to illuminate, cause to be bright; to emit light

   ብሩህ (F ብርህት) PASS PTCP bright, shining; cheerful, happy

   ብርሃን (PL ብርሃናት) light (*lit.* and *fig.*)

በረከ (IMPF ይብርክ, SUBJ ይብረክ) G to kneel, bend the knee

   አስተብረከ CGT to kneel, fall on one's knees

   ብርክ (PL አብራክ) knee

ባረከ L to bless, worship, greet, say farewell to (COMP or ላዕለ)

   ቡሩክ (F ቡርክት) blessed; fortunate, happy, excellent, outstanding

   በረከት (PL በረካታት) blessing

በረቀ G (IMPF ይብርቅ, SUBJ ይብረቅ) to lightning, flash like lightning

   ምብረቅ (PL መባርቅት) lightning

ብሩር (PL ብሩራት) silver

ብርት copper

ተባረየ GLT to follow successively, to do by turns, alternate with one another

    አብሬት alternation, successive turn(s); round or tour of duty or office

ብስራት/ ብስራት good news, gospel

በጽሐ G (IMPF ይበጽሕ, SUBJ ይብጻሕ) to arrive; to come to pass; to happen to (COMP, ላዕለ, or ዲበ); to appear, result in, be accomplished

    በጽሐት arrival

ቤት (PL አብያት) house; room; generation; tribe

በተከ G (IMPF ይበትክ, SUBJ ይብትክ) to break (COMP)

    ተበትከ GT to break

    ብቱክ (F ብትክት) PASS PTCP broken

    ብትከት fracture, rupture, breaking

በትር (PL አብትር) staff, branch, scepter; tribe, race, offspring

[ብ-ው-አ] ቦአ G (IMPF ይበውእ, SUBJ ይባእ) to enter, penetrate, frequent, intermingle, have intercourse (ውስተ, በ-)

    አብአ CG to bring/lead/take (COMP) in; to introduce, insert (COMP)

    በአት (PL በአታት) entry, entrance, entering; cave, lair, den, cell

    ሙባእ/ ምብዋእ (PL ሙባአት) place of entry; act of entering

    መባእ (PL መባአት) offering, gift, oblation

[ብ-ው-ሕ] ቦሐ G (IMPF ይበውሕ, SUBJ ይባሕ) to receive authority, permission

    አብሐ CG to allow, permit (COMP) to do something (SUBJ); to give authority, grant power

    ተበውሐ GT PASS; also: to have power over someone (ላዕለ, ዲበ, ቡ-)

    አስተበውሐ CGT to ask for permission

    ብዉሕ ለ- it is permitted for (someone) to do something (SUBJ)

    ብውሕ one who has the power, permission

    መብሕት power, authority, permission

በየነ D to discern (COMP), distinguish

    አበየነ CD to make (COMP) clear, evident

በየጸ D to separate, distinguish, discern

    ተባየጸ GLT to become companions

    ቢጽ (SING or COLL; PL አብያጽ) friend, comrade, companion; neighbor; single individual

በዝኀ G (IMPF ይበዝኅ; SUBJ ይብዛኅ) to increase, to be many, much, numerous, abundant

    አብዝኀ CG to multiply (COMP), make numerous; to produce a lot of, have a lot of

    ብዙኅ (F ብዝኅት) many, much, numerous, abundant

    ብዝኅ (PL ብዙኃን) multitude, large number or amount

    መብዝኅት major part, majority; most of

    መብዝኅቶ ADV often, frequently

ቤዘወ Q to redeem (COMP)

    ተቤዘወ QT to redeem oneself; to be redeemed

    ቤዛ ransom; as PREP in exchange for

    ቤዛዊ redeemer

    መቤዛዊ IDEM

ድ D

ዳእሙ ADV just, merely, only; also CONJ furthermore, moreover; rather, but, on the contrary

ዲበ PREP (W/ CLIT PRON: ዲቤ-) on, upon, onto, against, concerning, on account of

    ቡዲበ IDEM

    እምዲበ from on, from upon

ደብር (PL አድባር) mountain; monastery

ደብተራ (PL ደባትር) tabernacle, (royal) tent, hut, pavilion, sanctuary

ዴገነ Q/L to pursue, chase, persecute, track (COMP) (COMP or ድኅሬ, እምድኅሬ [እም+ድኅሬ])

ደሐረ G (IMPF ይዴህር, SUBJ ይድሐር) to divorce, repudiate

ድኅነ G (IMPF, SUBJ ይድኅን) to escape safely (from: እም); to be safe, to be spared, unharmed; to be saved (in the religious sense)

    CG አድኀነ to save, keep safe, rescue; to save

    ዳኅን ADJ safe, whole, sound, unharmed

መድኃን = መድኃኒ savior, redeemer

መድኃኒት salvation, safety, redemption

ድኅረ (w/ CLIT PRON: ድኅሬ-) PREP behind, in back of, past (time); ADV afterward, late, finally, at last

    በድኅረ IDEM

    እምድኅረ PREP from behind, after (of time)

    እምድኅረዝ after this, afterwards

ደኃሪ ADJ (F ደኃሪት) last, final; NOUN end, finish, exit

ደክመ (IMPF ይደክም, SUBJ ይድክም) to become tired, weary, weak, feeble, ill

አድለቅለቀ Q to shake, quake, tremble; also CAUS

    ድልቅልቅ violent motion, storm, tempest; earthquake

ደለወ G (IMPF ይደሉ, SUBJ ይድሉ) to be suitable, fitting, correct, proper, correct for (COMP) to do (SUBJ ±ከመ)ʼ; worthy of (enclitic pronoun)

    አድለወ CG to please, satisfy (COMP or ለ-); to adulate, flatter

    ተደለወ DT to prepare oneself, get ready; to live in luxury

    አስተደለወ CDT to prepare (COMP), make (COMP) ready

    አስተዳለወ CDLT IDEM

    ድልው· (FS ድሉት) ADJ worthy, deserving, successful; proper, prepared

    መድልው· (PL መድሊዋን) hypocrite; unjust official or judge

ደም (PL ደማት) blood

ደምፀ G (IMPF ይደምፅ, SUBJ ይድምፅ) to sound

    ድምፅ sound, noise

አድመመ CG (rare) to astonish, stupefy

    ተደመ GT = ተደመመ DT to be astonished, amazed, stupefied

    መድምም ADJ marvelous, astonishing; NOUN miracle, marvel

ደመነ D to cloud over, obscure; to become cloudy

    አደመነ CD IDEM

    ድሙን (F ድምንት) PASS PTCP cloudy

    ደመና (PL ደመናት) cloud(s)

    ደመንጊን rather cloudy

ደመቀ G (IMPF ይደምቅ, SUBJ ይድምቅ) to grind up, crush

ደመረ D to insert, mix in, join together, unite

    ተደመረ DT PASS; also: to be married (ምስለ)

    ድሙር (F ድምርት) PASS PTCP mixed, united, joined

    ዴማሬ union, joining, uniting

    ትድምርት union, marriage

ደንገፀ Q to be astonished, stupefied, amazed, disturbed in mind, terrified, upset; to tremble, quake, panic

    አደንገፀ CQ to astonish, amaze (COMP)

    ድንጉፅ (F ድንግፅት) PASS PTCP astonished, amazed, terrified

    ድንጋዔ astonishment, amazement, terror

    መደንግፅ ADJ astonishing, amazing, terrifying

ድንግል (PL ደናግል) virgin; monk, celibate

    ድንግሊና virginity

ደነነ (IMPF ይደንን, SUBJ ይድነን) G to stoop down, bow down, be submissive

ደንቀወ Q to be hard of hearing

    ድንቅው· (F ድንቁት) PASS PTCP hard of hearing; slow-witted, dense

ደቀቀ G (IMPF ይደቅቅ, SUBJ ይድቅቅ) to be small, be a child, be thin

    አደቀቀ CG to crush, pound, grind; weaken

    ደቂቅ (COLL) children; offspring, progeny

    ደቅ (COLL) children and/or servants

ደቀሰ D to sleep

    ድቃስ sleep

ደርግሐ a patch, mend

ደርግሓ a patch, rag, small piece of cloth, new piece of cloth

ዶርሆ (PL ደዋርሁ) chicken, hen, rooster

ደወል (PL አድወል) region, district, territory

ደወየ G (IMPF ይደዊ, SUBJ ይድወይ) to be sick, ill

    ድዉይ/ድውይ· (F ድውይት) PASS PTCP sick, ill

    ደዌ (PL ደዌያት) sickness, illness, disease

አድያም (PL አድያማት) area, region, environs, neighborhood, adjacent district

Gloss Lexicon

ደየነ D to judge, condemn, punish, condemn, convict, damn

ደይን judgment, punishment, condemnation, *esp.* of the Last Judgment

ፀ D

ፀዕር see ጸዕረ

ፀብዕsee ጸብእ

ፃዜ moth, worM

ፀፈረ G (IMPF ይፀፍር, SUBJ ይፀፍር) to weave, plait

ፅፉር (F ፅፍርት) PASS PTCP woven, plaited

ፅፍሮ plaited work

ፅፍረት NOUN weaving, joining, plaiting

አስተፃግዐ CLT to place on a bed or litter

ፅግዕ, ፅገዕ pillow, mattress

መፃጉዕ a paralytic, bedridden person

ፀግበ see ጸግበ

ፀጋም the left hand or side, north

ፀሐይ/ ፀሐይ (PL ፀሐያት) sun

አፅምአ CG to listen to, to hear

ፀመደ G (IMPF ይፀምድ, SUBJ ይፀምድ) to join, bind together, yoke

ተፀምደ GT PASS; also: to dedicate oneself to, pursue assiduously, submit oneself to, minister to

ፅሙድ (F ፅምድት) PASS PTCP joined, connected; zealous, assiduous; as NOUN: devotee, disciple, servant

ፅምድ yoke, pair

ፅጉድ sectarian, zealot, devote

መፅመድ rope, thong

ፀመረ G (IMPF ይፀምር, SUBJ ይፀምር) to join, affix, connect, attach

ተፃመረ GLT to associate with (one another)

ፀመረ = G

ፅምረት NOUN joining, connecting

መፅምር / መፅመር (PL መፃምር መፅምርት) partner, mate, companion, spouse

ፀምር wool

ምፅንገዕ railing, railed enclosure; a place where one leans or reclines

ፀንሐ see ጸንሐ

ፀንሰ G (IMPF ይፀንስ, SUBJ ይፀንስ) to become pregnant (by እም-); to conceive (a child: COMP)

ፅኑስ (F ፅንስት) PASS PTCP pregnant

ፅንስ pregnancy

አፀርዐ CG to cease, stop, be at rest; to bring (COMP) to a stop; to neglect

ፅሩዕ (F ፅርዕት) PASS PTCP inert, at rest, brought to a stop

ፅርዐት cessation, rest

ፀረፈ / ፀረፈ G (IMPF ይፀርፍ, SUBJ ይፀርፍ) to blaspheme, slander, vilify, abuse, revile against (ላዕለ, ለ-, or COMP)

ፅሩፍ (F ፅርፍት) PASS PTCP blasphemous, wicked, impious

ፀራፊ blasphemer

ፅርፈት (PL ፅርፈታት) blasphemy, abuse

ፀርቅ (PL አፅርቅት) patch, tatter

አፀረረ CG to be hostile

ተፃረረ GLT to act hostilely toward, be an enemy of

ፀር (PL አፅራር) enemy, adversary

ፀራዊ ADJ enemy, hostile

አፀወሰ CD to weaken, cripple, maim

ፅዉስ/ፅውስ (F ፅውስት) PASS PTCP weak, crippled, maimed, paralyzed, twisted, lame, defective, castrated

ጼወወ Q/L to take captive, lead away captive, deport, exile, seize (goods)

ጼውዉ / ጺውዉ captive, exiled

ጼዋ, ጺዋዌ, ጊዋዌ captivity, exile, imprisonment

ፍ F

ፈደፈደ Q to become numerous, abundant, to increase; to surpass, be superior

አፈደፈደ CG CAUS; to surpass (someone: COMP) in (something: COMP)

ወዘይፈደፍድ እምዝኍቱ and whats more

ፈድፋደ ADV exceedingly, very much, greatly

ፈደየ G (IMPF ይፈዲ, SUBJ ይፍዲ) to pay back, to pay a debt

    ፍዳ repayment, retribution; punishment, revenge

    ፈዳይ / ፈዳዩ one who pays back, repays

ፈፀመ G (IMPF ይፈፅም, SUBJ ይፍፅም) = ፈፀመ D to stop up, obstruct

    ተፈፅመ GT PASS, also: to be speechless

    ተፈፀመ DT = GT

ፈፀነ G (IMPF ይፈፅን, SUBJ ይፍፅን) to have a fever, be feverish; to shiver

    ፈፀንት fever

ፍሕም (PL አፍሓም) carbon, coal

ፈኈረ G (IMPF ይፈኈር, SUBJ ይፍኈር) to espouse, become engaged to (COMP woman)

    ፍኈርት fiancée

    ፈኃሪ fiancé

ፈከረ D to interpret, expound, explain, comment

    ፍካሬ explanation, interpretation, exposition

    መፈክር interpreter, expounder; soothsayer, prophet

ፍልፍል / ፈልፈል pepper

ፈለግ (PL አፍላግ) river, brook; valley

ፈለሰ G (IMPF ይፈልስ, SUBJ ይፍልስ) to separate, go away, depart, emigrate; to secede, be transformed, be changed, withdraw, split off from (እምነ)

    አፍለሰ CG to send away, deport, exile, remove, banish, transplant, separate

    ተፋለሰ GLT to wander as exiles from one place to another; to pass from one generation to another

    ፍሉስ (F ፍልስት) PASS PTCP exiled, in exile

    ፍልሰት wandering, travel; exile; death; assumption (into heaven)

    ፈላሲ an exile

ፈለጠ G (IMPF ይፈልጥ, SUBJ ይፍልጥ) to separate, divide, segregate, put into a separate group or category; to distinguish, discern

    አፍለጠ CG to speak distinctly, to make a distinction

    ተፋለጠ GLT to separate from one another

    ፍሉጥ (F ፍልጥት) PASS PTCP separate, distinct

    ፍልጠት separation, division, distinction

ፈነወ D to send, dismiss, send off, see off

    ተፋነወ GLT to bid farewell to

    ፍኑው (F ፍኑት) sent

    ፍኖት (PL ፍናው, ፍናዋት) road, way, path

    ፍና way, path, part, side, place, circumstance, concept

    ፍና፡ሰርክ towards evening, early evening

ፈቀደ G (IMPF ይፈቅድ, SUBJ ይፍቅድ) to want, wish, desire, require, be in need, permit, supervise, consider, regard, value, care for, take care of, survey, review, muster, number, enumerate

    ፈቃድ (PL ፈቃዳት) desire, wish, will, intention, liking, content, pleasure, goodwill, permission

    በፈቃዱ of his own accord

    ዘእንበለ፡ፈቃድ involuntarily

አፍቀረ CG to love, cherish, value, seek, regard, consider, seek, desire, wish for, number

    ተፈቅረ GT PASS of CG

    ተፋቀረ GLT ተፋቀረ to love one another; make friends

    ፍቁር (F ፍቅርት) PASS PTCP beloved, loved

    ፍቅር love

ፈርሀ G (IMPF ይፈርህ; SUBJ ይፍራህ) to be afraid; to fear; to revere (COMP or እም-)

    ፍርሀት (PL ፍርሀታት) fear, dread, awe; fearfulness, timidity

ፈረስ (PL አፍራስ) horse

ፈረየ G (IMPF ይፈሪ, SUBJ ይፍረይ) to bear fruit, be fruitful

    ፍሬ (PL ፍሬያት, ፍርያት) fruit (lit. and fig.), blossom, bud

ተፈሥሐ DT to be glad, be cheerful, merry, enjoy oneself, comforted, rejoice (in: በ-, በእንተ, ላዕለ, ዲበ)

    ፍሡሕ (F ፍሥሕት) PASS PTCP happy, joyous, rejoicing

    ፍሥሐ joy, happiness

    ትፍሥሕት (PL ትፍሥሕታት) IDEM

ፍሥሐ Passover

ፍሥሕ / ፍሥሐት (PL ፍሥሓታት) narrow passage, ravine, steep place, heap of earth, mound, shrine on an elevated place, high place, fortified place

ፈጸመ D to complete, finish, end, consume; to fulfill, perfect, satisfy, accomplish; to finish doing (INF)

    ተፈጸመ DT PASS; also: die right away, be affected

    ፍጹም (F ፍጽምት) PASS PTCP done, accomplished, completed, fulfilled, consummated; perfect, whole, complete

    ፍጻሜ consummation, end, completion, perfection

    ተፍጻሜት IDEM

ፈትሐ G (IMPF ይፈትሕ, SUBJ ይፍታሕ) to open, loosen, untie, release; to absolve, forgive (sins); to pass judgment, arbitrate, decide, interpret

    አፍትሐ CG to bring (COMP) to judgment

    ተፋትሐ GLT to be separated from one another; to engage in a legal case

    ፍቱሕ (F ፍትሕት) PASS PTCP open; absolved, forgiven

    ፈታሒ (PL ፈታሕት) judge

    ፍትሕ precept, law; judgment, decision

ፈተለ G (IMPF ይፈትል, SUBJ ይፍትል) to twist, spin

    ፍቱል (F ፍትልት) PASS PTCP spun, twisted

    ፈትል (PL አፍታል, አፍትልት) thread, cord

    ፍትሎ twisted work

ፈተነ G (IMPF ይፈትን, SUBJ ይፍትን) to investigate, explore; to examine, test

    አፍተነ CG to hand (COMP) over for examination, allow (COMP) to be examined

    ፍቱን (F ፍትንት) PASS PTCP investigated, examined, tested

    ፈታኒ examiner, tester

ፈተተ / ፈተ G (IMPF ይፈትት, SUBJ ይፍትት) = D to break (bread); to distribute (COMP), give out

    ፍት (PL ፍተት) part, portion, morsel; gift

    ፍትት (PL ፍተታት) IDEM

ፈተወ G (IMPF ይፈትው, SUBJ ይፍተው) to desire strongly, covet, lust for

    ፍቱው desired, desirable, pleasing, pleasant

ፍትወት (PL ፍትወታት) desire, lust, craving; the thing desired, pleasure

    መፍትው it is necessary, fitting, proper, obligatory (foll. by SUBJ ±ከመ)

ፈጠነ G (IMPF ይፈጥን, SUBJ ይፍጥን) to be quick, swift

    ፍጡን (F ፍጥንት) PASS PTCP swift, quick

ፈጠረ G (IMPF ይፈጥር, SUBJ ይፍጥር) to create, produce; to devise, fabricate, contrive, inscribe, make incisions on the flesh

    ፍጡር (F ፍጥርት) PASS PTCP created

    ፍጥረት the act of creation; what is created, creatures; nature, character; kind, species

    ፈጣሪ creator (always refers to God)

ፈወሰ D to cure, heal (COMP) from (እም-)

    ፈውስ (PL ፈውሳት) cure, healing; medicine, medication

    መፈውስ physician

ፈያት (COLL) thieves

    ፈያታዊ a thief

ገ G

ገዐዘ G (IMPF ይገዕዝ, SUBJ ይግዐዝ) to migrate; to be free (i.e., not enslaved)

    ግዕዝ (PL ግዕዛት) mode of life, manner; nature, quality, essential nature

    በግዕዘ PREP in accord with the view of; (2) ordinary mode of church singing

    ግዕዝ (PL አግዓዚ) Ethiopians

ገብአ G (IMPF ይገብእ, SUBJ ይግባእ) to come/go back, to return

    አግብአ CG to bring/ lead/take (COMP) back; to turn back; restore, restitute, put up, recover, hand over, betray (COMP)

    ተጋብአ GLT to gather, assemble; come together; to be turned back, collected

    አስተጋብአ CGLT to gather, assemble, collect, cause to be gathered, call up (spirits), bring together, recover, heap up, sum up, take up, cause (a city) to surrender (COMP)

ገብረ G (IMPF ይገብር, SUBJ ይግብር) to act, work, function;

to make, create, fashion, produce, prepare; to do, perform, enact, carry out, achieve, execute, procure, observe (ordinances)

> አግበረ CG to make or order (COMP) to do or make (COMP)

ገብር (PL አግብርት) servant

ግብር (PL ግብራት, ግብር) deed, act; work, task, business; religious service, liturgy; product, artifact, creation; as ADV necessarily, out of necessity

ገባሪ (PL ገበርት) maker, fashioner, craftsman

ምግባር (PL ምግባራት) action, practice, behavior, custom(s); business, activity, workmanship

ግብጽ Egypt

ገደፈ G (IMPF ይገድፍ, SUBJ ይግድፍ) to throw, cast; to throw away, discard; to lose by waste or neglect

> ግዱፍ (F ግድፍት) PASS PTCP thrown, cast; discarded; lost, rejected

ጐድጐደ Q to knock (on a door)

ተጋደለ GLT to struggle, contend, *esp.* in religious sense of struggling against temptation

> ገድል (PL ገድላት) a struggle, contest (*esp.* spiritual); title of works dealing with the lives of saints and ascetics

ገዳም (PL ገዳማት) wilderness, uninhabited place, plain, field, forest, desert

ገፍዐ G (IMPF ይገፍዕ; SUBJ ይግፍዕ) to harm, injure, oppress, afflict, treat violently, vex, wrong, push

> ተጋፍዐ GLT RECIPR; also: to collide, be crushed (by a crowd), press (upon)

ገፍትአ Q to destroy utterly, pervert, subvert, overturn, throw down; turn away

ጌገየ Q/L to err, go astray, get lost; to sin, commit error

> አንገገየ N to wander back and forth, hither and yon

> ጊጉይ (F ጊጊት) PASS PTCP lost, erring; sinful, wicked

> ጌጋይ (PL ጌጋያት) error, sin, crime, guilt

ገሀደ G (IMPF ይገሀድ, SUBJ ይግሀድ) to be revealed, become visible

> አግሀደ CG causative; to act or speak openly

> ግሁድ (F ግህድ) ADJ clear, manifest, open, obvious, visible

ገሀድ IDEM

ገሀደ ADV openly, manifestly, publicly

ግሀደት openness

ገሐፈ G (IMPF ይገሕፍ, SUBJ ይግሕፍ) to take away, out; to remove, disperse; to sweep away

> አግሐወ CG to take aside, divert, cause to turn aside; to remove, put aside, take away; to depart, withdraw

> ተግሕወ GT withdraw, retreat, retire, step aside, be aside, be detached, turn away, avoid, depart, refrain, separate oneself, recede, cease

ገልዐ (PL አግልዕት) a pot

ግልፍ (PL ግልፋት, አግላእት) carved work, idol, graven image, statue

ገለየ G (IMPF ይገሊ, SUBJ ይግሊ) to cut off, break off, separate, divide (COMP); to interpret, reveal (COMP)

ግምዔ (PL ገማዕይ) flask, container for oil

ገመደ G (IMPF ይገምድ, SUBJ ይግምድ) to cut down, cut in pieces, prune, amputate, prune, harvest

> ግምድ (PL ግምዳት) cut piece, slice

ገመል (PL ገመላት, አገማል) camel

አግመረ CG to perfect, finish, consummate; to include completely, comprehend, hold, encompass

> ተገምረ GT PASS of CG

> ግሙራ ADV always, altogether, completely, wholly, ever; w/ NEGATED VERB: (not) at all, never, by no means, e.g., ግሙራ፡ኢርኢነ "we have never seen"

> ልግሙራ ADV forever, always

ግንቦት Eth. month name: May 9–June 7

ጕንድ (PL አጉንድ) trunk of a tree; a restraining device, stock

ጐንደየ Q to last, remain; to delay, tarry, be slow in coming; with INF: to be tardy or late in doing, to be too long in doing

> አጐንደየ CQ to put off, delay, defer

> ተጐናደየ QLT to delay in doing (ላዕለ, ላዕለ + INF, or INF alone)

ጐንዲዮ ADV after a time

ጋኔን (PL አጋንንት) demon, evil spirit

   ዘጋኔን one possessed by an evil spirit

ገነት (PL ገነታት) garden; the Garden of Eden

ገነየ G (IMPF ይገኒ, SUBJ ይግናይ) to bow down; to submit, be submissive; to render humble thanks

   አገነየ CG CAUS; also: to subject (COMP)

   ተጋነየ GLT to confess one's sins, to seek pardon

   ግናይ humble thanks

ገነዘ G (IMPF ይገነዝ, SUBJ ይግንዝ) to prepare (a body) for burial

   ግኑዝ (F ግንዝት) PASS PTCP prepared for burial

   ግንዘት preparation for burial

   መግናዝ materials used in preparing a body for burial

ተጐርዐየ Q to strangle (or hang) oneself

   ጕርዔ (PL ጕራዌት) throat, neck

ገበፍ net

ገራህት (PL ገራውህ) field, arable land, farm, estate

ገረመ G (IMPF ይገርም, SUBJ ይግርም) to be awesome, fear-inspiring

   ገረመ D to frighten, terrify

   ተገረመ DT to be terrible, threatening, fearful

   ግሩም (F ግርምት) PASS PTCP awesome, terrible, fearsome, awe-inspiring

   ግርማ IDEM

   ግርማ / ግርጋ terror, awe; awesome nature

   ትግርምት threats, terrors

ገሰሰ G (IMPF ይገስስ, SUBJ ይግስስ) to touch, feel, handle

   ግሰት touch, touching

ገሠጸ D to admonish, scold, rebuke, chastise; to instruct, warn, correct, charge; to restrain

   ግሡጽ (F ግሥጽት) PASS PTCP well instructed, learned

   መገሥጽ teacher, instructor

   ተግሣጽ (PL ተግሣጻት) rebuke, reproach, admonition, instruction

ገጽ (PL ገጻት) face, appearance, person; type, sort; surface, direction, side; passage (of scripture)

ጐየየ / ጐየ G (IMPF ይጐዪ, SUBJ ይጉየይ) to flee

   ጐያዪ / ጐያዪ fugitive

   ጕየ flight

   ምጕያይ refuge, asylum

[ገ-የ-ስ] ጌሰ G (IMPF ይገይስ, SUBJ ይጊስ) to be or do something early in the day

   ጌሰም / ጌሰመ ADV tomorrow

ጊዜ (PL ጊዜያት) time, season, hour, moment [frequent in set phrases, as below]; also CONJ before verbs when, whenever

   ጊዜሃ at that time, right away

   ውእተ፡ጊዜ at that time

   ይእተ፡ጊዜ IDEM

   በጊዜ፡ጽበሕ in the morning

   በጊዜ፡ምሴት in the evening

   በጊዜሁ at its/the proper time

   በጊዜህ immediately, straightway

   በኵሉ፡ጊዜ always

ገዝአ G (IMPF ይገዝእ, SUBJ ይግዛእ) to serve at a feast

   ግዝእ / ገዝእ feast, banquet

   ገዛኢ (PL ገዛእት) waiter, attendant (at feast)

   ገዝአ IDEM

ገዝአ G (IMPF ይገዝእ, SUBJ ይግዛእ) to dominate, master

   እግዚእ (PL አጋእዝት, አጋእስት) lord, master, leader, chief

   እግዚእነ Our Lord

   እግዚእት lady, mistress

   እግዚእትነ Our Lady (i.e., Mary)

   እግዚአ፡ብሔር God (lit., the master of the land)

ገዘፈ G (IMPF ይገዝፍ, SUBJ ይግዝፍ) to be dense, stupid, dull, stout

   ግዝፍ / ግዘፍ density, dullness, stupidity

ገዘመ G (IMPF ይገዝም, SUBJ ይግዝም) to cut down (a tree); to fell; to cut, hew (wood)

ሀ H

-ሃ COMP used occasionally to mark proper nouns as the syntactic complement

-ሂ CONJ also, and, further, even, the very, for one's part (e.g., አነሂ I, for my part); added to INTER PRON to form indefinite, e.g., መኑሂ anyone, no one

-ሄ ADV there, here, away to

ኵልሄ everywhere

ሀጕላ G (IMPF ይሀጕል, SUBJ ይህጐል) to be lost, destroyed, perish, be deprived of (COMP)

ተሀጕላ GT to be lost, destroyed, perish, be deprived of

ሀገር (PL አህጉር) city, town; sometimes used vaguely for region, district, country, homeland

ሀለወ [ሀሎ] D to exist, be, be available, live

ሀለወ + IMPF of another verb expresses duration in the past or in the future

ሀለወ + CLIT PRON + SUBJ expresses an obligation or an instant future

ሀልዉ existing, who exists, who lives, that lasts, lasting, constant, that is present, who originates, that is true, that is exact

ሆሳዕና INT Hosanna! Save us! (Heb)

ሀውለየ Q to burn brightly

ህየ ADV there, in that place

(ህ-ይ-ድ) ሂደ G (IMPF ይህይድ, SUBJ ይሂድ) to rob, take by force, plunder, spoil, snatch away, confiscate, seize, wrong, ravish, bewitch

ሃይማኖት/ሀይማኖት faith, belief, religion

ሐ Ḥ

ሐብለየ Q to spoil, plunder, acquire by trickery, treat deceitfully, deal craftily, defraud, lie, suspect, be distrustful

ሕብልያ spoil, prey, booty

ሐደሰ D to renew, renovate, restore

ሐዲስ (F ሐዳስ, PL ሐደስት) ADJ new, recent, junior

ሕዳጥ see ኍዳጥ

ሐፀነ G (IMPF የሐፅን, SUBJ ይሐፅን) to nurse, rear, train, educate

ሕፃን (PL ሕፃናት) infant, very young child; young servant, page

ሕፅን (PL ሕፅን) bosom, womb, lap

ሕግ law, decree, canon, rule, rite, regulation, statute, norm, covenant, custom

ሐጕላ see ሀጕላ

ሐጕል destruction, end

ሐሊብ milk

ሐለየ G (IMPF የሐሊ, SUBJ ይሕሊ) to sing, celebrate with song

ማሕሌት (PL መሓልይ) song, canticle, hymn

[ሕ-ም-ም] አሕመ CG to afflict (COMP) with illness, pain, distress

ሕሙም ADJ ill, afflicted, distressed, unhealthy, diseased, suffering, distressed

ሕማም (PL ሕማማት) illness, pain, disease, affliction

ሕማሜ envy, avarice

ሐመር (PL አሕማር) boat, ship

ሐማት (PL ሐማታት) mother-in-law; daughter-in-law

ሐነጸ G (IMPF የሐንጽ, SUBJ ይሕንጽ) to build, construct, repair, erect

ሕቀ ADV a little, a little while; a short distance

ሐቁ (PL ሐቁያት) hip, loin, thighbone

ሐቅል (PL አሕቁል, አሕቃል) field, plain; desert, wilderness; district

ሐራውያ / ሐረውያ / ሐረዊያ (አሕርዉ) pig, wild boar

ሐሠየ / ሐሥየ G (IMPF የሐሢ, SUBJ ይሕሥይ) to make happy, give joy

ሐሤት ADJ joy, gladness, happiness

[ሕ-ው-ር] ሐረ G (IMPF የሐውር, SUBJ ይሐር, ይሑር) to go, go forth, depart, follow a way of life; have sexual intercourse

ሐዋርያ (PL ሐዋርያት) apostle, traveler, messenger, envoy

ሐይቅ (PL ሐይቃት) shore (of sea or lake)

ሐሰ (G IMPF ይሐይስ, SUBJ ይሐይስ) to blame, rebuke, revile

ሐሰት reviling, blaming

አስተሐየጸ CGT perceive, view, discern; observe closely, watch, spy, explore; lie in wait, be on the lookout for

አስተሐለየ CGLT IDEM

ሐይወ G (IMPF የሐዩ, SUBJ ይሕየው) to live, be alive; to revive, come back to life; to recover, get well

አሕየወ CG to restore to life; to heal, cure; to let live

ሕያው (F ሕያወት) ADJ alive, living

ሕይወት life, lifetime

ሕዝብ (PL አሕዛብ, ሕዘብ) people, nation, sect, multitude, crowd; Gentiles, pagans, heathens

ኀ ḫ

ኀበ (w/ CLIT PRON: ኀቤ-) PREP by, with, at, in the presence of, near; to, toward; in reference to; in comparison with; where

በኀበ IDEM, among, upon, in, wheresoever, before

እምኀበ from with, from the presence of; near; through the agency of, by means of; ADV where

ኀብአ G (IMPF የኀብእ, SUBJ ይኀብእ) to hide, conceal

ተኀብአGT PASS and REFLEX

ኅቡእ (F ኅብእት) PASS PTCP hidden, concealed; secret, arcane

በኅቡእ secretly, in secret

ምኅብአ (PL ምኅባኣት hiding place, hidden place; receptacle

ኀበረ / ኀበረ G (IMPF የኀብር, SUBJ ይኀብር) to be connected or associated with (ምስለ); to join, associate with; to conspire against (ላዕለ); to be in accord with, agree with (ምስለ, በ-); to share something (COMP) with (ምስለ); with INF or COORD verb: to do jointly, together

አኀበረ CG to associate (someone: COMP; with: ምስለ); to make a conspiracy; to be in agreement, accord

ተኀበረ GT to be associated with (ምስለ)

ኅቡር (F ኅብርት) PASS PTCP joined, associated

ኅቡረ ADV together, jointly, at one and the same time

ኅብረት union, joining, association; consensus, accord

ማኅበረ congregation, gathering; crowd, tumult; council; colleagues, associates; monastery, convent

ኀበዘ G (IMPF የኀብዝ, SUBJ ይኀብዝ) to bake

ኀባዚ baker

ኅብስት (PL ኅባውዝ) bread, piece of bread, loaf of bread

ኀደገ G (IMPF የኀድግ, SUBJይኀድግ) to abandon, desert, leave (behind, out, off), give up, let go, desist, cease, neglect, reject, forgive, divorce, dismiss, allow, permit, commit something to someone

ተኃደገ GLT to divorce

ኅዱግ (F ኅድግት) PASS PTCP left, abandoned, deserted; divorced

ኅድገት remission (of sins or debts)

ኅድጋት / ኅዳጋት divorce

ኀደረ G (IMPF የኀድር, SUBJ ይኀድር) to reside, dwell, inhabit (usually w/a PREP, but sometimes COMP); ላዕለ to reside in, possess (said of demons or spirits in a person)

አኀደረ CG CAUSATIVE, lodge, settle

ኅዱር (F ኅድርት) PASS PTCP residing, dwelling

ኅድረት NOUN residing, dwelling

ማኀደር (PL ማኀደራት, መኃድር) dwelling-place, residence; room, cell

ኅዳር Eth. month name: Nov. 10–Dec. 9

ኀዳጥ NOUN a small amount, a little; ADJ (PL ኀዳጥት) few

ኀፀበ G (IMPF የኀፅብ, SUBJ ይኀፅብ) to wash, wash away

ተኀፅበ GT to wash oneself (a part of the body may be added as COMP)

ኅፁብ (F ኅፅብት) PASS PTCP washed

ኅፅበት washing, ablution

ምኅፃብ (PL ምኅፃባት) bath, bathing place

ማኀፈድ tower

ኀፈረ / ኀፍረ G (IMPF የኀፍር, SUBJ ይኀፈር) to be ashamed of (በእንተ); to do something (INF or verbal noun or SUBJ); to fear, revere (እምነ)

ተኀፍረ GT to be ashamed, put to shame

ኀፍረት (PL ኀፍረታት) shame, impropriety, turpitude

ኁፉር (F ኁፍርት) PASS PTCP ashamed

ኀፋሪ ashamed; shameful

ኆኅት (PL ኆኃት, ኆዋኁ) door, doorway, gate, portal, leaf of door

Gloss Lexicon

ዐለፈ G (IMPF የዐልፍ, SUBJ ይዐልፍ) to pass by to pass through, among, away from; to leave; to perish

    ተኃለፈ GLT to wander to and fro

    ዐሉፍ (F ዐልፍት) PASS PTCP crossing, passing

    ዐላፊ (PL ዐለፍት) NOUN passer-by; ADJ transitory

    ዐላፊት (COLL) those passing by

    ምዕላ place for crossing or passing through

ዐልቀ G (IMPF የዐልቅ, SUBJ ይዐልቅ) to come to an end, be finished, consummated; to perish, disappear

    አዕለቀ CG to destroy, finish, consummate

    ዐልቀት end, consummation, completion; death

    ማዕለቅት end, completion; consummation, climax, death; performance, execution

ዐለቄ D to count, number, reckon

    ዑሉቅ (F ዕልቅት) PASS PTCP counted, numbered, reckoned

    ዑልቀ / ዐልቀ (PL ዑለቀ) number, sum

    ዑለቄ NOUN numbering, counting

ዐለት reed, cane

ዐለየ / ሐለየ D to think, ponder, meditate (about: COMP or በእንተ); to think up, devise; to decide (to do: ከመ + SUBJ); to take thought of, to take care of, look after (someone: CLIT PRON or በእንተ/ለ-)

    ዐሊና / ሕሊና thinking, faculty of thinking, mind, thought, understanding, intelligence, intellect, reasoning, reason, device, imagination, intention, conscience, proposal, opinion

ዐምስ (COMP ዐምሰ) F; ዐምስቱ (COMP ዐምስተ) M five

    ዐምስ F IDEM

    ኃምስ (F ኃምስት) ADJ fifth

    ዐምሳዊ (F ዐምሳዊት) IDEM

    ኃአሳይ (F ኃምሲት) IDEM

    ዐሙስ the fifth day (of week or month); five days

    ዐምስ ADV five times

    ዐምሳ fifty

ዐነቀ G (IMPF የዐንቅ, SUBJ ይዐንቅ) to choke, throttle

    ተዐንቀ GT PASS and REFLEX

ዔር (F ዔርት) ADJ good, excellent

ዒሩት NOUN excellence, goodness, virtue

ዐረየ G (IMPF የዐሪ, SUBJ ይዐረይ) to choose, select

    ዐሩይ (F ዐራት) PASS PTCP chosen, selected; pleasing, acceptable; an arbiter, mediator

ዐሰረ /ዐሥረ G (IMPF የዐስር, SUBJ ይዐሰር) to be in bad straits, wretched, miserable; to suffer loss, be reduced to poverty; to be dishonored, vilified, despised

    አዐሰረ CG to cause/inflict/afflict (with) any of the preceding states (COMP of person)

    ዐሱር (F ዐስርት) PASS PTCP wretched, impoverished, afflicted, vile, despised

    ዐሳር / ዐሣር (PL ዐሳራት) dishonor, abominable thing, humiliation, wretchedness, poverty, ignominy

ዐሠሠ G (IMPF የዐሥሥ, SUBJ ይዐሥሥ) to seek, look for, explore, desire, wish for, inquire about; to demand, require from (በ-ዐበ/እምነ); to study, pursue diligently

    ተዐሠ GT PASS and REFLEX

    ተዐሠሠ GLT to inquire about (COMP) collectively; to discuss (COMP) with one another

    ዐሣሢ pursuit

ዐሸ sand

ዐጺን (PL ዐጻውንት) iron; sword, weapon; tool, implement

ዐጸረ G (IMPF የዐጽር, SUBJ ይዐጽር) to be short

    አዐጸረ CG to shorten, diminish, subtract from

    ዐጹር (F ዐጽርት) PASS PTCP short, shortened

    ዐጺር (F ዐጽር) IDEM

ዐጸወ G (IMPF የዐጽም, SUBJ ይዐጹ) to castrate

    ዐጽው castrated; NOUN eunuch

ዐተመ G (IMPF የዐትም, SUBJ ይዐተም) to seal, close and seal

    ዐቱም (F ዐትምት) PASS PTCP sealed, signed

    ዐታሚ one who seals, signer

    ማዐታም / ማዐታምት a seal

ዐተወ G (IMPF የዐቱ, SUBJ ይዐቱ) to burn, be alight

    አዐተወ CG to light (a lamp); to burn, emit light

    ማዐቶት (PL መዐታው) lamp

ዐጥአ G to lack, not have, not find, to miss, sin fail, to be bereaved, to be destitute

አግጥአ CG to bereave, deprive (COMP); to cause (COMP) to sin

ተጐጥአ GT to lack, be wanting; to withdraw, escape; to be absent, lost

ጐጡአ (F ጐጥአት) PASS PTCP wanting, deprived, needy

ጌጢአት (PL ጐጣውአ) lack, fault, sin, trespass

ኃጥእ (F ኃጥአት; PL ኃጥአን) ADJ sinful, wicked; NOUN sinner

ጐጠት grain, seed

[ጐ-ይ-ል] ጌለ G (IMPF የጐይል, SUBJ ይጌል) to become well, strong

ጐየለ D to be strong, mighty, powerful; to prevail over, be superior to (COMP)

ተጐየለ DT PASS; also: to prevail, dominate; to act with force (good or bad sense) against; to take or do by force

ጐዩል (F ጐይልት) PASS PTCP strong, mighty, powerful, active, valiant, violent

ጐያል IDEM

ጐይል (PL ጐይላት) strength, power, might; army, troops; virtue, firmness

ጐየሰ D to be better, more outstanding; often impersonal: ይጌይሰኒ፡ከመ + SUBJ it is better for me that …

ጊሳን NOUN excellence

ከ K

-ኬ (± እንከ) ENCLITIC PART therefore, now then

ካዕብ (F ካዕብት) ADJ second, other

ካዕበ ADV again, a second time; further, moreover, twice

ምክዕቢት NOUN double, the double amount

ምክዕቢት ADV twofold, doubly; ምእተ፡ምክዕቢት a hundredfold

ከዐወ (IMPF ይክዐው, SUBJ ይከዐው) to pour out, spew out, spill (COMP)

ተከዐወ GT to pour out, be spewed out, be spilled

ከብደ G (IMPF ይከብድ, SUBJ ይክበድ) to be heavy, serious

አከብደ CG CAUSATIVE; also: to be burdensome

ክቡድ (F ከቢድ) PASS PTCP heavy

ከብድ heaviness

ከብድ the liver; the stomach

ከብካብ wedding, wedding feast

ከብረ G (IMPF ይከብር, SUBJ ይክበር) to be glorious, magnificent, great, famous, illustrious, precious

አክበረ CG to make or regard as glorious

ክቡር (F ክብርት) PASS PTCP glorious

ክብር glory, honor; splendor, magnificence

ከብተ G (IMPF ይከብት, SUBJ ይክብት) to hide, conceal, keep secret

ተከብተ GT PASS; also: to disappear

ከደነ G (IMPF ይክድን, SUBJ ይክድን) to cover, protect; to pardon (sins)

ክዱን (F ክድንት) PASS PTCP covered, protected

ኬድላን (PL ኬድላናት) covering; *esp.* tunic, garment

ክድነት protection

ክድላኒ protector

ከፈለ G (IMPF ይከፍል, SUBJ ይክፍል) to divide (up); to apportion, distribute; to make someone a participant/partaker in/of; IMPERSONALLY: to be one's portion (e.g., ኢከፈሎሙ it was not their portion = they were not worthy of it)

ክፉል (F ክፍልት) PASS PTCP divided

ክፍል (PL ክፍላት) part, portion, share

ክፋሌ partition, division, distribution, separation

ከፈር (PL አከፋር) container for measuring, a bushel

ከሀደ see ከሐደ

ከህለ G (IMPF ይክህል, SUBJ ይክሀል) to be able to do (INF); to prevail against, master (COMP or ምስለ)

ተክህለ GT(1) = G; (2) impersonal: to be possible for (COMP) to do (INF)

አክህለ CG to enable, make able

ተካህለ GLT to come to an agreement with (ምስለ)

ክሀሊ powerful, strong, capable

ክሀሌ፡ኵሉ omnipotent

ካህን (PL ካህናት) priest, clergyman

ክህነት priesthood

ከሐ, ከሓ, ከሐከ, ከሐሐ, ከሓሕ ADV thither, to that place; further on

ከሕደ G (IMPF ይከሕድ, SUBJ ይከሐድ) to deny, repudiate, renounce, reject, rebel, disown, be disobedient; to lack faith, be an unbeliever

    ከሓዲ (PL ከሓድያን) infidel, unbeliever, impious, apostate; rebel, disobedient, contentious

    ካሕድ lack of faith, impiety, heresy; disobedience, rebellion

    ከሕደት denial, apostasy, rebellion

ኮከብ (PL ከዋክብት) star; ኮከበ፡ምሴት evening star, ኮከበ፡ጽባሕ morning star

ኩል- QUANTIFIER: all, each, every (always with ENCL PRON)

    ኩሉ (COMP ኩሎ) is used in the sense of everything, everyone, anything, all; e.g. ዝንቱ፡ኩሉ all this

    ኩለንተ- (W/ CLIT PRON) all of, the whole of

    ኩሎ ADV altogether, completely; (not) at all

    ኩልሄ ADV everywhere, wherever

    በኩልሄ IDEM

ከልአ G (IMPF ይከልእ; SUBJ ይከላእ) to prevent, forbid, hinder (someone: CLIT PRON; from doing: INF); to withhold, deprive, restrain (something: COMP; from: እምነ)

    ተከልአ GT PASS; also: to abstain from (እምነ)

    ከልአት prohibition, prevention

ካልእ (F ካልእት) ADJ other, another, second; NOUN companion

    ክልኤ two, both

    ክልኤቱ (COMP ክልኤተ) M two, both, double

    ክልኤቲ (COMP ክልኤተ) F two, both

ከልብ (PL ከለባት, አክላብ) dog

ከልሐ D to cry out, shout

ከለለ D to crown, to surround like a crown

    ክሉል (F ክልልት) PASS PTCP crowned (with: በ-)

    ከላሌ NOUN crowning, coronation

    አክሊል (PL አክሊላት) crown, diadem

ከለሜዳ robe, vestment

ክልስስት (PL ከላስስት) bundle, sheaf

መክሊት (PL መካልይ) talent (measure of weight)

ከመ (w/ CLIT PRON: ከማ-) PREP like, as, even as, just as, as if, such; ከመዝ, ከማሁ like this, thus, in this way CONJ that (introducing a noun clause); so that, in order that (+ SUBJ); EXCLAMATIVE (e.g., ከመ፡ሠናይ፡ርእዩ "how fair is his appearance!"); ከመ፡ኢ- so that not, lest (+ SUBJ)

    በከመ PREP according to, in accordance with; CONJ according as, as

    ዘከመ CONJ how

    እምከመ CONJ as soon as, when

ከመ postpositive PART: even, only, not otherwise

ክንፍ (PL ክነፍ, አክናፍ) wing

ከንፈር (PL ከናፍር) lip; edge, hem

ኰነነ D to judge, condemn, punish, convict, pass judgment, torture, chastise; to rule, have power (over: comp or ለ-)

    ኩኑን (F ኩንንት) PASS PTCP judged, condemned, subject to punishment

    ኩነኔ (PL ኩነኔያት) judgment, trial, condemnation, punishment, law, rule, domain, ordinance

    መኰንን (PL መኳንንት) judge, administrator, high official, nobleman, dignitary

ከንቱ vanity, emptiness; COMP ከንቶ

    በከንቱ ADV in vain; fortuitously, without purpose, without reward or result

ኰረዐ G (IMPF ይኰርዕ, SUBJ ይኩርዕ) to strike someone's head with one's fists

ከርቤ myrrh

ምኵራብ (PL ምኵራባት) temple, shrine, synagogue

ከረመ/ ክርመ G (IMPF ይከርም, SUBJ ይክርም) to spend the winter; to belong to the previous year (wine)

    ከረምት winter; rainy season; year

ከርሥ (PL ከርሣት) belly, stomach, womb, abdomen, interior

ከሰድ / ክሰድ (PL ከሰዳት, ከሳውድ, ከሳውዕድ) neck

    ከሳድ ይቡስ stiff neck, stubbornness

ከሠተ G (IMPF ይከሥት, SUBJ ይከሥት) to reveal, uncover, lay (COMP) bare; to open (COMP)

    ክሡት (F ክሥትት) PASS PTCP uncovered, bare, visible, public; open

[ከ-ው-ን] ኮነ G (IMPF ይከውን, SUBJ ይኩን) to be, become, exist, happen, occur, take place, be permissible; ወከነ፡ሰ and when, and while; note that ከ-ው-ን may be used impersonally: (there) was X, or (it) was/became X (in which X may or may not have the dependent -a)

መካን (PL መካናት) place, locale, space, room, occasion

ኪያ- COMP PRON (emphatic), ኪያከ፡ሠመርኩ I am pleased with YOU

[ከ-ይ-ድ] ኬደ G (IMPF ይከይድ, SUBJ ይኪድ) to tread, trample on (COMP); to thresh (by treading)

ምክያድ sole of the foot, footprint; base; threshing floor

መከየድ / መካየድ IDEM; footstool

ተካየደ GLT to make a treaty, pact, covenant with (ምስለ or CLIT PRON); to promise; special use in hagiographa: the benefit promised by God to those who celebrate the commemoration of a saint

ኪዳን (PL ኪዳናት) pact, treaty, covenant; will, testament

ኪዳን፡ብሊት Old Testament

ኪዳን፡ሐዲስ New Testament

ል L

ለ- PREP to, toward, for, to the advantage of, with regard to; used in the periphrastic possessive construction: as in ቤቱ ለንጉሥ *lit.*, his-house to-the king = the king's house; prefixed to subjunctive to indicate wish or command, ለይኩን፡ብርሃን፡ let light exist!

ለለ Reduplication of the preposition gives it a distributive sense: ለለ፡ርእሱ for each one himself

ለአከ G (IMPF ይልእክ; SUBJ ይለአክ) to send a message/messenger, commission

ተልአከ GT be sent, commissioned; to serve, minister to, administer to (COMP)

መልአክ (PL መላእክት) angel, messenger; leader, ruler

ለዐለ (ይልዐል) G to be high, superior, elevated

ተልዐለ GT to rise, rise up, raise oneself, be raised, be lifted up, ascend, be superior, be exalted, be extolled

አልዐለ CG/CD lift up, raise up, elevate, exalt, extol

ላዕለ- (w/ CLIT PRON: ላዕሌ-) PREP above, against, on, upon, over, about, concerning

በላዕለ upon, on high, upon, in, among, by, through, against

ልብ (PL አልባብ) heart; mind, intellect, understanding, consciousness, ideas

ልብን balsam (tree or incense from the resin)

ለብሰ G (IMPF ይለብስ, SUBJ ይልበስ) to get dressed; to clothe (COMP, ለ-)

አልበሰ CG to clothe, dress (COMP-person) in (COMP-garment)

ልብስ (PL አልባስ) clothes, clothing; a garment

ለበወ D to comprehend, understand; to be intelligent; to be aware, conscious of (እም)

አለበወ CD CAUSATIVE; to instruct

ልጓም (PL ልጓማት አልጓም) bridle, rein, halter

ሌጌዎን Legion

ለህበ G (IMPF ይለህብ, SUBJ ይልሀብ) to burn, blaze, flame

ላህብ flame, heat glow

ልህቀ G (IMPF ይለሁቅ, SUBJ ይልሀቅ) to grow, grow up, grow old; reach manhood; ዘይልህቅelder

ሊቅ (PL ሊቃን, ሊቃውንት, ሊቃናት) elder, chief, master, magistrate

ልሂቅ (F ልሂቅት; ልህቅት) ADJ old, grown-up, adult, senior, presbyter

ለሊ- PRON -self (typically used in apposition to subjects), ወለሊሁኒ፡ውስተ፡ሐመር and he himself was in the boat

[ል-ል-ይ] አሌለየ CQ/L to spend the night; to rise while it is still dark

ሌሊት (PL ለያልይ) night

ለምጽleprosy, scab

ሊቅ (PL ሊቃን, ሊቃውንት, ሊቃናት) elder, chief, master, magistrate

ልሳን (PL ልሳናት) tongue, language, speech

ም M

-ም ENCLITIC PART for emphasis

ሚ- INTERROG PART what?

    ሚመጠነ how much?

    ሚጊዜ when?

    ሚኪ how?

ማእድ (PL ማእዳት) table, banquet, meal

ማእስ / ማዕስ (PL አምእስት) skin, hide, leather

ምእት (PL አምኣት) hundred

ማእዘ INTERR ADV when?

ተምዕዐ / ተምዐ GT to become angry, enraged

    ተማዕዐ GLT to get mad at one another

    አምዕዐ CG to enrage, provoke, irritate, inspire anger

    መዐት / መዓት wrath

ማዕድ see ማእድ

መዓልት see ወዐለ

ምዕረ ADV once, one time

አማዕረረ CQ to sweeten

    መዐር / መዓር honey; honeycomb

    መዐር IDEM

    መዐር፡ጸደና wild honey

    መዐር sweet

ምዕዘ G (IMPF ይመዕዝ, SUBJ ይምዐዝ) to smell good, be fragrant

    አምዐዘ CG to scent, perfume

    ተምዕዘ DT to be scented, fragrant

    ምዑዝ (F ምዕዝት) PASS PTCP fragrant, sweet

    መዐዘ scent, perfume, fragrance

መገበ D to administer, be in charge of (COMP); to surround and protect (with: በ-)

    ምግብ office, post, duty, ministry

    መጋቢ (PL መጋብያን, መገብት) administrator, guardian; a general designation for various types of rulers: prefect, proconsul, satrap governor

መጋቢት Eth. month name: Mar.10–Apr. 8

አመግዘአ CQ to fatten (cattle)

መግዘአ (PL መጋዝእት) fattened cattle, fatlings

ምድር (PL ምድራት, አምዳር) the earth; earth, ground, soil; land, field, region district, country

    ምድረ፡ጽባሕ eastern country

    አርዌ፡ምድር snake

    ምድራዊ (F ምድራዊት) worldly, of the world

መጸጸ G (IMPF ይመጽጽ, SUBJ ይምጸጽ) to ferment, be sour, acidic

    መጺጽ (F ምጽጽ) PASS PTCP fermented

መጸው spring (season)

መሀረ D to teach, instruct, train, discipline, educate (COMP or በ-, በእንተ)

    ተመህረ / ተምህረ DT to be taught, instructed; to learn (COMP)

    ምሁር PASS PTCP learned, expert in (COMP or በ-)

    መምህር (F መምህርት) teacher

    ትምህርት (PL ትምህርታት) what is taught, doctrine, teaching; study, learning

    መህሮት teaching, doctrine

ማህረከ Q to take captive, take as booty

    ምህርካ booty, spoils

መሐለ G (IMPF ይመሕል, SUBJ ይምሐል) to swear, take an oath

    አምሐለ CG to make swear, adjure

    ተማሕለ GLT to take a mutual oath, to conspire

    መሐላ oath, treaty

ተማሕለለ QT to beseech, supplicate

    ምሕላ supplication(s)

ምሕረ G (IMPF ይመሕር, SUBJ ይምሐር) to have mercy on, pity on, pardon (ለ-COMP or CLIT PRON)

    አምሐረ CG to move (COMP) to pity

    ተምሕረ GT to be shown pity/mercy

    አስተምሐረ CGT to be merciful

    ምሕረት (PL ምሥሪታት) mercy, pity

    መሓሪ (one who is) merciful

መሐወ G (IMPF ይምሑ, SUBJ ይምሑ/ይምሐው) to uproot, pluck out

    ተማሕዘ GLT to fall/be in love; to commit adultery

መሐዝ (PL መሐዛን) lover (M or F)

መሐዛ (PL መሐዛት) youth, a youth; lover (M or F)

ማሕዝን illicit affairs

ተመከሐ DT to boast

    ምክሕ NOUN boasting

    ትምክሕት IDEM

    መካሕ boastful

መከነ G (IMPF ይመክን, SUBJ ይምከን) to be sterile, childless

    መከን D to orphan

    አምከነ CG IDEM

    መካን ADJ sterile, childless, barren

    ምክነት childlessness

አመከነየ CQ to pretend, make excuses

    ምክንያት (false) excuse, pretext; reason, cause

መከረ G (IMPF ይመክር, SUBJ ይምከር) to plan, propose, decide on (COMP or SUBJ); to take counsel with (ምስለ)

    አምከረ CG to advise, give counsel to (COMP)

    ተማከረ GLT to take counsel together, to advise one another, consult, devise a plan, plot; to deliberate and decide (to do: SUBJ)

    ምክር plan, counsel, advice; consideration, deliberation; wisdom; opinion, point of view

    መካሪ counselor, advisor

    መምክር (PL መማክርት) IDEM

መከረ D to test, tempt, examine

    ተመከረ DT to be tested, tempted, tried

    አምከረ CD to test, try, tempt, examine, prove, explore (COMP)

    ምኩር (F ምክርት) PASS PTCP tempted, tried

    መከራ (PL መከራት) TEMPTATION, TESTING, TRYING, EXAMINATION

መልአ G (IMPF ይመልእ, SUBJ ይምላእ) (1) to be full, filled of/with (COMP or አምነ); to be fulfilled, completed; to abound, be abundant; (2) to fill (COMP) with (COMP, ላዕለ/ውስተ/በ-)

    ተመልአ GT to be filled with (COMP or በ-)

    ምሉእ (F ምልእት) PASS PTCP full of (አም- or COMP); abundant, copious; filling (COMP)

    ምልእ what fills

    በምልኡ w/CLIT PRON, fully, completely; e.g., በምልኡ he fully, he completely, በምልአሙ all of them, they together

መልአ see መልዐ

መልዐ D to set out, continue a journey, hurry, pass on hastily

መልገ G (IMPF ይመልግ, SUBJ ይምላግ) to tear out, uproot, draw out

    ምሉግ (F ምልግት) PASS PTCP uprooted, torn out

መለከ G (IMPF ይመልክ, SUBJ ይምልክ) to take possession of, occupy, rule

    ትመልከ GT PASS; also: to be made lord or divine

    አምለከ CG to worship God, to worship as a god (COMP or ለ-)

    ምሉክ (F ምልክት) PASS PTCP occupied, possessed, subject; pious

    መላኪ owner, ruler, heir

    ምልክና dominion, power, authority

    አምላክ (PL አማልክት) the Lord, god (PL connotes false gods)

    አምላካዊ divine

    መለኮት lordship, deity, divinity

    መለኮታዊ divine

    መምለኪ one who worships God or gods

ሚመ COORD either, or, whether

    ወሚመ IDEM

መኑ (COMP መነ) INTERROG PRON who?

    መኑሂ / መኑኒ anyone, no one

ምንዳቤ affliction, torment, distress, calamity, adversity, misery, hardship

መንገለ PREP (w/ CLIT PRON መንገሌ-) to, toward, in the direction of, beside, with regard to

    በመንገለ IDEM

    አምመንገለ from the direction of; on the part of

መነነ D to reject, repudiate, despise

    ምኑን (F ምንንት) PASS PTCP rejected, despised; unsuitable, worthless, vile

ምናኔ repudiation, rejection; worthlessness, wickedness

አመንሰወ CQ to lead to destruction/temptation

ምንስው· liable to temptation/punishment

መንሱት (PL መናስው·) temptation, danger; calamity, divine punishment

ምንሳዊ IDEM

ምንት (COMP ምንተ) INTERROG PRON what?

ምንተኑ why?

ለምንት why?

በምንተ why?

ምንትሂ / ምንትኑ anything, nothing

ሞቅሐ Q to put into chains/bonds, cast into prison

ሞቅሕ (PL መዋቅሕት) bonds, fetters, chains

ቤተ ሞቅሕ prison

ተመርዐወ QT to marry (a woman)

መርዓ wedding, marriage

መርዓዊ (PL መርዓዊያን) groom, son-in-law

መርዓት (PL መራዕው·) bride, daughter-in-law

መረገ G to plaster

ምሩግ (F ምርግት) PASS PTCP plastered

መርግ plaster

ተመርጐዛ QT to lean upon

ምርጉዝ staff

መርሐ G (IMPF ይመርሕ, SUBJ ይምራሕ) to lead (COMP), guide; to show the way to (CLIT PRON)

መርሕ (PL አምርሕት) leader, guide

መረ / መረረ G (IMPF ይመርር, SUBJ ይምርር/ይምሬር) to be bitter (*lit.* and *fig.*)

CG አምረረ to be bitter; to make bitter, exacerbate, aggravate; to behave bitterly

መሪር (F መራር) bitter

ምረር (PL ምሬራት) bitterness

ምሬት bitterness, anger, rancor; rebellion

ሜረት dirt, dust

መርታዊ ADJ dust, of dust

ተመረየ DT = ትማረየ GLT to divine, practice divination, soothsaying

ማሪ (PL ማርያን, ማሪይት) heathen priest, soothsayer

ሜስ (PL አምያስ) drink made from fermented honey, mead

መስሐ G (IMPF ይመስሕ, SUBJ ይምሳሕ) to dine, sup, feast, eat a mid-day meal

አምስሐ CG CAUS; also: to invite for a meal, prepare a meal

ምሳሕ meal, dinner; banquet, feast

መሲሕ (F ምሳሕ) PASS PTCP anointed; the Anointed, Messiah

መሲሓዊ ADJ Christian

ምስኪን pauper, poor person

ምስኪነት poverty

መስከረም Eth. month name: Sept. 11–Oct. 10

መሰለ G (IMPF ይመስል, SUBJ ይምሰል) to resemble, be like (COMP); to seem, appear as (COMP); also impersonal w/ CLIT PRON of patient: it seems to, e.g., መሰሎ it seemed to him

አምሰለ CG to regard as, hold (COMP) as equivalent to (COMP or ከመ)

መሰለ D to compare, liken, form, make a form, make an image, use a parable, speak in parables

ምስለ PREP (w/ CLIT PRON: ምስሌ-) with, in the company of, in addition to

ምስል (PL ምስላት, ምሰል, አምሳል) likeness, form, image; proverb, parable, similitude

አምሳል PL of ምስል; also: aspect, form, likeness, analogy; በአምሳለ in the manner of

ማሰነ L to be ruined, destroyed; to perish; to become corrupt, rotten

አማሰነ CL to corrupt, destroy, wipe out

ሙሱን (F ምስንት) PASS PTCP corrupt(ed)

ሙስና corruption (physical, moral), destruction

መሳኒ perishable, corruptible

ምስጢር (PL ምስጢራት) mystery; the Eucharist

መሰየ (ይምሰይ/ ይመሲ) G become evening

ምሴት (PL ምሴታት) evening, twilight

መሠጠ G (IMPF ይመስጥ, SUBJ ይምስጥ) to snatch (COMP), snatch away, seize and carry off by force

ተመሥጠ GT PASS and REFLEX

አምሠጠ CG to flee, escape

ምሡጥ (F ምሥጥት) PASS PTCP seized, snatched

መሣጢ (PL መሠጥ) rapacious, violent

መምሥጥ handle, lever

መጽአ G (IMPF ይመጽእ, SUBJ ይምጻእ) to come; to happen to, to occur to, to come upon

አምጽአ CG to bring, offer (COMP); to cause (COMP) to happen, bring about (COMP)

ምጽአት arrival, advent, coming

ምምጻእ place of origin

መጸወተ Q to give alms, practice charity

ተመጸወተ QT to receive alms

ምጽዋት act of charity, alms

ምት (PL አምታት) husband

መትሀ G (IMPF ይመትህ, SUBJ ይምታህ) to be deceptive in appearance

ምትህት (PL ምትህታት) phantom, fantasy, specter

መተረ G (IMPF ይመትር, SUBJ ይምትር) to cut, cut off (lit. and fig.); to decree

ምቱር (F ምትርት) PASS PTCP cut off, amputated; decided, decreed

ምትረት NOUN cutting (off)

ምታር fragment, segment

መጠነ PREP during, according to, about, at a distance (of), as long as, as large as

ዘመጠነ as great as

በሚመተን for how much?

አምጣነ CONJ as long as, as large as, as often as, as many as as much as, in accordance with, according to, in proportion to, to the extent of, in regard to, like, since

መጠወ D to surrender, hand over, grant, consign, present, transmit (COMP; to: CLIT PRON or ለ-)

ምጡው handed over, delivered

[ም-ው-አ] ሞአ G (IMPF ይመውእ, SUBJ ይማእ) to conquer, defeat, subdue

አምአ / አምአአ CG to make (COMP) victorious over (ላዕለ/ በ-)

ሙአት victory (for self); defeat (for another)

መዋኢ victorious, victor, conqueror

[ም-ው-ቅ] ሞቀ G (IMPF ይመውቅ, SUBJ ይሙቅ) to grow hot; to become intense (of the heat)

ሞቅ heat

ሙቀት heat

ሙውቅ (F ምውቅት) PASS PTCP hot

[ም-ው-ት] ሞተ G (IMPF ይመውት, SUBJ ይሙት) to die

አሞተ / አመተ CG to let die; to put to death; to have killed

ሞት death

ምውት (F ምውት; PL ምዊታን, ምውታን, ሙታን) dead

መዋቲ mortal

ማውታ corpse; the dead

ማይ (PL ማያት) water; liquid

[ም-ይ-ጥ] ሜጠ G (IMPF ይመይጥ, SUBJ ይሚጥ) to turn aside; to turn away (COMP), divert; to turn, direct; to return (COMP) to its original place, restore; to convert, transform (COMP) into (ለ-, ውስተ)

ተመይጠ GT PASS and REFLEX of G; also: to face about, return, go back, turn, turn back, turn away, turn against; to be converted (religious sense)

መዘነ / መዝነ G to laugh, laugh at, jeer at

ን N

ነ- INTRODUCTORY PART used to prepose and emphasize a pronominal element; inflected: ነየ as for me, behold me, ነዮ ... him, ነያ ... her, ነየነ ... us, ነዮሙ ... them (M), ነዮን ... them (F)

-ኑ INTERROG PART

-ኒ ENCLITIC PART also, even, the very, likewise, again; as for, as for one's part; added to INTERROG PRON to form INDEF PRON

ንእሰ G (IMPF ይንእስ, SUBJ ይንአስ) to be small, little (in size or importance); to be young

ንኡስ (F ንእስት) PASS PTCP small, little, young

ነአስ a young girl

ንእስ childhood, infancy

ምስቲት a little, a small amount

ንስቲተ ADV a little, for a little while

በበንስቲት፡ንስቲተ little by little, gradually, slowly

ንዕ- IMV: come; MS ንዕ, FS ንዒ, MP ንዑ, FP ንዓ

ነወ G (IMPF ይነዐው, SUBJ ይነዐው) to hunt; to catch birds

    ነዓዊ hunter

    ነዐዌ/ ናዐዌ hunting

አንብዐ CG to weep

    እንብዕ (PL አምባዕ) tear(s)

ነበበ G (IMPF ይነብብ, SUBJ ይንብብ) to speak, proclaim, tell to (ለ- or CLIT PRON); be eloquent

    ተነበ GT to be read, recited

    ተናበበ GLT to speak with someone (ምስለ, ኅበ, or COMP)

    CG አንበበ to read (COMP), chant, proclaim, recite; to study, meditate on (COMP)

    ንባብ speech; what one says, manner of speaking

    ነባቢ. garrulous, talkative, boastful; capable of speech, rational

አንበልበለ Q/N to flame

    ነበልባል flame

ነበረ G (IMPF ይነብር, SUBJ ይንበር) to sit, sit down; to stay, remain; to continue; to live, dwell

    አንበረ CG to set, place, deposit; to settle, cause to dwell

    ንቡር (F ንብርት) PASS PTCP sitting, seated, situated; residing; NOUN: resident

    ንብረት NOUN sitting down; session; position; condition, state; manner or mode of life; dwelling, abode

    መንበር (PL መናብርት) throne, seat, chair

    መንበርት state, condition, mode of life

    ምንባር (PL ምንባራት) place where something is put; place of residence; base, foundation

ነቢይ (PL ነቢያት, ነብያት) prophet

    ተነበየ DT to prophesy

    ትንቢት prophecy

ነድአ G (IMPF ይነድእ, SUBJ ይንዳእ) to drive (as cattle)

ነዳኢ. one who drives, expels

ነደደ / ነደ G (IMPF ይነድድ, SUBJ ይንደድ) to burn (SUBJECT is fire, flame, anger)

    አንደደ CG to set afire, ignite (COMP)

    ተናደደ GLT to burn with a mutual passion

    አንደደ CG to set afire, ignite (COMP)

    ተናደደ GLT to burn with a mutual passion

    ንዱድ (F ንድድት) PASS PTCP burning, flaming

    ነደት flame, burning

    ነድ flame

    ነደ IDEM

    ነዳዲ ADJ burning, blazing (of fire, wrath, lust)

    ምንዳድ furnace, oven, fireplace

ነደቀ G (IMPF ይነድቅ, SUBJ ይንድቅ) to build, erect

    ንድቅ building, structure, wall

    ነዳቂ builder

ነድየ G (IMPF ይነዲ, SUBJ ይንዲ) to be poor, destitute; to be deficient (in: በ-)

    አንደየ CG to reduce to poverty

    ንድት / ንድየት poverty

    ነዳይ ADJ poor, destitute, deficient; NOUN poor person

ነዕፀ G (IMPF ይነዕፅ, SUBJ ይንፃዕ) to strike, beat, knock down, trample

ነፍኀ G (IMPF ይነፍኅ, SUBJ ይንፋኅ) to blow, breath; to blow into, inflate

    ተነፍኀ GT to be inflated, to swell

    ንፍኀት inflation, blowing

ነፈቀ G (IMPF ይነፍቅ, SUBJ ይንፍቅ) to tear off, tear away, split, divide in two, separate

    ናፈቀ L to divide (usually in half, into two parts or factions); to be hesitant, doubtful, skeptical

    ተናፈቀ GLT to be divided, broken up into factions, be divided against oneself, be half-heated, be a heretic, be hypocritical

    ተነፍቀ GT IDEM

    ንፉቅ (F ንፍቅት) PASS PTCP divided, split

    ኑፉቅ hesitant, doubtful

    ነፍቅ compartment, box

ንፍቅ half, one of two parts

ኑፋቄ division, dissension, skepticism

መንፈቅ half, one of two parts; faction, sect, splinter-group; the half-way point

ነፍሰ G (IMPF ይነፍስ, SUBJ ይንፍስ) to blow (of wind or spirit)

   አንፈስ CG to breathe; to rest, find relief; to give (COMP) rest or relief

   ነፍስ (PL ነፍሳት) soul, spirit, breath; a person, life; self

   ነፋስ (PL ነፋሳት) wind, air, spirit

   ምነፈስ (PL መናፍስት) spirit; breathe, wind; a spirit or demon; essence

   መንፈሳዊ (F መንፈሳዊት) spiritual, of the spirit

ነፈጸ G (IMPF ይነፍጽ, SUBJ ይንፍጽ) to flee, escape

   ነፋጺ fugitive

   ነፋጺት remnant, what survives

ነገደ G (IMPF ይነግድ, SUBJ ይንግድ) to make a journey, to travel on business

   ንግድ travel, trade

   ነጋድ (PL ነጋዳን) a traveler, stranger, guest

   ነጋዲ traveler, merchant

   መንገድ public road, highway; trip, journey, pilgrimage

ነጐድ (PL ነጐዳዳት) thunder

ነገፈ G (IMPF ይነግፍ, SUBJ ይንግፍ) to knock off, shake off, dispel

   ተነግፈ GT PASS; also: to lose leaves

   ንጉፍ (F ንግፍት) PASS PTCP deciduous

ነግሀ G (IMPF ይነግህ, SUBJ ይንጋህ) to dawn, grow light

   አንግሀ CG to do something early in the day

   ነግህ early morning

ነገረ G (IMPF ይነግር, SUBJ ይንግር) to say, tell, recite, declare, indicate, inform (COMP; to: CLIT PRON or ለ-)

   ተነግረ GT to be told, spoken

   ተናገረ GLT speak to, with (ለ-, ምስለ, ኀበ, or COMP; about: በ-/በእንተ or COMP); to speak (a language: በ-)

   ነገር (PL ነገራት) speech, account, narrative, word, pronouncement, discourse; thing, affair, situation

አንገረገ Q/N to roll, spin

   ነገርጋር a type of epilepsy; rolling, spinning

አንገርጐረ Q/N to be angry, vexed; to murmur, mutter

ነግሠ G (IMPF ይነግሥ, SUBJ ይንግሥ) to become king, ruler; to rule over (ለ- / ላዕለ / ዲበ)

   አንገሠ CG to make (COMP) king over (ለ- / ላዕለ)

   ንግሥ reign, rule

   ንጉሥ (PL ነገሥት) king, ruler

   ንግሥት (PL ንግስታት) queen

   ነጋሢ (PL ነገሥት) king, ruler

   መንግሥት (PL መንግሥታት) kingdom, dominion; kingship, majesty

ናሁ INTRO PART behold!, now!

ንሕነ PRON 1CP we

ናሕስ (PL አንሕስት) roof, rooftop

ነሐሤ/ ነሐሴ Eth. month name: Aug. 7–Sept. 5

ንሕለ G (IMPF ይነሕል, SUBJ ይንሐል) to collapse, fall into ruin, be destroyed

   አንሕለ CG to knock down, destroy devastate, topple

[ን-ክ-ር] አንከረ CG to wonder, marvel, be amazed at (COMP or እምነ/በእንተ/በ-); to regard (COMP) as strange or marvelous

   ተናከረ GLT to repudiate, renounce, reject, estrange oneself, be alienated from (COMP)

   ነኪር (F ነካር; PL ነከርት) ADJ strange, alien, foreign; other, different; marvelous, wonderful

   መንክር (F ምንክርት; PL ምንክራት) ADJ marvelous, wondrous; NOUN miracle, marvel, wonder

አንኰርኰረ Q/N to roll

   ነኰርኰር NOUN rolling

   መንኰራኵር wheel

ትነአለወ QT to function as a shepherd, to tend flocks

   ኖላዊ (PL ኖሎት) shepherd

ነቅዐ G (IMPF ይነቅዕ, SUBJ ይንቃዕ) to split, burst, rupture

   አንቅዐ CG = bivalent of G ነቅዐ

   ንቁዕ (F ንቅዕት) PASS PTCP split, ruptured, cracked

ነቅዕ (PL አንቅዐት) fountain, source, spring

ንቄዐት split, crack, fissure

መንቅዐት thigh

አንቅሀ CG to awake, wake up, rouse, stir up

አንቀልቀለ Q/N to move, shake, quake; to shake, agitate (COMP)

ነቀልቃል motion, shaking, agitation

ነቊር one-eyed, blind

ነቀወ G (IMPF ይነቁ, SUBJ ይንቁ) = D to emit sound (subject may be bird or animal)

ነስሐ D to repent, do penance, regret, be sorry

 ተነስሐ DT IDEM

 ንሱሕ (F ንስሕት) PASS PTCP repentant

 ነሳሒ one who is repentant

 ንስሓ repentance, regret, penitence

ንስር (PL አንስር) eagle, vulture

አንሶሰወ Q/N to walk, stroll

ነሥአ G (IMPF ይነሥእ, SUBJ ይንሣእ) to raise, lift, pick up (COMP); to take, receive, accept (COMP); to capture (COMP); to take (a wife)

 ተንሥአ see ት-ን-ሥ-አ

 አንሥአ CG CAUS; also: to take up; to stir up, awaken, resuscitate

 ትንሣኤ resurrection

ነሠተ G (IMPF ይነሥት, SUBJ ይንሥት) to destroy, overturn, pull down, tear asunder, overthrow, abolish, demolish, annul

 ንሡት (F ንሥትት) PASS PTCP destroyed

 ንሥተት destruction

ነጸፈ G (IMPF ይነጽፍ, SUBJ ይንጽፍ) to spread, lay out

 ንጹፍ (F ንጽፍት) PASS PTCP spread

 መንጸፍ anything laid out: rug, covering

አንፍጸፈ Q/N to ooze, drip; to exude (COMP) in drops

 ነጸፍጻፍ juice, drops

 ጸፍጸፍ IDEM

ነጽሐ G (IMPF ይነጽሕ, SUBJ ይንጻሕ) to be pure, clean, cleansed

 አንጽሐ CG CAUSATIVE purify, make clean, cleanse, make pure, keep pure, consider pure, purge, pronounce clean, hold innocent, hold guiltless

 ንጹሕ (F ንጽሕት) PASS PTCP pure, clean; innocent, uncorrupted, sincere

 ንጽሕ purification, cleansing

 ንጽሕና purity, chastity, innocence

 መንጽሒ one who purifies

ነጸረ D to look, look up to, view, watch, regard, be on watch, observe, consider, examine, survey, look at (COMP or ውስተ, ኀበ)

 ተናጸረ GLT to look at one another

 አንጸረ CG to look

 አንጸረ ADV opposite, toward, in front of

 ንጸሬ are look, glance, viewing; sight (ability to see)

አንጠዐ CG to tear off/apart

ነጠፈ G (IMPF ይነጥፍ, SUBJ ይንጥፍ) to strain out

 ንጡፍ (F ንጥፍት) PASS PTCP strained, pure

 መንጠፍት strainer, sieve

መንጦላዕት (PL መንጠዋሌዐ) veil, covering

ነዋ INTRODUCTORY PART equivalent to ናሁ

[ን-ው-ኀ] ኖኀ G (IMPF ይነውኀ, SUBJ ይኑኀ) to be high, lofty; to be tall, long; to be distant, far off

 አኖኀ / አንኀ CG to extend, put forth (e.g., one's hand); to lengthen, make long(er); to raise high, elevate, exalt

 ነዋኀ (F ነዋኀት) ADJ high

[ን-ው-ም] ኖመ G (IMPF ይነውም, SUBJ ይኑም) to sleep

 ንዊም / ንውም (F ምውምት) PASS PTCP (one who) is sleeping

 ንዋም sleep

ንዋይ (PL ንዋያት) vessel, utensil, instrument; property, possessions, wealth, estate, fortunate, money; male genitals

ነየ see ነ-

ናዘዘ L to console, comfort

 ናዛዚ consoler, comforter

 ኑዛዜ consolation, comfort

ናዝራዊ (F ናዝራዊት) ADJ Nazarite

ፐ P

[none]

ጵ P

ጵጉሜን Eth. month name: Sept. 6–Sept. 10

ጲላጦስ Pilate

ጳጳስ (PL ጳጳሳት) bishop

    ሊቀ፡ጳጳሳት archbishop

    ጵጵስና the office of ጳጳስ: episcopacy, see

ጴጥሮስ Peter

ቀ Q

ቋዕ (PL ቋዓት) raven, crow

ቀብአ G (IMPF ይቀብእ, SUBJ ይቅባእ) to smear, anoint

    ተቀብአ GT PASS and REFLEX

    ቅቡእ (F ቅብእት) PASS PTCP smeared, anointed

    ቅብእ (olive) oil, ointment, butter

    ቅብአት anointing

ተቀበለ DT to go out to meet; to welcome, accept, receive

    ቀበላ a meeting, encounter

ቀበረ G (IMPF ይቀብር, SUBJ ይቅብር) to bury, inter

    ቅቡር (F ቅብርት) PASS PTCP buried

    ቀብር burial, funeral

    መቅበርት (PL መቃብር, መቅበርታት) grave, tomb, sepulcher; PL also = SG

ቆብር (PL ቆበራት) blackness, darkness

ቀብጸ G (IMPF ይቀብጽ, SUBJ ይቅብጽ) to be discouraged, be in distress

    ቅቡጽ (F ቅብጽት) PASS PTCP discouraged, despairing

    ቅብአት despair

ቀድሐ G (IMPF ይቀድሕ, SUBJ ይቅዳሕ) to draw water

    ቀዳሒ drawer of water; cupbearer

    መቅድሕት water-jar

ቀደመ G (IMPF ይቀድም, SUBJ ይቅድም) to go before, precede (CLIT PRON or ለ-/እምነ); with INF or COORD verb: to do beforehand, to do first

    አቅደመ CG to put or place first; to happen/exist first/ previously/ beforehand; with inf or COORD verb = G in same usage

    ተቀድመ GT to occur first/beforehand

    ተቀደመ GLT to go/come out to meet

    ቀዳሚ NOUN (PL ቀደምት): beginning; first or best of something; the ancients, men of old, those who came before; nobles, princes; ADJ: first, previous, prior, antecedent; ADV: at first, in the beginning, previously

    ቀዳሜ, ቀዳሚሁ ADV IDEM

    ቀዳሚት NOUN beginning

    ቅድመ PREP before (of place), in the presence of; በቅድመ IDEM; እምቅድመ from before, from the presence of; before (of time), prior to; CONJ (with SUBJ) before; ADV previously, beforehand

    ቀዲሙ ADV first, at first, previously, before this

    እምቀዲሙ IDEM; also used as a noun in a few fixed expressions: መዋዕለ ቀዲሙ days of old; ዘቀዲሙ things of old

    መቅድም NOUN beginning

    መቅድመ ADV first, beforehand

ቀደሰ D to sanctify, ordain, dedicate, consecrate, make or regard (COMP) as holy; to perform sacred offices

    ቅዱስ (F ቅድስት) holy, sacred, dedicated, consecrated; as NOUN: saint, esp. in titles

    ቅድሳት holiness, sanctity, sacredness, sanctuary

    ቅድስነ IDEM

    ቅዳሴ (PL ቅዳሴያት) sanctification, consecration; the sacred service or liturgy

    መቅደስ temple, sanctuary

ቅፍርናሖም PN Capernaum

ቃል (PL ቃላት) voice, sound, word, saying, discourse, expression, maxim, saying, thing

ቀኅልዔ (F ቀኅልዔ; PL ቀኅልዔያት) servant, domestic

ቀለደ G (IMPF ይቀልድ, SUBJ ይቅልድ) collect water, draw water

    መቅለድ (PL መቃልድ) bucket, bowl, basin, cup

ቀለለ G (IMPF ይቀልል, SUBJ ይቅልል)= D to be light, easy, swift, slight, rapid

አቅለለ CG to lighten, diminish a burden; to make swift, agile; to scorn, disdain, make light of

አቀልለ CD to consider light, to lighten

አስተቃለለ CGLT to lighten; to scorn, disdain, despise, revile

ቀሊል (F ቀላል) light, swift

መቅለሊ one who lightens or alleviates

ቀንአ G (IMPF ይቀንእ, SUBJ ይቅናእ) to be zealous, eager; to envy, be jealous of (person: ለ-; thing: እምነ); to emulate, imitate (COMP)

አቅንአ CG to incite to zeal or imitation

ተቃንአ GLT to be jealous of one another

አስተቃንአ CGLT to cause to be mutually envious

ቀንእ = ቅንአት jealousy; zeal; emulation, intense hate or love

ቀናኢ one who is jealous, zealous

ቀናናዊ ADJ Canaanite

ቁንቁኔ moth, worm

ቁንጽል (PL ቄናጽል) wolf, fox

ቅናት (PL ቅናታት, ቅናውት) belt, girdle, sash

ቀነየ G (IMPF ይቀኒ, SUBJ ይቅኒ) to acquire, buy, to reduce to servitude, to subject, rule; to force to work

አቅነየ CG IDEM

ተቀንየ GT PASS of G; also: to render service, attend, serve, minister to, worship, perform religious services, till (the land), be in bondage

ቅኑይ (F ቅኒት) PASS PTCP subject, servant, slave

ቅኔ servitude; service, ministry; task, office, function

ቅንየት domination, dominion, subjection

ቀርበ G (IMPF ይቀርብ, SUBJ ይቅረብ) to draw near, approach, be connected, be like, be celebrated

ተቃረበ GLT RECIPR; also: to have sexual intercourse

ቅሩብ (F ቅርብት) PASS PTCP near, nearby, adjacent; at hand, nigh (of time)

በቅሩብ PREP near

ቀርባን (PL ቀርባናት) offering, sacrifice

ምቅራብ neighborhood, vicinity

ተቃረነ GLT to oppose, resist

ቀርን (PL አቅርንት) horn (of animal), horn (blown in battle, etc.); tip, end

ተቃራኒ contrary, resisting, opposing

መስተቃርን IDEM

ቄረ/ ቄረረ G (IMPF ይቄርር, SUBJ ይቀርር) to be cold, cool; to cool (of anger)

ቄሪር (F ቄራር) cold, cool

ቍር cold, coldness

ቀረጸ G (IMPF ይቀርጽ, SUBJ ይቅርጽ) to incise, sculpt

ቅርጸት / ቃርጸት the stroke of a letter; stroke, mark, incision

ቀሰመ D to season, make tasty

ቅሱም (F ቅስምት) PASS PTCP well seasoned, tasty

መቅስም (PL መቃስም) highly seasoned food

ቀሲስ (PL ቀሳውስት) priest, presbyter, elder

ቀስት (PL አቅስስት, አቅስት) bow

ቀስታም bow, shepherd's crook, rod

ቀሠፈ G (IMPF ይቀሥፍ, SUBJ ይቅሥፍ) to beat, whip; to afflict, punish

ቅሡፍ (F ቅሥፍት) PASS PTCP beaten, whipped, afflicted

ቅሥፈት punishment, affliction

መቅሠፍት (PL መቅሠፍታት) punishment, beating, whipping; divine punishment

ቀሠመ G (IMPF ይቀሥም, SUBJ ይቅሥም) to pick (fruit), gather, collect, harvest

ቀሥም (PL አቅሣም) harvest, picking; the crops harvested

ቀሣሚ / ቀሣም a picker of fruit

አስተቀጸለ CDT to crown (someone: CLIT PRON) with (COMP)

ቀጸላ crown, diadem

ቄጽል (PL አቀጽል) leaf, foliage

ቀጸረ G to enclose or fortify with a wall

ቅጽር / ቀጽር (PL አቅጻር) wall, enclosure, fortification wall

ቀተለ G to kill, murder, slay, execute, slaughter, attack, engage in combat, fight, wage war with (COMP or ምስለ)

ቀ

ተቃተለ GLT to fight or kill one another; to fight with (ምስለ or COMP)

ቀትል NOUN killing, murder; battle, fighting

ቅትለት murder, killing

ቀታሊ (PL ቀተልት) murderer, killer

ቀተረ D to seal, lock

ቅቱር (F ቅትርት) PASS PTCP locked, sealed

ቀትር noon, midday

ቀጢን (F ቀጣን; PL ቀጠንት) fine, delicate; NOUN fine clothes

ቅጥነት fineness, delicacy

ቀጢን (COLL) servants, domestics

መቅጠን (PL መቃጥን) fishhook, line with hook

ቀጥቀጠ Q to grind; to break

ቅጥቁጥ (F ቅጥቅጥት) PASS PTCP ground, broken

ቅጥቃጤ NOUN grinding, breaking, destruction

[ቅ-ው-ም] ቆመ G (IMPF ይቀውም, SUBJ ይቀም) to arise, stand; to stand, take a position; be in charge, be set up, be established; to come to a halt, stop, remain, abide, last, endure

ተቃወመ GLT to oppose, withstand, take a stand against (COMP or ምስለ/ ላዕለ/ ቅድመ); to stand up for (ለ-)

አቆመ / አቀመ CG to set up, establish; to confirm the truth of; to accomplish; to cause to cease (e.g., rain)

ቆም stature, height

ቀመት nature, state, condition

ቀዋሚ standing, stable; NOUN patron, protector

ምቅዋም (PL ምቅዋማት) location, place where one stands or stops

ተቋም pedestal, lampstand

[ቅ-ይ-ሕ] ቄሐ G (IMPF ይቀይሕ, SUBJ ይቂሕ) to grow red

ቀይሕ / ቀየሕ (F ቀያሕ) red

ቀሐት redness

ር R

ርእስ (PL አርእስት) head; top, summit; chief, leader; capital, chapter; with CLIT PRON: self

ርእየ G (IMPF ይሬኢ, SUBJ ይርአይ) to see, look, look at, regard, contemplate, consider, take notice of, explore

ተርእየ GT to appear, seem

አርአየ CG to show (COMP) to (COMP); to reveal, make (COMP) manifest

አስተርአየ CGT to appear, become visible; to make (COMP) visible

ራአይ (PL ራአያት) vision, revelation; appearance, form, aspect

ርእይ appearance, seeing, vision

ርእየት appearance, form, aspect

ርዕደ G to tremble, quake, shudder, shake

ረዓድ trembling, terror

ርዕየ G (IMPF ይሬዒ, SUBJ ይርዐይ) to pasture, tend (herds, flocks); to graze (subject: flocks)

መርዔት (PL መራዕይ) cattle, flock, herd; pasture

መርዓይ IDEM

ምርዓይ a pasture

ረዓይ (PL ረዐይት) giant

አርባዕ (COMP አርባዐ) F; አርባዕቱ (COMP አርባዕተ) M four

ራብዕ (F ራብዕት) ADJ fourth

ረብዓዊ (F ረብዓዊት) IDEM

ራብዓይ (F ራብዒት) IDEM

ርብዕ F four

ርብዐ ADV four times

አርብዓ forty

ረበበ / ረበ G (IMPF ይረብብ, SUBJ ይርበብ) to expand (COMP), extend, spread out

ርበት expansion, extension

መርበብት net

ረባን (PL ረባናት) teacher, leader

ረብሐ G (IMPF ይረብሕ, SUBJ ይርባሕ) to gain (as) profit; to be profitable

ርባሕ / ረባሕ profit, interest, gain

ረድአ G (IMPF ይረድእ, SUBJ ይርዳእ) to help, aid, rescue, assist, protect (someone: CLIT PRON)

ረዳኢ helper, assistant

ረድኤት help, assistance; helper, assistant

ረድእ (PL አርዳእ, አርድእት) helper, assistant; disciple, follower

ተረድየ GT to lend at interest, receive interest

    ተራደየ GLT IDEM

    ርዴ interest

ረፍአ G to sew

    ርፍአት suture, sewing

    ረፋኢ tailor

    ርፉእ sewn work

    መርፍእ (PL መራፍእት) needle

ረፈቀ G (IMPF ይረፍቅ, SUBJ ይርፍቅ) to recline at a meal

    አርፈቀ CG to cause to recline at a meal

    ምርፋቅ a place to recline; a meal, party, symposium

    መርፈቅ threshold

ርግብ (PL አርጋብ) pigeon, dove

ረገፀ G (IMPF ይረግፅ, SUBJ ይርግፅ) to kick, trample

    ተራገፀ to kick one another; to writhe, toss convulsively, throw into convulsions

    አስተራገፀ CGLT CAUSATIVE of GT; to throw (COMP) into convulsions

ረገመ G (IMPF ይረግም, SUBJ ይርግም) to curse, execrate

    ርጉም (F ርግምት) PASS PTCP cursed, execrated

    ረጋሚ curser, execrator

    መርገም (PL መርገማት) curse, execration

ርህበ G (IMPF ይረሕብ, SUBJ ይርሐብ) to be wide, spacious, ample

    ርሑብ (F ርሕብት) PASS PTCP wide, spacious

    ረሒብ (F ረሐብ) IDEM

    ርሕብ width, breadth

    ራሕብ IDEM

    መርሕብ (PL መራሕብት) a wide place, street, forum, marketplace

ረሐነ G (IMPF ይረሕን, SUBJ ይርሐን) to spread (COMP) as a saddle, to saddle (COMP)

ርሕቀ G (IMPF ይረሕቅ, SUBJ ይርሐቅ) to be distant, remote, far off (both spatial and temporal)

ርሑቅ (F ርሕቅት) PASS PTCP far away, remote, distant, one who keeps away

    ርሑቀ = በርሑቅ ADV at a distance

    እምርሑቅ from afar

ርኅበ G (IMPF ይርኅብ, SUBJ ይርኃብ) to be hungry, hunger (for), desire to eat

    ርኁብ (F ርኅብት) PASS PTCP hungry, starving

    ረኃብ/ ረኃብ hunger, famine

አርኀወ CG to open

    ተርኀወ GT to open, be opened

    ርኁው (F ርኁት) PASS PTCP open

    መርኆ (PL መራኁት) key

ረከበ G (IMPF ይረክብ, SUBJ ይርከብ) to find, come upon; to acquire, invent, discover, perceive, suppose; with CLIT PRON for patient or experiencer: come upon, fall upon, come to pass, happen to

    ተረክበ GT PASS; also: to exist, be available, give an audience

    ተራከበ GLT to congregate; to join, associate with (COMP or ምስለ)

    አስተርከበ CGT to be at leisure (for); to be busy with, involved in; to be ready, convenient, opportune

    ርክበት NOUN finding; acquisition

    ምርካብ acquisition; pay, stipend

ረኵሰ G (IMPF ይረኵስ, SUBJ ይርኵስ) to be unclean, impure, polluted, contaminated; to be bad

    ርኩስ (F ርኵስት) PASS PTCP unclean, polluted, bad, abominable

    ርኵስ uncleanness, pollution; anything unclean, vile, abomination

አርመመ CG to be silent, keep silent, be tranquil, be at rest; to make silent, reduce to silence, astound

    አስተራመመ CGLT CAUS

    ተረመ GT TO be passed over in silence

    መርምም silent

    አርማሚ silent, not speaking

ረምሰሰ Q to grope, feel the way

    አረምሰሰ CQ IDEM

ረስዐ G (IMPF ይረስዕ, SUBJ ይርሳዕ) to forget; to be negligent; to err; to be impious, wicked, godless

    ተረስዐ GT PASS; also: to fall into error/ sin

    ራስዕ forgetful, negligent, impious

    ረሲዕ godless, impious, sinful

    ርስዐት forgetfulness, negligence, impiety

    ርስዓን, ርስዕና IDEM

ረስሐ G (IMPF ይረስሕ, SUBJ ይርሳሕ) to be unclean, filthy, polluted; to be subject to

    አርስሐ CG CAUS; also: to defile, pollute; to condemn, accuse

    ርሱሕ (F ርስሕት) PASS PTCP dirty, etc.; the accused, defendant

    ርስሐት (PL ርስሐታት) dirt, filth, pollution; crime, guilt

ረሰየ D to put, place, set; to impute (COMP) to (ላዕለ, ለ-); to make/regard (COMP) as/into (COMP or ከመ/ውስተ/ለ-); to make (COMP) do (SUBJ)

    ርሱይ (F ርሲት) PASS PTCP prepared, made ready, equipped

    ትርሲት adornment, equipment; adoption

ረሥአ G (IMPF ይረሥእ, SUBJ ይርሣእ) to grow old

    ርሥእ, ርሥእና, ርሥአን old age

ረትዐ G (IMPF ይረትዕ; SUBJ ይርታዕ) to become straight, be straightened, be right, be just, established, restored, well-ordered, successful, proper, righteous, truthful, sincere

    አርትዐ CG to make right, correct, straight, stable

    ርቱዕ (F ርትዕት) PASS PTCP just, righteous; straight, level, even; correct, proper, orthodox

    ራትዕ (F ራእዕት) just, righteous, truthful, sincere

    ርትዕ justice, what is right; truth

    መስተራት one who corrects, who straightens out; soldier of the guard; executioner

[ር-ው-ጽ] ሮጸ G (IMPF ይረውጽ, SUBJ ይሩጽ) to run

    ተራወጸ GLT run together, run as a group

    ረዋጺ swift, running

    ምርዋጽ distance run, course; race

ረወየ G (IMPF ይረዊ, SUBJ ይርወይ) to drink one's fill, to be satisfied with drink

አርወየ CG to give drink, water, quench third; to inebriate

አርያም (PL only) highest heaven, the heavenly heights

ስ S

-ስ - ENCLITIC PART of emphasis of contrast but, however, on the other hand

ሰአለ G (IMPF ይስእል, SUBJ ይስአል) to ask for (COMP; from someone: ኀበ, እም-, CLIT PRON)

    ተሰዐለ GT PASS; also: inquire, demand, ask

    ስአለት request, prayer, petition

ስአነ G (IMPF ይሰእን, SUBJ ይስአን) to be unable to do (INF), to be powerless, impotent, fail; to be in need of

    ተስእነ GT to be impossible

    ስኡን (F ስእንት) PASS PTCP impotent, powerless

    ስእነት impotence, inability

ሰዐት / ሰዓት (PL ሰዐታት / ስዓታት) hour, moment, time, season

ሰዐመ G (IMPF ይሰዕም, SUBJ ይስዐም) to kiss

    ስዕመት a kiss

ሰዐረ G (IMPF ይሰዕር, SUBJ ይስዐር) to remove, withdraw, cause to cease, undo, dismiss, destroy, violate, annul, dissolve, bring to an end, desecrate, fail to observe (a holiday), break (an oath)

    ስዐረት destruction, violation, annulment; dismissal, removal from office

ተሰብአ DT to become man, be incarnate

    ሰብእ (PL) people, men (PL of ብእሲ); man, mankind

    ትስብእት incarnation

ሶበ CONJ when, then

    ወከነ:ሶበ and when

    ይእተ:ሶቤ at that time

    ሶቤሃ ADV immediately, then, thereupon

ሰብእ humankind; also PL of ብእሲ.

ሰብዑ (COMP IDEM) F; ሰብዐቱ/ሰበዐቱ (COMP ሰብዐተ) M seven

    ሱብዕ F IDEM

    ሳብዕ (F ሳብዕት) ADJ seventh

    ሳብዓዊ (F ሳብዓዊት) IDEM

ሳብዓይ (F ሰቤዒት) IDEM

ሰቡዕ the seventh day (of week or month); seven days

ስብዐ ADV seven times

ሰብዓ seventy

ተሰብዐ GT DENOMINATIVE, it was made/done seven (times)

ሱብዕ (PL ሱብዓታተ) witchcraft, sorcery, spell, incantation

ሰብሐ D to praise, laud, glorify

ስቡሕ (F ስብሕት) PASS PTCP praised, glorified

ስባሔ praise, glorification, hymn

ስብሐት (PL ስብሐታት) praise, glory, majesty

ስብሓት IDEM

ሎቱ፡ስብሐት To Him be praise (formula after divine names)

ሰበከ G (IMPF ይሰብክ, SUBJ ይስብክ) = ሰበከ D to preach, proclaim, announce, cry out (COMP or በ-)

ስብከት NOUN preaching, proclamation; a preaching mission;

ሰባኪ preacher

ሰበረ G (IMPF ይሰብር, SUBJ ይስብር) to break (into pieces)

ተሰብረ GT PASS, also: to be overcome by disaster

ስቡር (F ስብርት) PASS PTCP broken

ስብር fragment, piece

ስብር IDEM

ስብረት NOUN breaking

ሰደደ G (IMPF ይሰድድ, SUBJ ይስድድ) to persecute; to drive out, banish, expel; to divorce (a wife)

ስዱድ (F ስድድት) PASS PTCP expelled, exiled

ስደት exile, expulsion; persecution

ስዳዲ persecutor; exorcist

ሲዶና PN Sidon

ስድስቱ (COMP ስድስት) M; ስሱ (COMP IDEM) F six

ስድስ F IDEM

ሳድስ (F ሳድስት) ADJ sixth

ሳድሳዊ (F ሳድሳዊት) IDEM

ሳድሳይ (F ሳድሲት) IDEM

ሰዱስ the sixth day (of the week or month); six days

ስድስ ADV six times

ስሳ sixty

ሰፍሐ G (IMPF ይሰፍሕ, SUBJ ይስፋሕ) to spread out, extend, expand; to spread (COMP) out, extend

ስፉሕ (F ስፍሕት) PASS PTCP spread out, extended; wide, spacious, ample; open, sincere, guileless; generous

ስፍሕ expansion, extension; width, expanse; sincerity; warp (of a loom)

ስፍሐት extension, width, capacity

መስፍሕ hammer, mallet; anvil

ሰፈነ G (IMPF ይሰፍን, SUBJ ይስፍን) to become strong, powerful; to exercise control, dominate, rule (over: ዲበ/ላዕለ or COMP)

ሰፋኒ ruler, controller, governor

መስፍን (PL መሳፍንት) ruler, governor, prefect, high official, judge

መስፍነ፡ምእት centurion

ምስፍና the office or status of a መስፍን

ስፍን INTERROG ADV how many? how many times?

ስፍንግ / ስፍነግ sponge

ሰፈረ G to measure out

ተሳፈረ GLT to mete out, distribute

ስፉር (F ስፍርት) PASS PTCP measured

መስፈርት (PL መሳፍር) a measure, specific amount

አስፈጠ CG to persuade, entice, seduce, deceive

ስፍጠት seduction, lure, enticement

ሰፋጢ seducer, deceiver

አስፈወ CD to promise something (COMP) to someone (COMP or ለ-)

ተሰፈወ DT to hope for, expect, look forward to (COMP)

ተስፋ (PL ተስፋት) hope, expectation, promise

ሰፈየ G (IMPF ይሰፊ, SUBJ ይስፊ) to sew

ሰፋዪ sewer, tailor, cobbler

መስፌ awl

ሰገደ G (IMPF ይሰግድ, SUBJ ይስግድ) to bow down, prostrate, adore, worship, pay homage to (ለ-/ቅድመ)

ስጉድ (F ስግድት) PASS PTCP prostrate (in a position of worship/adoration)

ስግደት prostration, act of adoration

ምስጋድ place of worship, shrine, mosque

አስገለ CG to divine, practice augury

አስተስገለ CGT IDEM; also: to consult diviners

ሰገል divination

መስግል (PL መስግላን) diviner, magician, soothsayer

ሰሐበ G (IMPF ይሰሕብ, SUBJ ይስሐብ) to pull, drag, draw; to attract to (ኀበ); to protract (ቃለ, ነገረ)

ስሕተ G (IMPF ይሰሕት, SUBJ ይስሐት) to err, to make a mistake, sin, do wrong, get lost; to stray (from a path or doctrine)

አስሐተ CG to lead astray; to lead into sin or error; mislead; to corrupt

ስሑት (F ስሕትት) PASS PTCP erring, led into error

ስሕተት (PL ስሕተታት) error, sin

ስሒት (PL ስሒታት) error, deceit

ስኂን frankincense

ሰከበ G (IMPF ይሰክብ, SUBJ ይስከብ) to lie down, be asleep, lie (with a woman)

ስኩብ (F ስክብት) PASS PTCP lying down

ምስካብ (PL መስካባት) place to lie down; bed, couch

አስካል (PL አስካላት) grape(s)

ሰከመ G to carry on the shoulders

ሰከረ G (IMPF ይሰክር, SUBJ ይስከር) to be intoxicated

ስኩር (F ስክርት) PASS PTCP inebriated, drunk

ሰከር intoxicating drink; intoxication

ሰከረት intoxication

ሰካሪ (PL ሰከርት) drunkard

ሰኰለ D to cease, come to an end, die out

ሰኰት / ስኰት (PL አስኰት) street, quarter

መስኮት (PL መሳክው) window

ሰለበ G (IMPF ይሰልብ, SUBJ ይስለብ) to take (COMP) away (from: CLIT PRON), deprive of, strip off

ስልበት NOUN depriving, taking away

ሰላም safety, peace, salutation

በሰላም safely, in peace

ሰላም፡ለከ Greetings!

ላዕሌሁ፡ሰላም May peace be upon him!

ስለን dill

ተሳለቀ GLT to joke, sport, play; to mock, make fun of (ላዕለ)

ስላቅ sport, play, mockery

መስተሳልቅ mocker, scorner

ሰለጠ G (1) to be whole, perfect; (2) to accept/bring back (something: COMP) whole/complete/in its entirety; to pay back; (3) to consummate, finish up/off

ሰለጠ D = G (2) and G (3); also: to be effective, to accomplish results

ተሰልጠ GT / ተሰለጠ DT to be finished, consummated

ስለጤ completion

ስም (PL አስማት) name; fame, reputation

ሰምዐ G (IMPF ይሰምዕ, SUBJ ይስማዕ) to hear, hear of, hear about (COMP); to heed, obey, listen to (COMP or ለ-)

ተሰምዐ GT PASS; also: to be spread (fame)

አስምዐ CG CAUS; also: to summon (COMP) as a witness

ተሳምዐ GLT to hear and understand one another, each other's language

ስሙዕ (F ስምዕት) PASS PTCP famous, illustrious; notorious

ሰማዒ ADJ hearing, listening to, obedient; NOUN (PL ሰማዕት) witness, martyr

ስምዕ (PL ስምዓት) rumor, report, testimony; martyrdom, martyrs

ስምዖን PN Simon

ሰሚ / ሰመክ fish

አስመከ CG to lean; to prop up, cause to lean

መስምክ / መሰምክት prop, support

ምስጋክ IDEM

ሴሜን the south

ሰማኒ (COMP IDEM) F; ሰማኒቱ, ሰማንቱ (COMP ሰማንት) M eight

Gloss Lexicon

ስምን F IDEM

ሳምን (F ሳምንት) ADJ eighth

ሳምናዊ (F ሳምናዊት) IDEM

ሳምናይ (F ሳምኔት) IDEM

ሰሙን the eighth day (of the month); eight days, a week

ስምነ ADV eight times

ሰማንያ eighty

ሰመየ G (IMPF ይሰሚ; SUBJ ይስሚ) to name, give a name, address, call, invoke, appeal to

    ስሙየ CG to be/become well known, famous, outstanding

    ስሙይ (F ስሚት) PASS PTCP named, called; famous, illustrious

    ስም (PL አስማት) name; fame, reputation

ሰማይ (PL ሰማያት) heaven, sky

ሰማያዊ (F ሰማያዊት) heavenly, divine, celestial

ተሰናአወ QLT to come to an agreement, be in accord

ስን (PL ስነን, አሰናን) tooth

ሰንበት (PL ሰንበታት/ሰናብት) sabbath; Sunday; week

    አሰንበተ CQ to observe the sabbath or Sunday

ስንዶን / ስንዱን fine linen

ተሰነነ DT / ተሳነነ GLT to enter into litigation with, to contend with

    ተስነን lawsuit, litigation, controversy

ሴናጴ mustard

ሰኑይ (F ሰኔት) the second day (of week or month), two days

    ሳኒት፡ዕለት the next day

    ሳኒታ IDEM; on the next day (or night)

ሰቀለ G (IMPF ይሰቅል, SUBJ ይስቀል) to suspend, hang up; to crucify

    ተሰቀለ GT PASS; also: to depend (on: በ-/ኀበ); to adhere, cling (to: ውስተ)

    ስቁል (F ስቅልት) PASS PTCP hanging, suspended, crucified; dependent

    ስቅለት crucifixion

    መስቀል (PL መሳቅል) cross

ሰቀላ (PL ሰቃልው) tent, tabernacle

ሰቈረ (ይስቍር) to pierce, dig out/through

    ስቁር (F ስቅርት) PASS PTCP perforated, excavated, breached

    ስቍረት aperture, opening

አስቆቀወ Q to lament, sing a dirge

    ስቆቃው dirge, lamentation

    መስቆቅው mourner; ADJ lamenting, mourning

ሶር (PL አስዋር) ox, steer

አስራብ (PL only) cataracts, downpours

ሱራፌል seraph, seraphim

ሲሮፊኔቃስ PN Syro-Phoenician

ሰረገላ / ሠረገላ (PL ሰረገላት) cart, wagon, chariot

አሰርገወ CQ to adorn, deck out, beautify

    ተሰርገወ QT PASS and REFLEX

    ስርጉ (F ስርጉት) PASS PTCP adorned, decorated, made beautiful

    ሰርጉ (PL ሰርጓት) adornment, beautification

ሰርሐ G (IMPF ይሰርሕ, SUBJ ይስረሕ) to labor to the point of exhaustion, to be afflicted with difficult tasks or duties

    አስርሐ CG to tire, exhaust; to cause or impose labor/misery

    ስሩሕ (F ስርሕት) PASS PTCP vexed, exhausted

    ስራሕ (PL ስራሓት) labor, bother, exhaustion, affliction

ሰርክ evening, twilight

    ሰርክ፡ሰንበት Sabbath evening

ሰረቀ G (IMPF ይሰርቅ, SUBJ ይስርቅ) to steal, plunder, rob

    ሰራቂ (PL ሰረቅት) thief

    ስርቅ / ስርቅ stolen object; theft

ሰረረ G (IMPF ይሰርር, SUBJ ይስረር) to fly

    ስሩር (F ስርርት) PASS PTCP flying, in flight

    ሰራሪ IDEM

    ስረት flight, flying

ሰረቀ G (IMPF ይሰርቅ, SUBJ ይስርቅ) to steal, rob, take away secretly, plunder

ሰርዌ (PL ሰራዊት) troops, army, cohorts; a military leader

ሰረየ G (IMPF ይሰሪ, SUBJ ይስረይ) to forgive, excuse, pardon

ሰሰለ D to withdraw, recoil, recede, pass away, be removed, depart, be separated

    አሰሰለ CD to remove, do away with, take away, take off, drive out, dismiss, shake off, lay aside

ሴሰየ Q/L to nourish, sustain, provide for

    ተሴሰየ Q/LT PASS

    ሲሳይ sustenance, food, provisions

    ሲሲት IDEM

ተሳተፈ LT to associate with (COMP or ምስለ); to share (something: በ-) with (someone: COMP)

    ሱቱፍ companion, partner

    ሱታፍ / ሱታፌ SING and COLL, companion, associate, consort

ሰትየ G (IMPF ይሰቲ; SUBJ ይስተይ) to drink

    ስቴ a drink (the act or what is drunk)

    ስታይ IDEM

    መስቴ IDEM

    ሰታይ / ሰታዬ a drinker, one who is fond of drinking

    ምስታይ a place for drinking, a watering place

አስጠመ CG to submerge, immerse, flood

    GT ተሰጥመ to sink

    ስጥመት submersion, sinking

    መስጥም ADJ submerging, flooding

ተሰጥወ GT to accept, receive, take; to comply with; to respond, answer, give heed

ሰወረ D to hide, cover over, conceal, protect

    ተሰወረ DT PASS and REFLEX

    ስዉር (F ስውርት) PASS PTCP hidden, covered, concealed

    ምስዋር hidden place, hiding place

[ሰ-ወ-ጠ] ሶጠ G (IMPF ይሰውጥ, SUBJ ይሱጥ) to pour

    ተወጠ GT PASS and REFLEX

    ስዉጥ (F ስውጥት) PASS PTCP poured

    ሱጠት NOUN pouring, emptying

ሰይፍ (PL አስያፍ, አሰይፍት) sword

ሰይጠን (PL ሰይጠናት) Satan; a devil, demon, adversary

ሠ Ś

ሠእን (PL አሣእን) shoe, sandal

ሡዕ / ሱዕ flax, tinder

ሠዐረ G (IMPF ይሠዕር, SUBJ ይሥዐር) to grow green, to grow

    ሣዕር (PL አሥዐርት) herbage, vegetation, grass

    ሥዑር (F ሥዕርት) PASS PTCP grassy, covered with vegetation

    ሥዕርት (PL አሥዕርት) hair (of head or body)

ሠዐየ G (IMPF ይሠዒ, SUBJ ይሥዐይ) to winnow

    መሥዒ (PL መሣዐይ) winnowing-fork

ሥጋ (PL ሥጋት) flesh, meat (human or animal); body; the flesh as opposed to the spirit

    ሥጋዊ of the flesh (not spiritual); carnal

አሥገረ CG / አሠገረ CD to cast (nets); fish; capture by trapping

    ተሠግረ GT to be captured, ensnared

    መሠግር (PL መሠግራን) fisherman, one who lies in ambush

    መሥግርት (PL መሣግር) snare, net, trap

    ሠገራት (PL) guards

    አሥጋሪ hunter, fisherman

ተሣሀለ GLT to show mercy (to: COMP); to forgive

    ሣህል mercy, kindness

    መስታሣህል merciful, lenient; seeking mercy or forgiveness

ሠሐቀ / ሥሐቀ G (IMPF ይሠሕቅ, SUBJ ይሥሐቅ) to laugh; laugh at, mock, ridicule (COMP or ላዕለ)

    ሣሕቅ / ሠሐቅ ridicule

    ምሥሕአቅ comedy theater

ሠኅተ / ሥኅተ G (IMPF ይሠኅት, SUBJ ይሥኅት) to be at ease, at rest, comfortable, well off

    ሠኅተ D / አሠኅተ CD to put at ease, allow to rest

    ሥኁት (F ሥኁትት) PASS PTCP relaxed, at rest, at ease

    ሣኅት tranquility, relaxation, rest

ሦክ (PL አሥዋክ) thorn, thornbush; sting

ሠለቀ G (IMPF ይሠልቅ, SUBJ ይሥልቅ) to grind, crush, peel

ሠላስ (COMP ሠላሰ) F; ሠለስቱ (COMP ሠለስተ) M three

Gloss Lexicon

ሥልስ F IDEM

ሣልስ (F ሣልስት) ADJ third

ሣልሳዊ (F ሣልሳዊት) IDEM

ሣልሳይ (F ሣልሲት) IDEM

ሠሉስ the third day (of week or month); three days

ሥልስ ADV thrice

ሠላሳ thirty

መሥልስት (PL መሣል) a kind of measure

ሠለጠ D to have power, authority

አሠለጠ CD / አሥለጠ CG to give power to

ተሠለጠ DT / ተሠልጠ GT to acquire power, authority; to rule

ሥሉጥ (F ሥልጥት) PASS PTCP powerful, in power

ሥልጣን (PL ሥልጣናት) power, authority

ሠምረ G (IMPF ይሠምር SUBJ ይሥመር) to take delight in, be pleased with (COMP or በ-)

አሠመረ CG to please, delight, give pleasure to (CLIT PRON or ለ-)

ሥሙር pleasing (to: ለ-, በኀበ, በቅድመ), nice, pleasant

ሥምረት good will, favor, approval, benevolence, delight, consent; በሥምረት with the consent of

መሥምር / መሥመሪ pleasing to (ኀበ, ለ-)

ሠኔ/ ሰኔ Eth. month name: June 8–July 7

ሠነቀ G (IMPF ይሠንቅ, SUBJ ይሥንቅ) to prepare provisions for a journey

ሠነየ D to be beautiful, fine, excellent, good, fitting, appropriate

አሠነየ CD to adorn (COMP), deck out, array; to make (COMP) good; to do (something: INF) well

አስተሣነየ CGLT to beautify, restore, adjust, improve

ሥኑይ (F ሥኔት) PASS PTCP adorned, decked out, lovely

መሠንይ / ምሥናይ the best (of), the best part (of)

ሥን beauty

ሠናይ ADJ (F ሠናይት) beautiful, fine, excellent, good (both physical and moral senses), proper, virtuous, prosperous

ሠቅ (PL ሠቃት, አሥቃቅ) sack, sackcloth

ሣቀየ L to afflict, vex, torment

ሥቃይ vexation, torment

መሠቄ goad; weavers comb

ሠርዐ G (IMPF ይሠርዕ; SUBJ ይሥራዕ) to put into order, arrange, prepare, regulate; to establish, set up, ordain, legislate, make a covenant

ሥሩዕ (F ሥርዕት) PASS PTCP arranged, ordered, established, ordained

ሥርዐት (PL ሥርዐታት) order, arrangement, disposition; decree, edict, command; law, statute; treaty, pact, testament; custom, habit, any fixed pattern

ሥርናይ / ስርናይ wheat

ሠረቀ G (IMPF ይሠርቅ, SUBJ ይሥርቅ) to rise, shine (of the sun)

ሠርቅ (PL አሠረቅ) rising (of heavenly bodies); the east; the new moon, the calendars

ሠረጸ/ ሠርጸ G (IMPF ይሠርጽ, SUBJ ይሥረጽ) to sprout

ሥርው (PL ሥርዋት, ሥረው, አሥራው) root; nerve, muscle, tendon

ሠርዌ (PL ሠራዊት) beam, timber

ሥራይ (PL ሥራያት) incantation, magic, charm, witchcraft, enchantment, poison, healing, medicine, cure, bandage

ሠጠቀ G (IMPF ይሠጥቅ, SUBJ ይሥጥቅ) to cleave, split; to cut, split (COMP)

ሥጡቅ (F ሥጥቅት) PASS PTCP cut, split

ሥጥቀት NOUN cutting, splitting; a cut, split

ሠጠጠ G (IMPF ይሠጥጥ, SUBJ ይሥጥጥ) to tear (apart), rend, tear asunder

ተሠጠ GT passive

ሥጡጥ (F ሥጥጥት) PASS PTCP torn, rent

ሥጠት tearing, rending; the part torn off, tatter, fragment

ሠውዐ G (IMPF ይሠውዕ, SUBJ ይሡዕ) to sacrifice, offer

ሠዋዒ (PL ሠዋዕት) priest, sacrificer

መሥዋዕት (PL መሥዋዕታት, መሣውዕ) sacrifice, offering, meat-offering, oblation

ምሥዋዕ/መሥዋዕ (PL ምሥዋዓት) altar

ሠወነ D to foam, drool

አሠወነ CD causative

ሠወየ G (IMPF ይሠዊ, SUBJ ይሥወይ) to ripen (of grain)

ሠዊት ear of grain, ear of corn, mature grain

[ሥ-ይ-ም] ሤመ G (IMPF ይሠይም, SUBJ ይሢም) to appoint (COMP patient) to (COMP position/location), designate, establish, promote, consecrate; to put, place, set

ሥዩም (F ሥይምት) PASS PTCP appointed, set, placed; NOUN appointee official, governor, prefect

ሢመት (PL ሢማት) ordination; office, position

መሣይምት (COLL) container(s), basket(s)

[ሥ-ይ-ጥ] ሤጠ G (IMPF ይሠይጥ, SUBJ ይሢጥ) to sell to (ኅበ, ለ-)

ተሣየጠ GLT to buy

ሤጥ price, value

ሠያጢ (PL ሠየጥ) seller, merchant

ምሥያጥ (PL ምሥያጣት) marketplace

ጽ Ṣ

ጼአ G (IMPF ይጻይእ, SUBJ ይጺእ) to rot

ጽዩእ (F ጽይእት) PASS PTCP rotten, decayed

ጺአት rot, decay

ጸዐደወ Q to be white

ጽዕድው· ADJ white

ጸዐዳ / ጸዓዳ (PL ጸዓድው·) ADJ white

ጸዐለ G (IMPF ይጸዕት, SUBJ ይጽዐት) to curse, revile

ጽዑል (F ጽዕልት) PASS PTCP despised

ጽዕለት NOUN cursing, reviling

ጸዓሊ curser, reviler

ጸዐነ D to load (an animal or vehicle)

አጽዐቀ CG to press in on, to confine

ጽዑቅ (F ጽዕቅት) PASS PTCP narrow, confined

ጽዕቅ confinement, press; need

መጽዕቅ ADJ pressing, confining

ጽዕረ (IMPF ይጻዕር, SUBJ ይጽዐር) G to be grieved, pained, afflicted

ጽዑር (F ጽዕርት) PASS PTCP grieved, pained, afflicted

ጸዐር pain, torment, grief, vexation, sorrow

ጸብአ / ፀብአ G (IMPF ይጻብእ, SUBJ ይጽባእ) to fight, make war with (COMP)

ተጻብአ GLT to fight one another (COMP or ምስለ)

ጸብአ (PL አጽብእ, ጸብአት) war, battle

ጸባኢ warrior, soldier

ጸባኢት army, troops; battle, fighting

አጽባዕት (PL አጻብዕ) finger, toe

ጸበ / ጸበበ G (IMPF ይጻብብ, SUBJ ይጽብብ) to be (too) narrow; to narrow, confine

ጸቢብ (F ጸባብ) narrow, confined

ጽበት narrowness

መጽብብ a narrow place, pass

ጸብሐ G (IMPF ይጻብሕ, SUBJ ይጽብሕ) to grow light, to dawn

ጸቢሐ at dawn

ተጻብሐ GLT to greet early in the day

ጽባሕ (PL ጽባሓት) morning, early morning, daybreak; east

ጽብሐ D to exact/collect taxes or tribute

ጸበሕት tribute, taxes

መጸብሕ (PL መጸብሓን) tax-collector

መጸብሒ IDEM

ምጽባሕ tax office

ጸበል dust

አጽበረ to work clay

ጽቡር clay, mud

ጸብን G (IMPF ይጻብን, SUBJ ይጽብን) to dip

ጸብን sauce, gravy

መጽብን dish, bowl

ጸደፈ G (IMPF ይጻድፍ, SUBJ ይጽድፍ) to rush, plunge headlong

ጸድፍ (PL አጽደፍ) precipitous place, precipice, abyss

ጸደለ G (IMPF ይጻድል, SUBJ ይጽድል) to shine, be splendid

አጽደለ CG to shine, emit light, gleam

ጽዱል (F ጽድልት) PASS PTCP shining, splendid

ጸዳል splendor, light, gleam

Gloss Lexicon

ጸደና wild bee, bee that lives underground

ጸድቀ G (IMPF ይጸድቅ, SUBJ ይጽደቅ) to be righteous, just, true, faithful

    አጽደቀ CG to make righteous, just; to declare just or innocent

    ጻድቅ (F ጻድቅት) ADJ righteous, just, true, reliable, faithful, innocent, saint

    ጽድቅ (PL ጽድቃት) justice; rightness, truth; righteousnss

ጸዳይ autumn

ጸፍዐ G (IMPF ይጸፍዕ, SUBJ ይጽፋዕ) to strike, slap, box

ጽፍነት pack, wallet

አጽፈቀ CG to make dense; to do something (INF) frequently

    ጽፉቅ dense, thick, crowded, pressed together; luxurious, frequent, abundant

ጽጉ (PL ጽጉጉ) street, marketplace

ጸግበ G (IMPF ይጸግብ, SUBJ ይጽገብ) to be sated, filled, satisfied; to be sick of something

    ጽጉብ (F ጽግብት) PASS PTCP sated, full, satisfied

    ጽጋብ satiety, abundance

ጸጉር hair; fur, feathers; fleece, fiber (of palm)

ጸገወ D to show grace or favor to (CLIT PRON or ለ-); to bestow gifts

    ጸጋ (PL ጸጋት) grace, favor, kindness; gift, payment, reward

    ጸጋዊ liberal, generous

ጸገየ G (IMPF ይጸጊ, SUBJ ይጽገይ) to flower, blossom

    ጽጉይ (F ጽጊት) PASS PTCP flowering, adorned with flowers

    ጽጌ (PL ጽጌያት) flower

ጸሕብ vessel, jar, pitcher, bowl

ጸሐደ G (IMPF ይጸሕድ, SUBJ ይጽሐድ) to be smooth, tender, soft

    አጽሐደ CG causative; to anoint

ጸሐፈ G (IMPF ይጸሕፍ, SUBJ ይጽሐፍ) to write, inscribe, describe, register

    ጽሑፍ (F ጽሕፍት) PASS PTCP written

    ጽሕፈት writing (act or product)

ጸሓፊ (PL ጸሐፍት) scribe, writer, secretary; learned person

    መጽሐፍ (PL መጻሕፍት) book, document; writing, inscription, volume, written deed, written characters, art of writing, epistle, Scripture

ጸሕል dish, bowl, platter

ጽሕቀ G (IMPF ይጻሕቅ, SUBJ ይጽሐቅ) to desire; to be eager for, pursue diligently; to take care of

    ጽሑቅ (F ጽሕቅት) PASS PTCP desirous, eager, concerned

    ጽህቅ desire, eagerness

ጽሕው serene

ጸልአ G (IMPF ይጸልእ, SUBJ ይጽላእ) to hate, be hostile toward (COMP)

    ተጸልአ GT PASS and REFLEX

    ተጻልአ GLT to behave in a hostile way toward one another

    ጽሉእ (F ጽልእት) PASS PTCP hated, hateful

    ጽልእ / ጸልእ hatred, hostility, enmity

    ጸላኢ (PL ጸላእት) enemy, hater, detractor

ጸለዕ (PL ጸልዓት) rock(s)

ጽሌ / ጸላ (PL ጽላት) tablet

ጸልሐወ Q to act treacherously

    ጽልሑው treacherous, guileful

    ጽልሑት treachery, guile, malice

ጸለለ D to float upon, hover, come to the surface (of water)

ጸለለ D to shade, cover

    አጽለለ CG to furnish shade; to seek the shade; to sit, live, dwell

    ጸሎ lampblack, soot

    ጽላሎት shade, shadow(s), darkness

    ምጽላል a shady place, shelter, booth, tabernacle

    መጸለት IDEM

ጸለመ / ጸለመ G (IMPF ይጸልም, SUBJ ይጽለም) to grow dark, be black; of eyes: to grow blind

    ጸልመ፡ገጹ he became angry

    ጽሉም (F ጽልምት) PASS PTCP dark, obscured, blinded

ጸሊም (F ጸላም) black

ጽልመት darkness

ጸለየ D to pray, supplicate, intercede, plead, make a vow

    ጸሎት (PL ጸሎታት) prayer(s)

    ምጽላይ place to pray, chapel

ጸምአ G (IMPF ይጸምእ, SUBJ ይጽማእ) to be thirsty

    ጽሙእ (F ጽምእት) PASS PTCP thirsty

    ጽምእ thirst

    መጻምእ something that causes thirst

ጸምሀየየ Q to wither, dry up

ጸመመ / ጸመ G (IMPF ይጸምም, SUBJ ይጽምም) to be deaf and dumb

    ተጸመመ GT to be made deaf, to feign deafness

    ጽሙም (F ጽምምት) PASS PTCP deaf and/or dumb

    ጽም ADV secretly, in secret, in private

    ጽሚተ IDEM

    በጽሚት IDEM

ጸመወ L to labor, toil

    አጸመወ CL to inflict harsh labor on

    ጻማ (PL ጻማት) labor, toil, work; device, artifice; strife, anxiety, mortification

ጼና smell, odor, perfume

ጸንዐ G (IMPF ይጸንዕ, SUBJ ይጽናዕ) to be strong, powerful, solid, valid, firm; to be lasting, enduring; to be hard, harsh, severe

    አጽንዐ CG CAUS; also: to grasp (COMP or በ-) firmly; to learn by heart (በልብ-)

    ጽኑዕ (F ጽንዕት) PASS PTCP strong

    ጸናዒ (PL ጸነዕት) strong, firm; fortified

    ጽንዕ, ጽንዐት hardness, firmness; strength, power, force

    ምጽነዕ (PL ምጽነዓት) firm base; firmament

ጽንፍ (PL አጽናፍ, ጽነፍ) edge, margin, hem; shore, bank; end, limit

    ጸናፊ ADJ exterior, extreme, outer

ጸንሐ G (IMPF ይጸንሕ; SUBJ ይጽናሕ) to wait, await, expect; to be imminent (COMP or ለ-); to lie in wait for, ambush

አጽንሐ CG to set traps or snares for; to promise (i.e. cause to expect); to prepare (COMP)

    ጽኑሕ (F ጽንሕት) PASS PTCP waiting, expectant; put aside, reserved

ጽንሓሕ sacrifice, offering

ተጸነሰ DT to be impoverished, reduced to poverty

    ጽኑስ (F ጽንስት) PASS PTCP poor, indigent, wretched

    ተጽናስ poverty, wretchedness; lack, deficiency

ጽርዕ / ዕርዕ Greece, the Greeks

    ዕርዓዊ ADJ Greek

አጽርዐ see አዕርዐ

ጸረበ G (IMPF ይጸርብ, SUBJ ይጽርብ) to hew, do carpentry

    ጽርበት woodwork, stonework

    ጸራቢ carpenter, craftsman, stonecutter

ጽርሕ (PL አጽራሕ, አጽርሕርት) room, chamber, house; bedroom

ጸርኀ G (IMPF ይጸርኅ; SUBJ ይጽራኅ) to cry, cry out, shout

    ጽራኅ a cry, shout

ጸሪቅ copper, small coin

ጸሪቀት thin disk, cake

ጻጾት gnat, flea

ጼው salt

ጸውዐ D to call, summon, invite, invoke; to proclaim; to shout, cry out

    ጽዉዕ (F ጽውዕት) PASS PTCP summoned, invited

    ጽውዐ call, summons, invitation

    ጽዋዔ IDEM

ጽዋዕ (PL ጽዋዓት) cup, goblet, chalice

[ጽ-ው-ም] ጸመ G (IMPF ይጸውም, SUBJ ይጹም) to fast

    ጽዉም (F ጽውምት) PASS PTCP fasting

    ጾም (PL አጽዋም, ጾማት) fast, fasting

[ጽ-ው-ር] ጾረ G (IMPF ይጸውር, SUBJ ይጾር / ይዱር) to carry, bear (lit. and fig.), wear

    ጽዉር (F ጽውርት) PASS PTCP bearing, burdened with (COMP)

    ጾር (PL አጽዋር) burden

    ጻዋር carrier(s), porter(s)

ጸዋሪ (F ጸዋሪት; PL ጸዋርት) one who carries, bears

[ጽ-ይ-ሐ] ጼሐ G (IMPF ይጸይሕ, SUBJ ይዲሕ) to make level, to pave (a road), sweep

    ጽዩሕ (F ጽይሕት) PASS PTCP level, even, paved; easy

    መጽያሕት highway

ት T

ተብዐ to be brave, manly

    ትብዕ, ትብዐት bravery, courage, virtue

    ተባዕት (PL አትቡዕ) NOUN a male

    ተባዕ, ተባዒ (PL ተባዕት) ADJ male, strong

    ተባዓዊ ADJ male, masculine

ታቦት (PL ታቦታት) ark (of Noah, of the Covenant)

ተፍአ G (IMPF ይተፍእ, SUBJ ይትፋእ) to spit

    ትፍአት spit, saliva

ተግሀ G (IMPF ይተግህ, SUBJ ይትግህ) to be wakeful, watchful, vigilant, attentive

    ትጉህ (F ትግህት) PASS PTCP wakeful

    ትጋህ vigilance, watchfulness

ትሕተ G (IMPF ይተሕት, SUBJ ይትሐት) to be humble

    አትሐተ CG CAUS; also: to subject (COMP)

    ተትሕተ DT to humble oneself, be submissive, to act or be inferior, lowly

    ትሑት (F ትሕትት) PASS PTCP humble, modest, obedient; lowly, ignoble

    ትሕትና humility, humbleness

    ታሕተ PREP under, below, beneath; ADV below, from below

    መትሕት lower or inferior part

    መትሕት PREP below, under, beneath

ታኅሣሥ Eth. month name: Dec. 10–Jan. 8

መትከፍ (PL መታክፍት) shoulder

ተከለ G (IMPF ይተክል, SUBJ ይትከል) to plant; to fix in, implant, establish, pitch (a tent)

    አተከለ CD to push, shove, hit

    ትኩል (F ትክልት) PASS PTCP planted; implanted, fixed

    ተከል (PL ተከላት, አትክልት) a plant, tree

መትከል (PL መታክል) stake, peg

ተኩለ (PL ተኩላት) wolf

አትከተ CG = አተከተ CD to wish to gain time

    ትካት antiquity, yore

    ዝትካት ancient, old, primeval, pristine

    እምትካት from of old, hitherto, once, formerly

ተክዘ D to be sad, grieved, distressed, troubled in mind, anxious, concerned, show care

    ትኩዝ (F ትክዝት) PASS PTCP sad

    ትካዝ (PL ትካዛት) sadness, grief, care, concern; business, task

ተለወ G (IMPF ይተልው, SUBJ ይትሉ) to follow, succeed, adhere to, accompany (COMP or ለ-)

    አትለወ CG CAUS; also: continue, proceed, add

    መትልው/መትለው ADJ following; NOUN that which follows, succession, order, order of succession/sequence; rest, remainder

ተንሥአ Q to arise, get up; to rise (from the dead); to rise up against (ላዕለ); derived from noun of root ን-ሥ-አ

ተርፈ / ተረፈ G (IMPF ይተርፍ, SUBJ ይትረፍ) to be left over, remain, survive

    አትረፈ CG to leave (as a remainder)

    ትሩፍ (F ትርፍት) PASS PTCP left, remaining; abundant; excellent, outstanding

    ትርፍት (PL ትሩፋት) virtue, excellence, perfection

    ትራፍ remainder, residue; overflow, abundance

    ትራፋተ፡ነገሥት the OT book of Chronicles (*lit.* the remainder or overflow from Kings)

    ተራፊ survivor

ተርጐመ Q to translate

    ትርጓሜ (PL ትርጓምያት) translation, interpretation

    መተርጉም translator, interpreter

ትስዑ / ተስዑ (COMP IDEM) F; ትስዐቱ / ተስዐቱ (COMP ትስዐተ) M nine

    ትስዕ F IDEM

    ታስዕ (F ታስዕት) ADJ ninth

    ታስዓዊ (F ታስዓዊት) IDEM

    ታስዓይ (F ታስዒት) IDEM

ተሱዕ the ninth day (of the month); nine days

ትስዐ ADV nine times

ትስዓ / ተስዓ ninety

ቴታን / ቶታን (PL ቶታናት) lace, thong, lace

ጠ Ṭ

ጣእጠአ / ጣዕጠዐ / ጣዕጥአ Q to be properly arranged, settled, inclined favorably

አስተጠዕጥአ CQT to arrange favorably, shape, fashion in an orderly manner

ጥዕመ / ጠዐመ G (IMPF ይጠዕም, SUBJ ይጥዐም) to taste, to experience (e.g., death); to be tasty, delicious

አጥዐመ CG CAUS; also: to make sweet, pleasant

ጥዑም (F ጥዕምት) PASS PTCP tasty, delicious, sweet, pleasant

ጣዕም (PL ጣዕማት) taste, flavor; sweet taste, pleasant taste; reason, good sense

ጣዖት (PL ጣዖታት) heathen idol(s)

ጥዕየ G (IMPF ይጤዒ, SUBJ ይጥዐይ) to be healthy, well

ጥዑይ (F ጥዒት) PASS PTCP well, healthy (of person or place), sound, sane

ጤዒና good health

ጠበበ / ጠበ G (IMPF ይጠብብ, SUBJ ይጥበብ) to be wise, prudent; to be skilled, expert

ተጠበበ DT to be crafty, cunning

ጠቢብ (F ጠባብ) wise, wise man, scholar, clever, prudent, expert, skilled, craftsman, artisan, sober, philosopher, magician

ጥበብ (PL ጥበባት) wisdom, prudence, skill, experience, intelligence, cunning, ruse, ability

ጠብዐ G (IMPF ይጠብዕ, SUBJ ይጥብዕ) to be willing, ready (to do something)

አጥብዐ CG CAUS; also: to do something willingly (with foll. verb); to persevere, be constant, firm, undeterred

ጥቡዕ (F ጥብዕት) PASS PTCP willing, quick, eager, ready, undeterred, bold, persevering

ጠብሐ G (IMPF ይጠብሕ, SUBJ ይጥባሕ) to make an incision; to sacrifice

ጥብሕ sacrifice, sacrificial victim

ጥብሐት sacrifice

መጥባሕት (PL መጣብሕ) knife, sword

ጠቢቅ (PL ጠቢቃተ) plate, platter (of food)

ጠፍአ G (IMPF ይጠፍእ, SUBJ ይጥፋእ) to be put out (light), extinguished; to perish, vanish, be lost, fail

አጥፍአ CG CAUS; also: to destroy, blot out

ጥፍአት extinction, destruction, loss

ጠፈረ G (IMPF ይጠፍር, SUBJ ይጥፍር) to roof over, put up a ceiling

ጠፈር roof, ceiling, wooden floor, firmament

ጠለ G to be moist

ጥሉል (F ጥልልት) PASS PTCP moist, rich, fat, prosperous

ጠል dew

መጥለሊ ADJ moistening, refreshing

ጠሊ (F ጠሊት; PL አጣሊ) goat

ጠመቀ G (ይጥምቅ) = አጥመቀ CG to baptize, dip, immerse

ጥሙቅ (F ትምቅት) PASS PTCP baptized

ጥምቀት baptism

መጥምቅ baptizer

ምጥማቅ place for baptizing, baptistry; pool

ጥንት beginning

ጥቀ ADV very, extremely, greatly, completely; exactly, accurately; still, even

ጥቀ PREP near, beside

በጥቀ IDEM

ጠቀበ G to sew, attach by sewing, sew together, stitch, patch, mend

ጥቅበት sewing, stitch

ጥቅምት Eth. month name: Oct. 11–Nov. 9

ጥቅም wall, city wall, fortification wall

ጥር Eth. month name: Jan. 9–Feb 7

ጢሮስ PN Tyre

እጥረየ CG to acquire, possess

ጥሪት possession, property, wealth

[ጥ-ይ-ስ] ጤሰ G (IMPF ይጠይስ, SUBJ ይጢስ) to smoke

ጢስ smoke

ጠየቀ D to examine, observe closely, scrutinize, investigate, explore; to ascertain by examining

    ተጠየቀ DT PASS; ALSO: TO SEEK CERTAINTY, TRY TO MAKE SURE

    አጠየቀ CD to inform someone (COMP) of something (COMP)

    ጥዩቅ (F ጥይቅት) PASS PTCP precise, accurate; certain, sure

    ጥዩቀ precisely, accurately, certainly

ው W

ወ- CONJ and

ውእቱ (COMP ውእተ) PRON MS he
    DEM MS that; that one

ወዐለ / ውዕለ G (የዐል) to pass the day, remain

    ወዓሊ attendant, servant

    ዕለት (PL ዕለታት) day; time

    መዐልት/መዓልት (PL መዋዕል) day, daytime

    መዋዕል (PL መዋዕላት) period, era

ውዕየ G (የዐይ) to burn up, be consumed by fire

    CG አውዐየ to burn up (COMP); to burn, scorch

    ውዑይ (F ውዒት) PASS PTCP hot, burning

    ዋዕይ fire, heat, burning

    ውዕየት NOUN burning, conflagration

ወድአ D to finish, complete; used as an auxiliary verb in the sense of "already"

ወድቀ G (IMPF ይወድቅ, SUBJ ይደቅ) to fall, fall down, collapse, to go to ruin, sink, become decayed, throw oneself (into)

    አውደቀ CG to drop, let fall; to throw down, cast down; to fell, hew down

    ውዱቅ (F ውድቅት) PASS PTCP fallen, lying fallen

    ድቀት fall, ruin, collapse

    ድንቀተ ADV suddenly, unexpectedly

ወደየ G (IMPF ይወዲ SUBJ ይደይ) to put, place, set, put under, lay, throw

    አስተዋደየ CGLT to bring charges, accuse, slander, abuse

    ውዴት charge, accusation

    ሙዳይ (PL ሙዳያት) a container of any sort; basket, hamper

ወፅአ G (IMPF ይወፅእ, SUBJ ይፃእ) to go/come forth, emerge; to leave, depart from, to spring from, originate from

    አውፅአ CG to bring/lead/take (COMP) forth; to expel, put forth, produce (COMP); to cause (COMP) to pay

    ውፁእ (F ውፅአት) PASS PTCP departing; emerging; lacking in

    ፅአት exit, departure, exodus

    ሙፃእ place of exit, source

ወፈረ G (IMPF ይውፍር; SUBJ የፍር) to go to a field, go to the countryside, feed in a pasture

    ወፍር the countryside, fields, farms, farmland

    ሙፋር farmland, pasture

ወገረ G (IMPF ይወግር, SUBJ ይገር) =ወገረ D to throw, cast (COMP); to stone someone (COMP)

    ወግር (PL አውግር) heap, mound, hill

    ምግርት sling

አውገዘ CG to curse (COMP), lay a ban on, banish, expel

    ተዋገዘ GLT to alienate oneself from (COMP)

    ውጉዝ (F ውግዝት) PASS PTCP cursed, banned

ወሀበ G (IMPF ይሁብ; SUBJ የሀብ) to give, grant, confer upon, offer, bestow, deliver, transmit, allow, permit something (COMP) to (COMP)

    ህብት (PL ህብታት) gift

    ወሃቢ one who gives, donor; ADJ generous

ውኅዘ/ውሕዘ G (የኅዝ) to flow, flow out, flow with (COMP), run down, pour down (tears)

    ወሒዝ (PL ወሓይዝት) river, stream; flow, current

    ውሕዘት flow, flowing

    ሙሓዝ/ሙኃዝ aqueduct, canal, channel (of water); river, brook

ውኅደ G (የኅድ) to be few, small

    ውኁድ (F ውኅድት) PASS PTCP few, small, scanty

    ውኅደት paucity, scantiness

ውኅጠ / ወኅጠ G (የኅጥ) to swallow

ተወክፈ GT = ተወክፈ DT to accept, receive, take unto oneself; also PASS of same

    ውኩፍ (F ውክፍት) PASS PTCP accepted, acceptable, agreeable, pleasant

ተወከለ DT to trust or have faith in (በ-/ዲበ or CLIT PRON)

    ውኩል (F ውክልት) PASS PTCP trusting, confiding, dependent

    ትውክልት trust, faith, confidence

ወለደ G (IMPF ይወልድ; SUBJ ይለድ) to bear (a child); to beget (COMP) by (በነበ); to conceive; to bring forth (COMP)

    ተዋለደ GLT to procreate; to increase, flourish, multiply by procreation

    አውለደ CG to beget; to cause to bear

    ወልድ (PL ውሉድ) son, child, boy, lad, disciple, servant; PL also used as singular

    ወለት (PL አዋልድ) daughter, girl, maidservant

    ውሉድ (1) PL of ወልድ; (2) syn. of ወልድ in singular; (3) PASS PTCP (F ውልድት) born, begotten

    ልደት birth

    ወላዲ (F ወላዲት, PL ወላድያን) parent

    ሙላድ place of birth, native land

    ትውልድ (PL ትውልዳት) offspring, family; race, tribe, family, species; generation

ወለጠ D to change, alter, transform

    ውሉጥ (F ውልጥት) PASS PTCP changed, transformed, different

    ውላጤ change, alteration, transformation

    ታውላጥ change; exchange, price

ወንጌል gospel

    ወንጌላዊ (F ወንጌላዊት) ADJ gospel; NOUN evangelist

ወቀረ G = ወቀረ D = CG አውቀረ to dig, excavate

ወቀሠ G (IMPF ይወቅሥ, SUBJ ይውቅሥ) to reprimand, reproach; to accuse, condemn

    ተዋቀሠ GLT to contend, contradict; to defend a case; to bring into judgment, go to court

ወረደ G (IMPF ይወርድ, SUBJ ይረድ) to descend, come down, go down

    አውረደ CG to bring/send/lead (COMP) down

    ርደት descent

    ሙዓድ place of descent, downward slope

ወርኅ (PL አውራኅ) moon, month

    ወርኃዊ lunar

ወርቅ gold, money

ወረቀ G (IMPF ይወርቅ, SUBJ ይውርቅ) to spit

    ምራቅ spittle, saliva

ወረሰ G (IMPF ይወርስ, SUBJ ይረስ) to inherit

    ተወርሰ GT to gain by inheritance, gain possession of

    ተዋረሰ GLT to inherit (jointly or singly)

    ወራሲ heir

    ርስት (PL ርስታት) inheritance

    መዋርስት (PL መዋርስት) heirs

ወረወ G (IMPF ይወሩ, SUBJ ይውሩ) to throw, cast

    ተወርወ GT PASS and REFLEX

ወሬዛ (PL ወራዙት) a youth, young man

    ውርዛዌ youth, manhood, maturity

    ውርዙት IDEM

አውሰበ CG to marry

    አስተዋሰበ CGLT to give someone in marriage, to marry off

ወሰደ G (IMPF ይወስድ, SUBJ ይሰድ) to lead, conduct, bring, take (COMP) to (ነበ /ውስተ / ለ-)

ወሰከ D to add (COMP) to (ዲበ / ላዕለ); to increase, augment (COMP)

    ተውሳከ addition

ወሰነ D to delimit, mark off, define

    ወሰን boundary, limit

ውስተ (CLIT PRON: ውስቴት-) PREP in, inside, into, to, toward, at, among, by

    በውስተ IDEM

    እምውስተ from in, from within

ውስጥ interior, middle

አውሥአ CG to respond, answer; to take up a discourse, speak; chant

    ተዋሥአ GLT to speak against, contradict; to dispute, argue (with: CLIT PRON or ለ-)

አውተረ CG to continue, persevere in, be assiduous in (COMP or INF); to direct (hands, eyes) to (ኀበ / ላዕለ / ለ-)

    ወትረ ADV always, perpetually, continuously, assiduously

ወጠነ G (IMPF ይወጥን, SUBJ ይጠን/ይውጥን) = D to begin, comment, set forth (COMP or SUBJ or INF)

    ጥንት NOUN beginning

ወውዐ D to shout

    ውውዓ a shout, cry

ወይ interjection woe! alas!

ወይን (PL አውያን) vine, wine, grapes

    አጸደ ወይን vineyard

ይ Y

ይእቲ (COMP ይእተ) PRON FS she

    DEM FS that, that one

ይእዜ (±ኒ) ADV now

    እምይእዜ from now on

    እስከ፡ይእዜ up until now

ያዕቆብ PN Jacob, James

የብሰ G (IMPF ይየብስ, SUBJ ይይብስ) to be dry, arid, dry up, be withered

    ይቡስ (F ይብስት) PASS PTCP dry, arid; paralyzed, stiff

    የብስ dry land, the dry ground

አይድዐ to inform, inform, declare, announce, tell someone (COMP)

ይሁዳ PN Judah

ዮሐንስ PN John

ዮጊ ADV perhaps, by chance, perchance

የካቲት Eth. month name: Feb. 8–Mar. 9

ዮም ADV today; on this day (of the year)

የማን the right (side or hand)

    ይምን IDEM

    ይምነ ADV on/to the right

    ይሙነ ADV rightly, correctly

ዮናናዊያን PN the Greeks

ዮርዳኖስ PN Jordan

ዮሴፍ PN Joseph

የውሀ / የውሐ G (IMPF ይየውህ, SUBJ ይይውህ) to be gentle, mild, modest, submissive, innocent, simple; to please, charm, persuade, entice

    የውሀት mildness

    የዋህት IDEM

    የዋህ ADJ mild, gentle

    የውህና mildness

ዘ Z

ዘ- REL who, that, which; CONJ that, the fact that

    ዘዘ DISTRIBUTIVE

ዛ- DEM FS this

ዝ- (COMP ዘ-) DEM MS this

ዚአ- The relative form before an attached pronoun; e.g., ዚአሁ that is his

ዘብሐ G (IMPF ይዘብሕ, SUBJ ይዝባሕ) to slaughter, sacrifice, offer sacrifices

ዘብዴዎስ PN Zebedee

ዘበጠ G (IMPF ይዘብጥ, SUBJ ይዝብጥ) to beat, whip (COMP)

    ዘባጢ ruffian, fighter

    ዝቡጥ (F ዝብጥት) PASS PTCP beaten

    ዝብጠት NOUN beating, whipping

ዘፈር (PL አዝፋር) hem or fringe of a garment

ዘገበ G (IMPF ይዘግብ, SUBJ ይዝግብ) to store up, accumulate, hoard; to store away, hide

    መዝገብ (PL መዛግብት) treasure, wealth; storeroom, magazine

ዝሐነ G (IMPF ይዘሕን, SUBJ ይዝሐን) to be calm, tranquil

    ዝሑን (F ዝሕንት) PASS PTCP calm, tranquil

    ዛሕን calm, tranquility

ተዘነረ / ተዝነረ DT to boast; to brawl

    ዝኑር (F ዝኑርት) PASS PTCP boastful, arrogant; quarrelsome

    ትዝንርት NOUN boasting, insolence; strife, brawling

ዝንር tomb, monument

ዘከረ G (IMPF ይዘክር, SUBJ ይዝከር) = ዘከረ D to remember, mention

    ተዘከረ DT = G

    ዝኩር (F ዝክርት) PASS PTCP mentioned, remembered

    ዝክር mention, memory; commemoration

    ተዝካር memorial service or holiday, commemoration; memory; memorandum, notation

ዝኩ (COMP ዝኩ) MS that (ADJ or PRON)

    ዝክቱ ዝኮቱ IDEM

ዘለፈ G (IMPF ይዘልፍ, SUBJ ይዝለፍ) to admonish, reproach

    ዘላፊ reproach, admonition, reprimand

አዝለፈ CG to continue, persevere in (COMP verbal noun or COMP INF)

    ዝሉፈ, ለዝሉፉ ADV continuously, continually, perpetually, forever

    ዘልፈ ADV IDEM; always, regularly, frequently, often; perpetually; ኢ ... ዘልፈ never

    ዘዘልፍ ADJ perpetual

ዘልገሰ Q to be afflicted with a dreadful disease (leprosy)

    ዝልጉስ leprous

    ዝልጋሴ leprosy

ዜማ melody, tune, song

ተዘምዳ GT to be related

    ዘመድ (PL አዝማድ) family, kin, relatives, clan; tribe, kind, sort, species; SG and PL forms are used interchangeably

    ትዝምድ family, tribe, race, species

ዘመረ D (1) to make music; to play instruments, sing; (2) to state or proclaim authoritatively, to bear witness to

    አዘመረ CG = D (2)

    ዘሙር authority, witness

    ዝማሬ psalm, hymn

    መዝምር psalmist

    መዝሙር (PL መዝሙራት) psalm, the psalter; chorus of singers

    ምዝጋር authority, witness

ዘመወ D to commit adultery; to have illicit intercourse with (ምስለ or COMP)

    ዝሙት fornication, adultery, harlotry

    ዘማ whore, adulterer, fornicator; applied to both males and females

    ዘማዊ IDEM; applied to both males and females

ዘነብ tail

ዘንመ G (IMPF ይዘንም, SUBJ ይዝንም) to rain

    አዝነመ CG to bring rain, cause to rain

    ዝናም (PL ዝናማት) rain

ዘንገዐ Q to be insane, mad, crazy

    ዝንጉዕ mad, raving; stupid, inept

ዘንጐጐ Q to ridicule, hold in scorn

ዝንቱ (COMP ዘንተ) DEM MS this

ዜነወ L/Q to inform, tell, announce, bring tidings, declare, narrative, proclaim, relate, report, make known, make inquiries

    ዜና (PL ዜናት) news, report; narrative, story, account; pronouncement

ዝቅ (PL ዝቃት) skin bottle, leather bag

ዘርአ, ዘርዐ G (IMPF ይዘርእ, SUBJ ይዝራእ) to sow, scatter (seed)

    ዘርእ / ዘርዕ (PL አዝርእት) seed; progeny, offspring

ዘረወ G (IMPF ይዘሩ, SUBJ ይዝሩ) to scatter, disperse, distribute

    ዝሩው scattered, dispersed

    ዝርወት dispersion

    ዘራዊ (one) who scatters, disperses; prodigal

ዛቲ (COMP ዛተ) DEM FS this

ዝየ ADV here; በዝየ IDEM; እምዝየ from here, hence